Madame de Pompadour's Protégé

Madame de Pompadour's Protégé

Henri Bertin and the collapse of Bourbon absolutism *c.*1750–1792

Gwynne Lewis

EMLYN
Publishing

First published in the United Kingdom in 2011
by Emlyn Publishing

ISBN 978-0-9567923-0-3

Produced by
The Choir Press, Gloucester
www.thechoirpress.co.uk

Contents

Part One

The Minister, the Monarch and the Mistress

Chapter One

Henri Bertin: The Rise of a Provincial Robe Noble

At the end of November 1759, Louis XV appointed Henri Léonard Jean-Baptiste Bertin to the prestigious office of *contrôleur général des finances de France* (finance minister). He did so on the advice of his sometime mistress and, at times, de facto 'first minister', madame de Pompadour. Henri's appointment was an appropriate reward, not only for his loyal service to the monarchy during the 1750s, but also for the contribution of his fiercely ambitious father, Jean Bertin II, a robe noble from the small city of Périgueux, situated some hundred kilometres north-east of Bordeaux. In the pursuit of what he deemed to be the best interests of his family, Jean Bertin would sacrifice, in the most tragic fashion, the military career, indeed the life, of Louis-Mathieu, marquis de Fratteaux, the eldest of his sons, who refused to follow the administrative career path designated by his father. Following his resignation from the army, Louis-Mathieu would be embroiled in a series of picaresque adventures before being kidnapped by his own father and thrown into the Bastille in 1752, where he was left to rot until his death, twenty-seven years later. The *affaire Fratteaux*, involving as it did Louis XV and Pompadour, developed into an international scandal that has attracted scant attention from historians. The consequence of this tragic affair must have affected Henri Bertin, at least until the death of his elder brother; it would certainly ensnare him in the web of patronage woven by madame de Pompadour. By the time of her death in 1764, Bertin had become almost indispensable to Louis XV, whom he continued to serve until Louis' own demise a decade later. During this period, he not only held the high-ranking official post of secretary of state, but also the unofficial post of 'Keeper of the King's Purse and Personal Secrets', and it was in this latter capacity, during the early years of his career, that he would gain the support and favour of both Louis XV and madame de Pompadour.

The humiliating defeat of France by the British during the Seven Years' War (1756–63) would mark an historic turning point in the balance of European, and to a certain degree, world power. On a personal level, it would provide Henri Bertin, strengthened from December 1763 with his authority as secretary of state and a department specially created for him by Pompadour and Louis, with the opportunity of implementing a number of reforms that would provide much of the ideological sub-structure of the 'Grand Design' – the political and socio-economic project to reform Bourbon absolutism, which he would develop over the years with the unflagging support of his close colleague and friend, Jacob-Nicolas Moreau, government propagandist and subsequently royal historiographer. It is not our intention to provide a comprehensive biography of Bertin's 'life and times':[1] our principal concern will be to record and evaluate Bertin's significant contribution to the ideological, political, and economic reforms that were introduced following the disasters of the Seven Years' War. The 'Grand Design', as we have chosen to describe these reforms, was influenced by the intensifying opposition to the crown of the thirteen French parlements of the realm, informed by Enlightenment theories of political and socio-economic reform; they would seek to adapt the antiquated governance of Bourbon absolutism to the exigencies of a more democratic and egalitarian age. We need, however, to provide a relatively brief résumé of Bertin's formative years if we are to comprehend fully his particular commitment to this reforming mission.

* * *

Although the Bertin family had worked consistently, and very successfully, to add a noble veneer to their family shield over the centuries, the male line had emerged from solid Périgourdin, bourgeois stock. Périgueux, the province's administrative centre, was situated on the old Roman route that crossed southern France from Bordeaux to Lyon. Its citizens had continually been dragged into the bloody conflicts that constituted two 'Hundred Years' Wars' – the first fought between the Capetians and the Plantagenets that led to the Treaty of Paris in 1259, the second the struggle between the French and the English monarchies, ending with the battle of Castillon in 1453.[2] By1431, when Joan of Arc was burned at the stake by the English, Périgueux had become a frontier city situated between the English enclave of the Guyenne, extending from Bordeaux down to Bayonne, and the territory governed by the French king, Charles VII, covering most of the centre and south of the country. Today, Périgueux is the chef-lieu of the department of the Dordogne, and still a very popular pole of attraction for the British.

At the beginning of the sixteenth century, Joseph Bertin, his wife and their two sons, Etienne and Pierre, were living in a suburb of Périgueux, Saint-Laurent-du Manoir, 'the cradle of the Bertin family'. Little is known about Joseph Bertin save for his will, dated 15 December 1507, which makes no claim to noble status. It was his son, Etienne, who was destined to lay the foundations stones of the '*noble* House of Bertin'. During the 1550s, he rose to become the mayor of Périgueux, while his brother, Pierre, was managing an inn on the outskirts of the city. It was a time when successful, bourgeois citizens like Etienne Bertin received their just rewards in the Périgord: mayors of important towns and cities, for example, were granted minor noble status (*noblesse de cloche*), Périgueux having won the right to ennoble its officials as a reward for its historic resistance against English invaders. Henri Bertin would never forget the historic Périgourdin link between bourgeois success, recognition by the king, and patriotic sentiment, even if, for many sword nobles (*noblesse de l'épée*), the 'municipal nobility' (*noblesse de la cloche*) would continue to

5

represent the lowest of the ennobled low. By the end of the
sixteenth century, the professional career choices and achievements of Etienne Bertin and his son, François, had largely determined the future shape of the Bertin dynasty. Like so many
successful bourgeois families in early modern France, it would
seek to exchange its financial success for the glittering noble
prizes to be won either by purchasing an expensive, but
ennobling, royal sinecure (that of *sécretaire du roi* was widely
coveted, and the most expensive), or by serving as a magistrate
on a regional or provincial seat of government, which increased
the chances of becoming a minister of the crown. The particular
history of the Bertin family confirms the validity of Robin Briggs'
comment on French seventeenth-century society that: 'In practice
wealth did confer social mobility; the reason society was not more
fluid was primarily the success of the possessors of wealth in
hanging on to it, combined with an economic situation that made
rapid accumulation difficult'.[3]

There was certainly no stopping the rise of the Bertins who
would explore every opportunity, and employ every appropriate expert, to add the odd cubit to their purchased noble stature.
They would concentrate on the acquisition of noble land and the
purchase of ennobling royal offices, as well as marriage into the
traditional nobility of the blood. The enterprising François I, for
example, had not only acted as a property speculator, but also
a purchaser of royal offices. On 10 February 1574, he had
acquired the position of *conseiller aux Requestres du Palais à
Bordeaux*. As was the custom of the time, he passed this office
on to his son, François II. By the end of the sixteenth century,
the latter would be referred to as the 'noble François de Bertin',
the two letters of the particle 'de' carrying far greater weight in
terms of *ancien régime* social prestige than its minor grammati-
cal function might suggest.[4]

During the seventeenth century, the Bertins would continue to
pursue their interest in the acquisition of property and ennobling
offices; they also added an industrial dimension, in the form of
two ironworks, to their portfolio. These wider options are best

reflected in the career of Jacques de Bertin, François II's son who became a lawyer in the parlement of Bordeaux as well as a consul on the municipal council of Périgueux. Jacques exhibited those streaks of ruthlessness and devotion to the Bourbon monarchy that would become characteristic of Henri Bertin's father and grandfather. During the fiscal riots of the mid-1630s, it was Jacques de Bertin, not the mayor of Périgueux, who restored order by executing the ringleaders of a popular revolt in the city. During the national revolt of the Fronde during the 1650s, when even princes of the blood took up arms against the monarchy, he played a prominent role in ultimately securing the town of Périgueux for the crown. It was the bourgeoisie, not the popular masses or the nobility of the sword, who proved to be the most loyal servants of the monarchy on this occasion, as they had been when the city had been besieged by English invaders in the fifteenth century. We shall see in subsequent chapters how the 'Grand Design' to save the Bourbon monarchy would draw upon this family history lesson when, during the pre-Revolutionary crises of the 1770s and 80s, Bertin would advise Louis XVI to tap into the patriotic veins of the bourgeoisie and the *noblesse de robe* rather than into those of the endangered aristocracy of the sword. The House of Bertin would triumph during the eighteenth century by remembering the debt it owed to those bourgeois ancestors who anchored their fortunes to the fate of the Bourbon dynasty, receiving its due reward in the form of lucrative state offices and, ultimately, the high office and ennoblement it had always coveted. We shall see that Henri Bertin together with his colleague, Jacob-Nicolas Moreau, believed that, suitably reformed, the Bourbon monarchy could be an 'attendant lord' at the birth of the eighteenth-century bourgeoisie.

*   *   *

But it all took time. At the beginning of the eighteenth century, the Bertins had not yet made their mark on the national stage. They were just 'an honourable family, which continued to grow in numbers and wealth, a united and tightly-knit group living on land stretching along the banks of the rivers Manoire and de l'Isle to the river Garonne, whose leading figures had been attached, for two centuries, to its birth-place in the humble parish of Saint-Laurent'.[5] Two formidable individuals, Jean Bertin I and Jean Bertin II, Henri Bertin's grandfather and father, were to place the Bertins securely on the national stage, shifting the focus of their activities from Périgueux to the very gates of Versailles. Henri Bertin's carriage would pass through those gates, setting him on the path to a career as a royal minister that would last from the 1750s into the Revolution of 1789.

Jean Bertin I began to 'nationalise' the family's interest in commerce and industry when he decided to take a more active interest in the iron industry: his grandson, Henri, would exhibit a particular interest in mining throughout his time as secretary of state (1763–80). The ownership of mines or glassworks did not lead to the loss of noble status during the *ancien régime*; involvement in the actual manufacture, or retailing, of products was quite another matter. As the industrial sector expanded, especially under Louis XV, the number of noble, and ennobled, iron-masters would increase. The necessary raw materials, coal and wood suitable for early furnaces, could often be found on noble land. Jean Bertin I managed the family's two iron-forges in the 1700s, the first on his noble fief of Saint-Martin, the second, in the hamlet of Sainte-Marie-de-Chignac on the bank of the river Manoire (another energy source). Both places, in fact, were situated within the 'cradle of the Bertins' around Saint-Laurent-du-Manoire.

Through contacts established in Bordeaux and Versailles, Bertin I began to win contracts for the supply of iron to produce cannons for the French navy. One of these contacts was François d'Hautfort, the baron de Segonzac and owner of the sizeable *forge d'Ans*, who had won a contract to supply the port of Rochefort with 100 cannons. Was it his relationship with successful industrialists such as d'Hautfort (a baron no less!), that prompted Jean Bertin I to purchase in 1692 the royal offices of *commissaire des armes de la Manufacture de Périgueux* as well as that of *commissaire aux revues et logements des gens de guerre*, offices that transformed him into one of the crown's military officials in the Périgord?

One thing is certain, Bertin was determined to benefit from the craze for royal offices that Louis XIV was creating in order to pay for his seemingly endless wars. In just six years, Bertin had sold the above offices to a neighbour and purchased, for the high price of 33,000 *livres*, membership of the royal taxation office for the district of Bordeaux, accompanied by the very prestigious post of *conseiller commissaire général, trésorier de France*.[6] Jean Bertin I was now well advanced in this process of incremental ennoblement (contemporaries referred to it as 'nobility on the quiet'!): by 1702, he was employing the title of écuyer (squire) to describe his status, as he had every right to do. The particular history of the Bertin family confirms the validity of Robin Briggs' general comment on French society at the end of the seventeenth century: 'Royal finance, taxation, and the sale of offices have been the central themes of this book, not just for their importance as props of absolutism, but because they influenced the development of French society as a whole'.[7]

It was now time for Jean Bertin I to enter one or more of his sons into the marriage stakes in order to find a suitable bride. Jane Austen, in one of the most frequently quoted opening lines of a novel, wrote in *Pride and Prejudice* that 'It is a truth universally acknowledged that a single man in possession of a good fortune must be in a want of a wife.' For Jean Bertin, however, a cut or two above the gentry, it was more a case of 'a married man in possession of a good fortune must be in need of a *noble* daughter-in-law'. He did not have too much difficulty finding a suitable candidate: on 17 August 1705, he married off his son, Jean Bertin II, to Lucrèce de Saint-Chamans. As they sipped their white Bordeaux, none of the guests needed to ask whether or not the Saint-Chamans were 'vrai' or 'faux' nobles. The bride was descended, on her mother's side, from the Grimoard family, which could boast a sword noble heritage dating back to 'time immemorial'; her dowry included the tenth-century noble fief of Fratteaux that

9

formed part of the estate of des Vivans. The marriage was a classic example of new (robe noble) money marrying into an old (sword noble) family. However, such marriages were not always 'made in heaven', and when the great crisis occurred in the 1740s over which of the brothers should inherit the lion's share of the family fortune, the ensuing fracture between the Bertin and the Grimoard clans would leave wounds that never really healed. The eldest son, Louis-Mathieu, who received the title of marquis de Fratteaux from his mother, would chose to follow the military *noblesse de l'épée* tradition of the Grimoards; his younger brother, Henri, the administrative *noblesse de robe* tradition of the Bertins. The former would end his life in the Bastille; the latter would become a favourite of madame de Pompadour, a family metaphor perhaps for the decline of the sword nobility and the rise of the administrative robe nobility during the eighteenth century. The recurrent hostility during the second half of the eighteenth century between 'robe and sword' would threaten the foundations of the 'Grand Design', which projected, along with other attacks upon the traditional nobility, such as the abbé Coyer's work, *La Noblesse commerçante* (1756), a vision of a more cohesive noble 'class', as opposed to an anachronistic noble 'caste'.

In the early days, however, the Bertin–Grimoard marriage had been a cause for celebration: it had strengthened the Catholic credentials of the Bertin family. Etienne Bertin, the mayor of Périgueux between 1550 and 1552, had championed the Catholic cause during the conflict with local Protestants ('les malheureux huguenaux') during the sixteenth century Wars of Religion. Jean Bertin I was no exception to this family rule, dying a faithful member of the Roman Catholic Church. His grandson, Henri, would be regarded as a sometime supporter of the Catholic *dévot* faction at the court of Louis XV. He would also count a bishop, an abbé, and a nun amongst his brothers and sisters. He would attach religious devotion to the 'Grand Design', although his Catholic variant would carry rather less weight as time passed as he succumbed, in no small measure, to the influence of the more deist wing of the Enlightenment, and reacted, adversely, to what

10

he regarded as the more retrograde policies of the papacy. But if Henri's grandfather had consolidated the provincial power-base of the Bertin family, it was his father, Jean Bertin II, who transferred it to the national stage. He drew upon the wealth and experience inherited from his forbears, continuing the policies of investing the family fortune in noble land and royal offices, but shifting some of his attention to high finance. In 1711, he paid 90,000 *livres* to purchase the position of *trésorier particulier des Invalides de la Marine des port et amirauté de Bordeaux* as well as 30,000 *livres* for the post of *contrôleur particulier des Invalides de la Marine*. These were expensive offices, available only to the very rich. A few months later he sold them to pay for the more prestigious position of *conseiller en la Cour du Parlement de Bordeaux*. His status as a successful robe noble was now uncontested, the notarial records of the period describing him as 'Puissant Seigneur Messire Jean de Bertin, chevalier'.[8]

The Bertins had arrived on the national stage. Over the next few years, our 'Puissant Seigneur' would spend more time in Paris than in Périgueux; more time orbiting the world of Parisian finance than its provincial satellites. His personal ambition, coupled with the feverish financial circumstances of the Regency period (1715–23), combined to provide Jean Bertin II, along with tens of thousands of equally avaricious speculators, with the opportunity of striking it very rich indeed. The death of Louis XIV in 1715, and the consequent shift of commercial interest from the killing fields of Europe to mythical El Dorados overseas, fuelled by the financial frenzies of the South Sea Bubble in England as well as by John Law's *Système* in France, opened a new chapter in French economic history. In December 1719, Jean Bertin confirmed that he was well placed to tackle whatever lay ahead with his successful application for the office of *president trésorier de France*, a position his father had held for over twenty years. He was now moving in the right salons, those frequented by bankers and rich, royal tax farmers (*fermiers généraux*); the same circles, it should be noted, in which a certain Jeanne Poisson, the attractive and distinctly 'pushy' mother of the future

11

madame de Pompadour, could often be found. The first links in the social chain that was to unite the Pompadours and the Bertins were being forged.

* * *

The duc d'Orléans (Regent of France between 1715 and 1723) helped John Law to open his first bank in the rue Saint-Avoie in June 1716. A year later, Law had founded his Mississippi Company in the American colonies: it was situated within the vast royal concession known then, in honour of Louis XIV, as 'Louisiana'. A Scots adventurer and financial wizard, Law exercised a remarkable degree of influence over the intelligent, but equally adventurous, Regent, who gave him permission to open a Royal Bank in Paris on 4 December 1718. By the summer of 1719, Law had acquired almost complete control of government finances, along with those of many overseas companies, including the *compagnie de Sénégal* in West Africa and the *compagnie des Indes*. His infamous *Système* included the issue of shares floated on unsubstantiated promises of the untold wealth that was only waiting to be discovered in Louisiana. Investors, including several princes of the blood, were now eagerly exchanging their gold and silver for Law's bank notes and shares. By the end of 1720, however, Law's bubble had burst. Those who had got out in time had made personal fortunes. Among their number was a certain Jean Bertin II who had rented an apartment in the rue Richelieu, not far from Law's bank, to oversee, almost literally, the safety of his investments.[9]

The bold but reckless Law *Système* constitutes a landmark in French economic and social history: on a more personal level, it provided Jean Bertin II with the funds he required to extend the 'noble House of Bertin'. He embarked upon a major campaign to acquire properties that would bring him and his family both wealth and improved noble status. On 20 December 1719, he purchased the splendid *comté de Saint-Gérand-de-Vaux* in the Bourbonnais from one of the oldest noble families in France, the

Rohan-Soubise. The acquisition of this property enabled its proud owner to use the title of 'comte'. Just over a month later, Bertin bought (in his mother's name) the noble fief of Bellisle from the Segonzac family, for the knockdown price of 6,412 *livres*. This was the very same family that had assisted his father in his quest to become a successful iron-master. The crowning achievement of Jean Bertin II's campaign, however, was the purchase, in January 1720, of the *seigneurie de Bourdeille* from the Jumilhac-Cubjac family, which had not only fallen on bad times, but was also about to become one of the many victims of the Law crash. Bertin bought this medieval/Renaissance property for the massive sum of 523,000 *livres*! Why did he pay this high price for an estate that, although it exercised authority over fourteen parishes, provided rather poor returns in terms of feudal dues and rents? It is possible that the Bertins did not consider themselves to be, first and foremost, 'feudal' nobles, but more concrete considerations must be taken into account: Bourdeille was relatively close to home territory in Saint-Laurent; then there was the enticing prospect that the purchase could be, indeed was, paid for, in part, with Law's rapidly depreciating paper money, bequeathing a legacy of hatred between the Jumilhac-Cubjacs and the Bertins that would last into the Revolution of 1789; finally, Bourdeille was both a *comté* and a *baronnie*, conferring upon its new owner the much-coveted title of 'premier baron du Périgord'. For many robe nobles, the finery of feudalism could occasionally be used to increase family status.[10] In 1742, a document concerning yet another property acquisition would describe Bertin II, rather grandiloquently, as a *'haut et puissant seigneur, conseiller du roi en tout ses conseils, maître des requêtes, baron et comte de Bourdeille, seigneur de Brantôme'.*[11] By this time, however, this 'high and mighty seigneur', who had opened the gates of Versailles for his family, could see a very black cloud approaching on the horizon as he looked out of the window of his fine château – his eldest son, Louis-Mathieu, had rebelled against his father's authority, launching a national scandal that was to bring his favourite son,

Henri Bertin, into contact with Louis XV and madame de Pompadour.

*   *   *

Jean Bertin II's noble bride presented him with no fewer than sixteen children, although only eight girls and six boys would reach adulthood. It was not surprising, perhaps, that Lucrèce died, in 1754, at the relatively early age of forty-nine. We do not know what degree of affection Bertin *père* bestowed upon his children; we do know that some, if not all, were treated as pawns on the family chessboard. There is nothing unusual about noble fathers dictating the fate of their offspring in the eighteenth century, it just seems that Jean Bertin II was more dictatorial than most. On 2 April 1707, his first son was born. He was Louis-Mathieu, the future marquis de Fratteaux, whose life was to be ruined by his father because he refused to move to the square assigned to him on the family chessboard. Two of the girls who were born became nuns, while one boy, Louis-Augustin, became an abbé; Charles-Jean obtained the bishopric of Vannes in Brittany, another reminder that the Bertins were dedicated Catholics. Henri, the future minister of the crown who would walk the corridors of power with Pompadour, was one of the last of the Bertin brood, born on 24 March 1721.[12]

It is somewhat surprising that the eldest son of the Bertins, Louis-Mathieu, should have ended his days in the Bastille, virtually forgotten by his contemporaries and posterity whilst his much younger brother, Henri, was fêted in his heyday as a protégé of the famous madame de Pompadour, and is now, rather belatedly, recognised as one of the foremost administrators of his time. Part of the answer to this apparent mystery is to be found in the authority that was vested in the eighteenth century head of state, Louis XV, as well as in the head of a provincial noble family, Bertin *père*. In a profoundly hierarchical and patriarchal society, they frequently wielded more power than was good for themselves or for their families. Relations between Bertin père and his first-born son, Louis-Mathieu, appear to have deteriorated seriously not long after the latter had reached his teenage years. This is evident from a reading of two rare pamphlets: *An address to those in power occasioned by the violence to which the marquis de Fratteaux has been a sacrifice*, and the more informative and revealing account, *The Unfortunate oficer* [*sic*], *or the history of M. Bertin, marquis de Fratteaux*. Both were published in London, the first in 1752, and the second, which was also translated into French, a year later. Since Louis-Mathieu was imprisoned in the Bastille from 11 April 1752, *The Unfortunate oficer* was probably written by the comte d'Hauteville du Tertre, a friend of the marquis, from notes prepared by the marquis and smuggled out of the Bastille by du Tertre. This publication is both rare and quite extraordinary, as two of the experts who have studied it, Georges Bussière and André Bourde, agree. The former tells us that 'if all the details of the *Histoire* were true, I would be dealing with the plot of a novel whose reality would be *as interesting as any fictional work* [emphasis added]'; according to André Bourde, the *Histoire* 'looks forward to the work of Alexandre Dumas and Walter Scott … It is a *tragi-comédie-policière*, a fore-runner of the *roman noir*'.[13] There can be no doubt, as we shall see below, that Louis-Mathieu's actions during the 1740s and early 1750s does indeed provide excellent material for a Dumas novel – violent clashes with his father; imprisonment in France, followed by colourful adventures in Spain and England; the father's use of royal arrest warrants (*lettres de cachet*) to recapture his son, who, by this time, had metamorphosed into a combination of Don Quixote and d'Artagnan; widening divisions within the Bertin family; and, finally, widening international repercussions involving the governments of England and France as Louis-Mathieu was kidnapped in England and transported to the Bastille.

It was the military tradition of his mother's aristocratic family that had first turned Louis-Mathieu against his father. The latter had predestined him for a place among the elite of the *noblesse de robe*; his son opted for the *noblesse de l'épée*. The *Histoire* informs us that the boy was born to follow a military career, 'that he was attracted to it, and that he had the ability to make a success of it'.

The *Histoire* also suggests that it was only the pressure exerted upon him by his father's mistress that had induced Bertin *père* to purchase the post of a cadet officer in the famous regiment de Noailles for his son (the influential maréchal de Noailles would become one of Henri Bertin's protectors at court). What makes subsequent events more tragic is the fact that Louis-Mathieu's army career appears to have been highly successful. It is recorded that he served, with distinction, in both the War of the Polish Succession (1733–5) as well as in the War of the Austrian Succession (1740–48), his bravery being recognised by his promotion to the rank of captain and the award of the coveted *croix de Saint-Louis*.[14]

Throughout this prolonged period of military service, several attempts appear to have been made to bridge the widening gap between the expectations of Bertin *père* and the martial exploits of his warrior son. In 1733, for example, the Bertin family's financial adviser, Louis-Augustin Bertin, abbé de Brantôme, tried to get Louis-Mathieu more closely involved in family affairs by seeking his advice on several legal cases, but attempts at reconciliation failed. The response to poignant pleas addressed to his father – 'Ah! father, father how have I wronged you? Why are you trying to destroy me?' – was, 'I never wish to see your face again!' The year 1733 represented a low watermark in the stormy relations between father and son, Louis-Mathieu actually being imprisoned by the government, on the request of his father, for several months. It was around this time that Bertin *père* began to give credence to rumours that the marquis de Fratteaux was something of a changeling; and / or that his behaviour towards his father could only be explained by the onset of mental instability. Given that there was no history of madness in the Bertin family, Bertin *père* argued, the real Louis-Mathieu must have died as a result of his nurse's negligence, and one of her own offspring substituted for him. To add some credibility to this claim, evidence of madness was allegedly discovered in the nurse's family. If there was any truth in all of this, then Bertin *père* could not possibly make the marquis de Fratteaux his 'universal heir'!

All very convenient, but, as we shall discover, totally unfounded.[15]

There can be little doubt that the steady career advancement recorded by Louis-Mathieu's much younger brother Henri helped to fuel the explosive relationship between Bertin *père* and his eldest son. While the former was serving his country, the latter was pursuing an apprenticeship in the arts and crafts of becoming an administrative robe noble and a government minister. Is it any wonder that Louis-Mathieu became increasingly consumed with jealousy and anger? Henri had commenced his legal studies in Paris in 1737. Just over three years later, he had been admitted to the bar of the Bordeaux parlement (16 January 1741); his father had purchased a similar office in the same parlement some thirty years earlier. To further his career, Bertin *père* provided the substantial sum of 50,500 *livres* for his son to purchase the office of *conseiller de sa Majesté en son Grand Conseil*. Bertin *père*'s campaign on behalf of Henri's career continued in 1744 with a letter to the *contrôleur général*, Philibert Orry, who just happened to be a family friend, requesting the transfer of his own prestigious government post of *maître des requêtes* to Henri. It cost 70,000 *livres*, but the 'master-builder' was in a hurry; Louis-Mathieu was threatening court action to obtain recognition of his 'natural rights'. Fortunately, Louis XV's government was desperate for hard cash to pay for its participation in the War of the Austrian Succession. Family ambition and royal debt combined to secure a happy outcome for Henri Bertin – and the Bourbons.[16]

In 1747, Louis-Mathieu resigned from the army at the age of forty. The major cause of his resignation was probably the signing of his father's last will and testament on 3 July 1746. The will was legal confirmation of all Louis-Mathieu's fears – half of his father's estate was to be divided equally between all the Bertin children; the other half to be bequeathed to Henri Léonard. Henri was also designated as Jean Bertin II's 'universal heir concerning all my possessions, present and future'. As for Louis-Mathieu, he was to receive his share of the money earmarked for all the family, as well as the noble fief of Fratteaux. Excluding Henri, it was a better deal than any of his siblings received, but it was, nonetheless, small beer compared with Henri's inheritance. For one thing, Louis-Mathieu, as we have noted above, had long regarded himself as 'the marquis de Fratteaux' since the estate to which this noble fief was attached belonged to his mother's side of the family and, in his opinion, this had to be recognised, whatever the law said. Although he had harboured few illusions about his father's intentions, this legal expression of his hatred opened a completely new chapter in the family saga that would eventually assume an international dimension. It seems that Bertin *père* had been expecting trouble from the beginning of his marriage to the aristocratic Lucrèce de Saint-Chamans. The marriage contract had contained a clause giving him the right to donate half of his entire estate to one of his children, 'subject to the restriction that I chose a male child of my own choosing'. To drive the point home, one of the stipulations of his 1746 will was that Louis-Mathieu might even lose what had been bequeathed to him if he contested the right of his much younger brother to assume the role of 'universal heir'.[17]

But Louis-Mathieu had been contesting his father's decisions for over twenty years, and it can hardly be imagined that the will provided any grounds for a change of heart. As the *Histoire* informs us, Louis-Mathieu had always fought for his rights: 'This was his "crime", and the only "crime" with which he is charged'.[18] The problem was, however, that law, custom, and precedents were not entirely on his side. Detailed regional studies indicate that the rule of primogeniture was not always observed by heads of households in the Périgord, or indeed in many other regions of the south, during the eighteenth century. Margaret Darrow, referring to Revolutionary criticisms of *ancien régime* inheritance laws, writes that 'In conjuring up eldest sons who lolled in luxury while their brothers languished in poverty, the advocates of equal inheritance exaggerated both the prevalence of primogeniture and the degree of inequality that resulted from the *faculté de tester* [the right of the individual to bequeath his property by written testament to whom he chose]'. The will drawn up by Louis-Mathieu's grandfather is a case in point. He had chosen Bertin père as his 'universal heir', although he was not the eldest (male) child. If the 'universal heir', was not the eldest son, however, he was usually given the most important family fief as compensation, the property that symbolised the antiquity or lineage of the household (the *préciput*). The *préciput* was the homage that supporters of equal inheritance paid to the ancient tradition of primogeniture, and Louis-Mathieu's father had recognised this, reluctantly one suspects, by legalising his son's claim, through his mother's relatives, to the noble fief of Fratteaux.[19]

For a year or so after his will was published, Bertin père used the 'gift' of the Fratteaux fief to bring his errant son on side. Would the marquis like his father to arrange the legal transfer of the *terre et château de Fratteaux* to him? The property is not yours to dispose of, Louis-Mathieu replied, since it forms part of the seigneurial estate of des Vivans, which has already been bequeathed to me by my mother's family.[20] Sons were not slaves to their father's every whim, Louis-Mathieu added, 'everyone knows that a person must be free to choose his own career'. Had he not proved that he had been born for the état of a soldier? The obdurate Louis-Mathieu was echoing the opinions of a more enlightened age when he argued that personal 'serfdom' belonged to the past. Why, he had been asked, did he not prove his loyalty to the family by making a simple renunciation of his rights as the first-born son? The answer to this question was that 'it was Nature that had assigned him to his place as the first-born son; he could not, indeed, must not renounce his rights ... individuals must remain within the estate determined for them by divine providence. These rules were also dictated by Reason; to think of violating them was the real crime. Even threats of death would not shake his resolve on this matter'.[21]

How many *philosophes*, from Diderot to the marquis de Sade, would burn the eighteenth-century midnight oil trying to resolve the complexities and contradictions that are inherent in definitions of 'Reason' and 'Nature'? The thousands of definitions of these and other universal concepts contained in the first volumes of the *Encyclopédie*, which were published in the early 1750s, at the very time Louis-Mathieu was being imprisoned in the Bastille, would re-fashion the mental universe of the eighteenth-century cultural and intellectual world, a world in which the radical ideas of a global Enlightenment clashed with the traditional values of an aristocratic, hierarchical and ecclesi- astical society. Louis-Mathieu, who frequently appealed to concepts of aristocratic *vertu*, lived in both worlds, a stance that was apparently acceptable to the Bourbon state, but which the reformist Henri Bertin would seek to challenge. Colin Jones, who rightly associates the changes wrought by the radical world of the Enlightenment with the emergence of an increasingly capitalist and consumerist society, as indeed did the abbé Coyer and Bertin, has noted that 'The state found itself facing two ways on the issue of noble virtue, locating it both in the archaic values of a warrior elite [those espoused by Bertin *mère*] and then again in the merit of outstanding figures, noble or non-noble, who contributed to society's prosperity'.[22] The Bertin family saga provides us with a microscopic example of the macroscopic change that was occurring throughout Europe, and, as we shall see in our final chapter, the wider world. Henri Bertin, influenced by the indus- trial and commercial tradition of the Bertins, would, as a minister of the crown, be willing to engage with the contemporary conflicts engendered by the emerging capitalist world, while Louis-Mathieu chose to cling on to the more traditional military values espoused by his mother's aristocratic, Grimoard family.

The bitter divisions created by Bertin *père* eventually led to 'scènes terribles' within the Bertin household. Both Bertin *père et fils* resorted to occasional violence, accompanied by mutual accu- sations of attempted murder. The *Histoire* records a violent confrontation between father and son in the château de Bourdeille, during which Bertin *père* allegedly lost all control, shouting that whilst Louis-Mathieu may have seen many people blown to bits by cannon balls during his army career, he would finish his son off with a shotgun![23] On 11 October 1748, Bertin *père*, weary of these continual confrontations, obtained a royal warrant empowering the local police to re-arrest Louis-Mathieu and hand him over to the *Frères de charité* in the town of Cadillac near Bordeaux.[24] This escalation of the affaire reveals the reservoir of power that Bertin *père* could draw upon through his contacts with ministers at Versailles. That power, however, had to be used wisely. Royal arrest warrants (*lettres de cachet*), which allowed successful applicants to imprison their enemies without costly and lengthy court trials, had become the target of many reformers who were determined to defeat 'Bourbon despotism'. Louis-Mathieu himself condemns the use of royal arrest warrants, describing them as 'emetics', employed by those who acquired them to 'flush out' their enemies. In this respect, the *affaire Fratteaux* may be said to have made an early contribution to the increasing attacks on 'ministerial despotism' that were to punctuate the second half of the eighteenth century.[25]

On a more personal level, Louis-Mathieu's arrest and imprisonment by a *lettre de cachet* escalated the quarrel between the paternal and maternal sides of the Bertin family. His mother's friends organised a petition to the king, signed by over thirty members of the nobility of Guyenne, as well as by army colleagues of the marquis. In their *requête au roy*, dated 22 September 1749, they complained that Jean Bertin's pursuit of his son was 'humiliating for the entire family': it was, after all, a question of family honour, and family honour was one of the foundation stones of the *noblesse de l'épée*. The petitioners asked Louis XV to appoint independent commissioners, answerable to the parlement of Bordeaux, to resolve the *affaire Fratteaux*. A family quarrel over a will drawn up by a robe noble in the Périgord was rapidly being transformed into a national scandal that would ultimately ensnare Louis XV and madame de Pompadour.[26]

No immediate action was taken, which is hardly surprising. Weighed in the balances of state power, the family and friends of the Saint-Chamans clan could not hope to tip the scales against Jean Bertin II, who had spent a lifetime cultivating friends in high places. In the first place, there was his son, Henri, the beneficiary of his largesse and influence. Only a few weeks after the king had received the *requête du roy* from Louis-Mathieu's supporters, Henri had become one of the presidents of the king's *Grand Conseil*. Then there was the *contrôleur général*, Orry. He had purchased the estate and château of Saint-Gérand from Bertin *père*, and organised the eventual transfer to Henri of the royal offices that Bertin had bought over the years. Finally, there was the minister of the King's Household, the comte de Saint-Florentin. He was a notorious *roué*, a childhood friend of Jean Bertin, and a favourite of Louis XV. Ministers of the King's Household were usually involved in preparing royal arrest warrants, and it has been estimated that Saint-Florentin had issued thousands during his lengthy spell in office. He would perform the function of mentor during Bertin's apprenticeship as 'Keeper of the King's Purse and Personal Secrets'.[27]

If his maternal relatives had transformed the *affaire Fratteaux* into a national scandal, it was Louis-Mathieu himself who made the fatal decision to take his case into the international arena. His father, exploiting the support he had received from the king, had recruited a number of retainers and spies to track his son's every move following his release from imprisonment in Cadillac. Fearful of more draconian action on the part of his father, Louis-Mathieu now decided to flee abroad, first across the Pyrenees to Spain, then across the Channel to England. This marked the beginning of a personal odyssey that would throw the marquis into the company of a motley crew of ex-army colleagues, card-sharps and crooks, and agents of the French and English governments, as well as spies in the pay of his father. Through all these escapades, the reckless marquis de Fratteaux would never lose his almost manic resolve to right the wrongs he felt that he had suffered at the hands of his father: an admirable trait, perhaps, but one that would eventually lead him to his fatal involvement with madame de Pompadour.[28]

* * *

The marquis de Fratteaux first set foot on English soil at the beginning of January 1750, determined to devote all his energies to the task of obtaining revenge against his father and younger brother. The *Histoire de M. Bertin* records in considerable detail how Louis-Mathieu's obsessive search for justice doomed him, in just over a year, to be transported back to France, ultimately to his death cell within the infamous Bastille. Throughout his exile in London, he would be obliged to walk on extremely thin foreign ice, pitting his wits not only against his father but also against agents of the English and French governments. Fortunately, relations between these two countries during the build-up to the Seven Years' War was not exactly cordial, whilst a twenty-year military career, which had seen the marquis fight on many of the battlefields of western and eastern Europe, had inoculated him against dangerous situations and dangerous colleagues. But then Louis-Mathieu's bravery had never been in doubt; it was his judgement and common sense that had been damaged beyond repair. Having familiarised himself with the topography and the various ethnic communities of the city, he chose to join the sizeable French community in Soho, many of them descendants of Protestants who had emigrated from France at the time of Louis XIV's Revocation of the Edict of Nantes in 1685. Peter Ackroyd's celebratory biography of London explains how Soho in the 1750s fitted the marquis de Fratteaux's requirements like a glove: By 1688 over eight hundred of the empty and newly built houses had been filled with Huguenots, who characteristically transformed the ground floors into 'genuine French shops', cheap cafés and restaurants, 'like those near "the barrier" in Paris'. So by degrees this emerging region of London came to be compared with the French city. The *Histoire* is suffused with the atmosphere of freedom and unfamiliarity, first created by the Huguenots, that lingered on in Soho. Few places on earth could have been more suitable for the asylum-seeker from the Périgord.[29]

From January 1750 to April 1752, he surrounded himself with 'a society of swindlers, dubious characters, and pamphleteers among whom we find the occasional English or French informer'.

Prominent among these informers was a defrocked monk named Daniel de Souchard, referred to in the *Histoire* under his pseudonym of 'Dagès'. He had been despatched to England by Louis-Mathieu's father to spy on his son, a task he accomplished with professional expertise. Dagès would play a central role in Louis-Mathieu's eventual downfall, prompting the distraught and all too gullible marquis to describe him as 'this scoundrel, this monster, this anti-Christ ... an infernal demon'. Playing Iago to Louis-Mathieu's Othello, Dagès managed to secure a position as one of Louis-Mathieu's 'secretaries', chiefly responsible for organising the marquis' publicity campaign against his father and his friends 'in high places'.[30]

No sooner had Louis-Mathieu settled in Soho than he was surrounded by a swarm of scribblers eager to satisfy his penchant for expressing exaggerated opinions in exaggerated prose style. Roy Porter has highlighted the importance of 'this emergent culture industry' in England, the thousands of freeborn Englishmen who were creating 'self-identities as critics, knowledge-mongers and opinion-makers, addressing a growing public, and used as well as abused by the authorities'. Between 1660 and 1800 over 300,000 separate book and pamphlet titles were published in England, amounting to perhaps 200 million copies all told. Censorship was the rule in France, but in England, too, the 1750s heralded a new era in the triangular relationship between government, the press and authors. The first volume of the *Encyclopédie* was published in 1751; the appointment of the liberal minister, Chrétien-Guillaume de Lamoignon de Malesherbes, as the government's *Directeur de la librarie* ensured that it would not be the last, despite the ferocity of the attacks targeted at its editors, Denis Diderot and Jean Le Rond d'Alembert. The massive publishing enterprise of the Encylopédie immeasurably increased the number of self-proclaimed '*philosophes*' and associated 'scribblers' in France. It was this mini-revolution in the 'emergent culture industry' that provided Louis-Mathieu with the oxygen of publicity required to transform a family quarrel into an international scandal.[31]

24

On 15 January 1751, Louis-Mathieu's 'secretariat' circulated a memoir to the French court, a limited edition of just 120 manuscript copies. Its main purpose was to prepare the ground for the marquis' eventual return to France. In the pursuit of this objective, signed copies were sent to the comte de Saint-Florentin, the archbishop of Sens, as well as to the president of the parlement of Bordeaux. The *affaire Fratteaux* had not disappeared, much to the despair of Louis-Mathieu's father. Louis-Mathieu's next, and most fatal, step was to launch an attack on Louis XV and his mistress, madame de Pompadour. In a letter despatched to France on 20 March 1751, Louis-Mathieu, in typically grandiose style, accused Pompadour of preventing the king from appointing commissioners to deal with his case, as laid out by his supporters in the *requête au roy* of 22 September 1749. Did she, Louis-Mathieu asked, 'at the risk of scandalising the whole of Europe for centuries to come … and despite his full awareness of my innocence, really want to stop the king appointing commissioners to deal with an affair that pertains to his *gloire*, and to prevent him appointing them in accordance with the *requête* of the nobility of Guyenne?'. Louis-Mathieu continued with the dire warning that if she refused to intervene on his behalf he was 'going to be poisoned or strangled in France, threats that have been made against me, on several occasions'. He did not think that she was capable of turning a blind eye to these threats, and 'I will never think so!' Georges Bussière's comment on this extraordinary accusation against madame de Pompadour was short and to the point: 'The marquis de Fratteaux was lost beyond recall'.[32]

Louis-Mathieu had chosen a very unpropitious time to attack the king's mistress and increasingly influential adviser. In the spring of 1749, she had engineered the downfall of the comte de Maurepas, one Louis XV's most powerful ministers. Maurepas, a man of intelligence and sharp wit, had objected to the growing interference of Louis' mistresses, especially Pompadour, whom he dismissed as a bourgeois upstart. Exploiting the current vogue for publishing scandalous satirical verses against court favourites, he foolishly supplied the French equivalent of the

Grub Street press with a few lines that poured ridicule on Pompadour. The lady was not amused, and having recently reached an unwritten agreement with Louis XV, whereby she would turn a blind eye to his attraction for the opposite sex if he would recognise her attraction for wielding political power, she used her newfound authority to get rid of Maurepas, one of her most dangerous opponents.[33] It would be some time, however, before this most talented of royal mistresses would feel secure enough to dismiss full-frontal attacks, such as those launched by the marquis de Fratteaux in 1751, with the contempt she felt they deserved. But, something would have to be done about this troublesome exile, especially since her protégés, Jean Bertin II and his favourite son, Henri, were asking her to act on their behalf. The response of Louis XV and madame de Pompadour would eventually bind Henri Bertin closer to both of them.

We have also uncovered evidence that Jean Bertin II's expertise in tracking down his own son was used by Pompadour during the early 1750s to defend herself against her enemies, at home and abroad, specifically in the 'Melotta Ossonpi' affair. One of the spies she employed was none other than the 'anti-Christ' and 'infernal demon' whom Bertin had hired to mastermind the downfall of the marquis de Fratteaux in England, Daniel de Souchard, or 'Dagès' as the unfortunate marquis knew him. The 'Melotta Ossonpi' affair involved a scandalous libel against the marquise's mother, the society beauty, madame de Poisson, née La Motte, a lady, it was claimed, who was no better, and possibly worse, than she should have been (crossword addicts may have spotted the fact that 'Melotta Ossonpi' is an anagram of 'Poisson' and 'La Motte'). Always vulnerable to attacks upon her family, Pompadour ordered one of the king's ministers, the comte d'Argenson, to conduct an enquiry into the firm, based in Amsterdam, that published the libel – Marc-Michel Roy.[34] Bertin *père*, one of Louis XV's councillors, was chosen to head this enquiry, and it was Bertin who contacted Daniel de Souchard, who would operate on this occasion under the pseudonym of 'd'Alphonse'! It is clear from the comte d'Argenson's correspondence that de Souchard, described as a government spy working in England and Holland, corresponded directly with Bertin *père*. The '*affaire Ossonpi*' provides instructive parallels with the *affaire Fratteaux*. The author of the Ossonpi libel was tracked down by 1753 and locked up in the Bastille until 1784, five years after Louis-Mathieu's death in the same prison.[35] When confronted with attacks on the king or his mistress, the full, brutal force of *ancien régime* law was frequently invoked.

It was distinctly unfortunate that the marquis de Fratteaux's uncompromising attack on Pompadour should have been made at the very time that she was transforming herself from a mistress to assume a more front-line role on the political stage. Louis-Mathieu's accusations called into question her ability to offer the king sound advice, which was the last thing she wanted to hear at this sensitive stage of her political career. Regarding herself as a member of the intelligentsia, a friend of Voltaire and madame de Geoffrin, Pompadour was happy to ignore the publication of serious literary and scientific works that challenged received wisdom, but not scurrilous attacks on herself and the king. Encouraged by Jean Bertin II, madame de Pompadour now ensured that the marquis de Fratteaux would be dealt with mercilessly and expeditiously. The *affaire Fratteaux* was now an *affaire d'état*.

The immediate problem, however, given that England had no extradition treaty with France, was how to attract the marquis de Fratteaux back to his homeland. It was eventually decided to kidnap him. In anticipation of a successful outcome to this risky venture, Bertin père had been given a *lettre de cachet* on 25 March 1752 that could be used to arrest his son as soon as he set foot on French soil. After one abortive attempt, Louis-Mathieu was finally arrested in London on Friday, 7 April, as a debtor. In true cloak and dagger fashion, Louis-Mathieu was bundled into a carriage and driven to the banks of the Thames. His captors then transferred him to a boat moored under London Bridge. From this historic landmark, he was transported to Gravesend, where he was obliged to wait for another boat that took him across the Channel to Calais, finally arriving in France on Easter Sunday.

There to greet him, armed with their *lettre de cachet*, was a fifty-strong detachment of mounted police. The marquis was shackled in irons, transported to Paris, and incarcerated during the night of 11 April in the Bastille. He was only forty-five years of age, but he would never see the Périgueux, or any other town, again: 'The doors closed on him like the gravestone of a tomb.'[36]

* * *

On 4 August 1754, Louis-Mathieu's father died in his impressive Parisian *hôtel* on the banks of the Seine, which was only a short walk from the Bastille. Whether or not he died a contented man we shall never know, but he had lived long enough to see his favourite son, Henri Léonard, installed as intendant of Roussillon through the patronage of a king's ex-mistress. In 1759, that son would hold the prestigious ministerial post in Louis XV's government of *contrôleur général*, again an honour conferred upon him through the good offices of madame de Pompadour. As for Jean Bertin's eldest son, Louis-Mathieu, there was now the prospect, at least, of an early release from the Bastille. We learn from the governor's reports that, just three days after his father's death, Louis-Mathieu set fire to the bedclothes and furniture in his cell. Fearing the consequences, he had begged his guard to intercede on his behalf with the governor, explaining that 'he was a most unfortunate and miserable human being who has more right to justice than anyone this century' and that he now 'wished to place his fate in the Lord's hands'.[37]

One thing was certain – the Lord's self-appointed dispenser of justice on earth, Voltaire, would not take up his case. Voltaire, like Henri Bertin, was also a suitor for the patronage of madame de Pompadour at this time. In 1749, he had left France to accept, for personal and political reasons, the position of Chamberlain and 'poet-in-residence' in Potsdam. By the spring of 1753, his hopes of converting Frederick the Great into his version of a 'philosopher-king' had faded and he was desperate to return. He knew that most ministers would not welcome him back, but he decided to put his faith in Pompadour's hands. In January 1754, Voltaire's eldest niece and sometime mistress, madame Denis, informed him that she had seen madame de Pompadour who told her that Louis XV was not in favour of the great man's return from exile. Voltaire replied that this news was 'an overpowering thunderbolt [that] 'has upset all my plans and hopes'.[38] The king's reaction serves as a reminder that Louis XV was far from being a pawn in the delicate hands of madame de Pompadour. Her first concern would always be to get Louis 'on-side'; after all, her position would have been perilous without his support. One could say very much the same about the relationship between Henri Bertin and Louis. Indeed, as we shall see in the following two chapters, Louis XV, Pompadour and Henri Bertin were in the process of creating a royal 'triumvirate' that would last almost until Pompadour's death in 1764.

Voltaire's disappointment, however, could hardly be compared with that experienced by the distraught marquis de Fratteaux. It could not have been many months before he realised that his case was far too explosive for madame de Pompadour and his brother, Henri, to countenance his release. On 17 September, Louis-Mathieu managed to escape from his cell and reach one of the inner courtyards, after a cleaner had forgotten to lock his cell door. The marquis was quickly recaptured and transferred to one of the most dismal cells in the Bastille. Situated beneath the roof of the ironically named *Tour de la liberté*, it had no fireplace, and very little light succeeded in filtering its way in from the gloomy corridors outside. On 8 November 1755, the prison records inform us that the marquis had asked for paper and ink, as well as a few books, so that he could embark on a literary project. His request, the last we find in the prison records, was granted and he was moved to a new cell. He was given copies of works by Corneille and Molière, as well as 'improving' religious publications'.[39]

There is a reference to 'Bertin de Frateaux' (*sic*) in *La Bastille dévoilée*, a work, published in 1789, which sought to discredit the illegal practices of *ancien régime* 'despotism'. The reference is brief, but reveals how Louis-Mathieu, incarcerated by the request of his family, had always been very closely guarded.[40] What this work does not record is the extraordinary fact that, after 1761, those ultimately responsible for his fate were to be none other than his own sister and brother-in-law! His sister, Anne, had married Antoine-Joseph Chapelle de Jumilhac, seigneur of Jumilhac and Cubjac. This was the same Jumilhac family that had been swindled, as they saw it, by Bertin *père* who had partly purchased his Bourdeille estate from them with John Law's worthless paper currency. However, in an eighteenth-century, French version of *Romeo and Juliet*, it appears that Antoine and Anne had fallen in love and married, despite the apparent misgivings of their respective families, although one suspects that Bertin *père*, who was hardly the man to sacrifice family interests to star-struck lovers, may have been using the marriage of his daughter to end the Jumilhac–Bertin feud. The relevant point for us is that Antoine-Joseph was appointed as deputy governor of the Bastille on 1 January 1758, and promoted to governor of the infamous prison on 27 May 1761. These events had little or nothing to do with coincidence: Henri Léonard Bertin had been appointed *lieutenant général de police de Paris* in 1757, an important post that included jurisdiction over the Bastille. From this time forward, Louis-Mathieu's fate was sealed. He would be left to rot in his Bastille cell until the day his corpse was carried out on 3 March 1779.

Louis-Mathieu Bertin, marquis de Fratteaux, was buried in the cemetery of Saint-Paul, a parish that was situated in the shadows of the Bastille. An autopsy, undertaken by Louis XV's own doctor, was carried out according to the wishes of his family. It revealed that the base accusation made by Louis-Mathieu's father concerning the alleged illegitimacy of his wayward son was totally unfounded. The body carried, on Louis-Mathieu's right side above his hip, the distinctive birthmark of the Bertin family.[41] The introductory verse of Louis-Mathieu's *Histoire de M. Bertin* had been chosen from the book of Jeremiah, chapter eleven, verse nine: 'They held counsel together and they said, "Tear him away

from the land of the living, so that his name shall be forgotten".'
'They', the triumvirate Louis XV, madame de Pompadour, and
Henri Bertin, were, in large measure, successful.

*   *   *

With his family skeleton safely locked away in the Bastille, Louis-
Mathieu's brother had been able to pursue a political career that
would fulfil his father's wildest dreams. Henri's rapid promotion
during the 1750s, from *maître des requêtes to contrôleur des finances*,
would be facilitated by the complicated machinery of patronage
and favouritism that characterised the court of Louis XV, especially during the reign of madame de Pompadour. From 1750 to
the death of Louis XV in 1774, advancement at court would
depend, more than ever, on whom one knew rather than what one
knew. It was best to know the way to Pompadour's apartment,
situated immediately above the king's after 1748, as she gradually
tightened her rather tenuous grip on power. A visit to the private
offices of very influential ministers, such as the duc de Richelieu,
could also prove advantageous. However, the frequently
contested and criticised transfer of authority from Louis XV to his
more iconic mistresses, madame de Pompadour in particular,
unquestionably weakened public confidence in Bourbon absolutism. Counter-balancing this decline in the personal authority
of the monarch, we find the parallel, and related, rise of the
modern, administrative, bureaucratic state. Henri Bertin would
make a significant contribution to this modernising process. The
accolade accorded to him by Michel Antoine, one of the most
respected historians of this period of French history, that Henri
Bertin was 'one of the great administrators' of the eighteenth
century, was well deserved.[42]

Bertin's credit at Versailles was immeasurably strengthened
through his friendship with Philibert Orry. Orry was an
important patron of the Bertin family: his own career had
provided the template for Henri Bertin to follow – *maître des
requêtes*, intendant of Roussillon, and *contrôleur général des*

finances. In 1744, Bertin *père* had relinquished control of offices he had purchased twenty years earlier, for which he had paid the princely sum of 70,000 *livres*. Following the customary practice of treating offices of state, including that of *maître des requêtes*, as family heirlooms, Bertin *père* persuaded Orry to transfer them to his son. By 1784, around 80 offices of *maître des requêtes* would be attached to the judicial and administrative apparatus of the state. These offices not only provided successful applicants with the status of robe nobility, which, thanks to his father, Bertin did not covet, but also the necessary experience if one wished to become an intendant, a consummation devoutly to be wished by many *maîtres des requêtes*.[43] Bertin was no exception to the rule, and, in November 1750, his hopes were realised with his promotion to the intendancy of Roussillon. Roussillon was, geographically, about as far away from Versailles as one could get, but, in terms of career advancement, Bertin had now joined that exclusive club of provincial *intendants* from whom so many ministers of the crown were chosen. It cannot be said that Bertin's experience as the king's representative in Roussillon, responsible, inter alia, for the implementation and management of a wide range of affairs, from the maintenance of public order and public roads to the provision of essential food supplies, was an unqualified success. Roussillon was a difficult province to administer; its native language and culture, its distance from Paris, fostered a spirit of independence and, occasionally, outright rebellion, that was almost Breton in character. On New Year's Day 1750, the imposition of a new tax (the *vingtième*) by a reforming *contrôleur général*, Machault d'Arnouville, provided the opportunity for provincial, predominantly noble, landlords to flex their muscles. Bertin, faced with a serious rebellion against state authority, was told by Machault to stamp the authority of central government on the rebels.

Bertin was learning his trade: the opposition of provincial and privileged groups to central government will become a central theme of this study – it would be a cross that Bertin would have to carry throughout his reforming career. Provincial governors and presidents of the twelve provincial parlements of the realm had their own local axes to grind, their own patrons at court. Herein lay one of the most important structural faults of the Bourbon system of *ancien régime* government. The example of 'the Roussillon rebellion', which dragged on for several years, provides us with a case in point. According to Bertin, the provincial governor of Roussillon, Mailly d'Harcourt, was actually encouraging resistance to the government's new tax proposals. The marquis d'Argenson suggests that Mailly, a proud man 'with unreasonable ambitions', was receiving advice and encouragement from his own nephew, Renè de Voyer d'Argenson, related to Mailly by marriage. In Bertin's corner, we find the influential court favourite maréchal de Noailles. Thus, the resolution of an administrative problem regarding the relationship between provincial and central government was being undermined at Versailles by a family dispute between court favourites. The conflict between the governor and the *intendant* of Roussillon was only resolved in March 1754 when an unsatisfactory, but not untypical, compromise was reached – both Mailly d'Harcourt and Henri Bertin were removed from office. However, Bertin would go on to compete for the glittering prizes at Versailles, whilst d'Harcourt's ambitions were never to be fulfilled. At Versailles, the influence of aristocratic individuals and cabals was being challenged, and leading that challenge, at times, was madame de Pompadour, who had moved on from the position of the king's mistress to become Louis XV's 'lady in the front office', and, for a while, his enforcer. Pompadour was now occupying the precarious 'no man's land' between royal ministers and a king, who, since the death of Cardinal Fleury in 1743, had chosen to be his own 'first minister'. In the notoriously unpredictable hands of Louis XV, politics would become increasingly impenetrable, essentially a matter of 'smoke and Versailles mirrors'.

Given the above, it would never be easy for Pompadour to wield a heavy stick: she would be obliged to flatter, rather than flatten, her many enemies. She needed the king's support to humiliate *les Grands*, such as the d'Argensons, whose bloodline may not have been unassailable, but who exhibited a Saint-Simonian detestation for the distinctly bourgeois origins of madame de Pompadour. The marquis d'Argenson thought that the maréchal de Noailles, a genuine 'Grand', had only sided with Bertin over the Roussillon affair because he wanted to undermine the influence of his brother at court, the royal minister, comte d'Argenson. Whether this was true or not, the key figure in determining the future careers of Harcourt and Bertin was undoubtedly Pompadour, who nursed a particular, and understandable, grievance against the d'Argenson clan. One only has to skim through the marquis d'Argenson's *Journal* to realise how much effort the author employed to undermine her position at court. It was, in fact, Pompadour who had instructed the maréchal de Noailles to sack d'Harcourt for undermining the king's authority in Roussillon. Touching up the portrait of Louis XV as an absolute monarch was one of Pompadour's principal tasks. D'Harcourt would have to be humiliated by being demoted to the position of *lieutenant-général* of Roussillon, whilst Henri Bertin, a devoted servant of the king, would receive further proof of Pompadour's patronage by being promoted to the intendancy of the Lyonnais, which included, of course, France's second city, Lyon. The marquis d'Argenson recorded, bitterly, in his *Journal* that 'the promotion of this magistrate [a dig at Bertin's *robe noble* status] would increase the mortification of our family'.[44]

The royal decree that installed Henri Bertin as a provincial *intendant* reveals the extensive power these royal officials wielded: his brief covered 'justice, police, and finances in the province of the Lyonnais'. In addition, Bertin was asked to pay particular attention to 'le bien du commerce', quite understandable given Lyon's reputation as a global textile centre. The Bertins had always evinced a profound interest in trade and industry, whether in textiles or iron production, and Henri's tireless efforts to promote the development of the Lyonnais region, facilitated as they were by the general expansion of the French economy, would hold him in good stead when his name was eventually touted at Versailles in 1759 for the enviable, if onerous, position of *contrôleur général des finances*.

By the mid-eighteenth century, the city of Lyon was being administered by representatives of the king, in the persons of the *gouverneur*, the duc de Villeroy and the *intendant*, Bertin. The Catholic Church, represented by the cardinal-archbishop, Pierre Guérin de Tencin, supported by the *chanoines-comtes de Saint-Jean*, was a power to be reckoned with, as were the *échevins* (municipal councillors), ensconced in the *hôtel de ville*, a power group that provided a voice for the rich, largely Protestant, financial and manufacturing elite of the city. Divided, as Lyon was, in matters of religion, politics, and commerce, an *intendant* had to tread very warily indeed, but Bertin was now an experienced practitioner of this administrative art. For example, he was keen, from the beginning, to show his support for the governor, the duc de Villeroy, who was a member of an influential aristocratic family. When dealing with the influential representatives of the Catholic Church in the Lyonnais, Bertin could draw upon his family's traditional attachment to the Roman faith, which explains why he appears to have had few major disagreements with either the cardinal-archbishop or with the aristocratic *chanoine-comtes de Saint-Jean*, important conduits between the mass of the Catholic population and the city authorities. As for the Protestant elite that dominated the *fabrique de Lyon* (the organisation that controlled the Lyonnais textile industry), we saw earlier how important industry and trade had been in the rise of the Bertin family. Henri Bertin, courting the assistance of the *Fabrique*, would work hard to improve communications between the Lyonnais and surrounding regions, especially those of Languedoc and the Bordelais, gateways for textiles and wines to the wider trading world. He would be assisted in this task by two important pioneers of French economic development: the first, Daniel Charles Trudaine, one of France's truly great servants of the French state; the second, Nicolas de Ville, a pioneering head of public works in Lyon.

Trudaine, who had taken charge of the famous *département des ponts et chaussées* in1743, had mapped out plans for two *grandes routes* from Lyon, the first to Montpellier in Languedoc, the second to Bordeaux in Acquitaine. Bertin was from Périgueux, which was situated on the main road from Lyon to Bordeaux, and he was naturally anxious to put his hometown on the map. Although his stay in Lyon would be far too brief to witness the completion of major works programmes, he did encourage the construction of a new road from the Beaujolais that served the expanding textile town of Thizy, as well as providing encouragement and support for Trudaine's more ambitious plans. Bertin also developed a close friendship with Nicolas de Ville, evidence of whose contribution to the architecture of Lyon is still visible today. The two men embarked upon the major project of safeguarding the city from the periodic flooding of many districts on the left bank of the river Rhône (Lyon is situated on the confluence of the Rhône and the Saône) by stabilising its course as it enters the city from the north-east. Before he left in November 1757 to assume the position of *lieutenant général de la police de Paris*, excavations of the bed of the Rhône had ensured that the river would follow (in the main) its original course.[45]

Bertin's brief career in the Lyonnais was undoubtedly successful, but what he lacked, in his opinion, was a wife. It was not, apparently, that he did not want to marry: marrying into a prestigious family would undoubtedly advance his career prospects, hence his advances to a mademoiselle de Gendre, related to the d'Argensons *and* the Noailles. Unfortunately, the young lady in question, or her parents, did not consider Bertin to be a sufficiently attractive suitor. Her subsequent marriage to the handsome, twenty-four-year-old comte de Cheverney (Bertin was in his mid-thirties at this time) appears to have left a permanent scar on Bertin's psyche. He seems to have been completely disillusioned by the entire affair, devoting the rest of his life to his career, his scholarly pursuits, and the interests of the Bertin family.

But these personal affairs do not explain why Bertin's reasonably successful work in the Lyonnais was halted after just a few years, nor why he should have then been promoted to the quasi-ministerial post of *lieutenant général de police de Paris* (he was not admitted to the powerful king's inner council until 1762). The following two chapters will address these questions by providing, in the first place, an assessment of Louis XV's performance as an absolute monarch, in particular, the impact of his private life and his relationship with madame de Pompadour upon the governance of France; and, in the second, an account of Bertin's appointment as *lieutenant général de police de Paris* that would complete the membership of the royal triumvirate, composed of Louis, Pompadour, and Bertin. The work of this triumvirate will provide us with a new angle of vision on the changing face of Bourbon absolutism as France entered the historic, and fateful, conflict of the Seven Years' War (1756–63).

Notes

1 By far the most scholarly and comprehensive account of Henri Bertin's career and family history was published by Georges Bussière in a series of studies (*c*.180,000 words) that were published in the *Bulletin de la Société Historique et Archaéologique du Périgord* (hereafter *BSHAP*) between 1905 and 1909. I am indebted to Mme Sophie Bridoux-Pradeau, secretary of the above society, for providing me with a detailed list of references relating to Henri Bertin and his family.

2 Joelle Chevé, *La noblesse du Périgord* (Paris, 1998), pp.14–15.

3 Robin Briggs, *Early Modern France, 1560–1715* (Oxford, 1998), pp.55–6; Bussière, *'Etude sur Henri Bertin'*, *BSHAP*, vol.32, pp.221–33.

4 Bussière, *'Etude sur Henri Bertin'*, *BSHAP*, vol.32 (1905), pp.237–9.

5 Bussière, *'Etude sur Henri Bertin'*, *BSHAP*, vol.32 (1905), pp. 243–4.

6 From 1667, the *livre* (occasionally referred to as the 'franc') became the national currency of France. By 1726, the English pound was worth *c*.24 *livres*. By the 1760s, a Parisian journeyman printer might earn 13 *livres* for a week's work, which meant that he would have received an annual salary of around 680 *livres* (if he worked every week). It has been estimated that, by the end of the century, a working man had to earn *c*.435 *livres* a year to maintain a family of four at subsistence level. The usual price of the daily bread ration was nine sous (there were 20 sous to the *livre*).

7 Briggs, *Early Modern France, 1560–1715*, p.202.

8 Bussière, *'Etude sur Henri Bertin'*, *BSHAP*, vol.32 (1905), pp.406–9.

9 Gwynne Lewis, *France 1715–1804: Power and the People* (London, 2004), pp.26–33.

10 *Archives départementales de la Dordogne*, 2E 130/7. The series 2E (especially folders 1–17) provide important information on the Bertin family from the sixteenth century to the Revolution of 1789.

11 The property in question was a noble hunting lodge, the *château des Ombres* in the Angoumois, which Bertin bought on 17 February 1742 for 18,000 *livres*. See M. H. de Montégut, *Histoire d'un vieux logis en Angoumois: le château des Ombres* (Paris, 1922), pp.32–3.

12 Bussière, 'Etude sur Henri Bertin', *BSHAP*, vol.33 (1906), pp.74–83.

13 In this chapter, we shall be using the French translation, now in the *Bibliothèque Nationale: Histoire de M. Bertin, marquis de Fratteaux avec des éclaircissements sur son enlèvement de Londres et les noms de ceux qui y ont participé, par le comte d'H**** (Paris, 1756).

14 Bussière, '*Etude sur Henri Bertin*', *BSHAP*, vol.33 (1906), p.74; André Bourde, *Le comte de H****, *Histoire de M. Bertin, marquis de Fratteaux* (*Imprimerie nationale*, 1994), pp.11–13.

15 *Bourde, Le comte de H****, p.3.

16 Bussière, '*Etude sur Henri Bertin*', *BSHAP*, vol.33 (1906), pp.79–83.

17 Bussière, '*Etude sur Henri Bertin*', *BSHAP*, vol.33 (1906), pp.83-6.

18 *Histoire de M. Bertin*, p.40.

19 Margaret Darrow, *Revolution in the House: Family, Class, and Inheritance in Southern France, 1775–1825* (Princeton, 1989), p.63; Chevé, *La noblesse du Périgord*, p.30.

20 *Histoire de M. Bertin*, pp.30–3.

21 *Histoire de M. Bertin*, pp.3–13.

22 Colin Jones, *The Great Nation: France from Louis XV to Napoleon* (London, 2002), p.332.

23 *Histoire de M. Bertin*, pp.30–3.

24 Bourde, *Le comte de H****, pp.10–29.

25 *Histoire de M. Bertin*, pp.48–9.

26 Chevé, *La noblesse du Périgord*, p.130. Bussière thought that the petition was important enough to be reproduced in its entirety, '*Etude sur Henri Bertin*', *BSHAP*, vol.33 (1906), pp.90–4.

27 Bourde, *Le comte de H****, pp.30–1.

28 *Histoire de M. Bertin*, pp.38–45.

29 Peter Ackroyd, *London: the Biography* (London, 2000), pp.532–3.

30 Bourde, *Le comte de H****, pp.55–7.

31 Roy Porter, *Enlightenment: Britain and the Creation of the Modern World* (London, 2000), p.73; Robert Darnton, *The Business of the Enlightenment, 1775–1800: A Publishing History of the Encyclopédie* (Cambridge, 1979), pp.9–11.

32 Bussière, *'Etude sur Henri Bertin'*, *BSHAP*, vol.33 (1906), pp.96–9.

33 André Picciola, *Le comte de Maurepas: Versailles et l'Europe à la fin de l'ancien régime* (Paris, 1999), pp.357–72.

34 Darnton, *The Business of the Enlightenment*, pp.18–19

35 Yves Combeau, *Le comte Pierre-Marc d'Argenson, Ministre de Louis XV* (Paris, 1999), pp.353–4.

36 Bussière, *'Etude sur Henri Bertin'*, *BSHAP*, vol.33 (1906), pp.101–3.

37 Bussière, *'Etude sur Henri Bertin'*, *BSHAP*, vol.33 (1906), pp105–10.

38 Ian Davidson, *Voltaire in Exile* (London, 2004), pp. 9–13.

39 Bussière, *'Etude sur Henri Bertin'*, *BSHAP*, vol.33 (1906), pp.105–10.

40 *La Bastille dévoilé*, 3 vols (Paris, 1789), ii, p.68.

41 Chevé, *La noblesse du Périgord*, p.132.

42 Michel Antoine, *Louis XV* (Paris, 1989), p.456. For an excellent résumé of the administrative system under Louis XV, see pp. 189–202.

43 John Lough, *An Introduction to Eighteenth Century France* (London, 1960), pp.116–17.

44 Marquis d'Argenson, *Journal et mémoires du marquis d'Argenson* (Paris, Renouard, 1866), vol.8, p.6, 8 May 1753.

45 Bussière, *'Etude sur Henri Bertin'*, *BSHAP*, vol.33 (1906), pp.242–327.

Chapter Two

Louis XV and Madame de Pompadour

In his sympathetic biography, Jean-François Chiappe concedes that Louis XV was 'full of contradictions ... an eminent strategist, exhibiting a steely courage in battle, yet afraid of catching a cold', someone 'who could be both aloof and familiar, an egoist who could also be generous, often affable, but always obsessed by his religious obligations, in short, everything and its opposite – a base-hearted king according to Saint-Beuve, a dazzling prince according to Pierre Gaxotte and Michel Antoine'.[1] Jonathan Dull, in his masterly, detailed study *The French Navy and the Seven Years' War*, argues that 'Louis XV's role in the war ultimately was heroic', yet, pursuing the antithetical approach of so many other historians, has to concede a few pages later that 'Lacking someone like Louis XIV with the strong self-confidence to impose his authority, the unity of the French government collapsed.'[2] The marquis d'Argenson, an enemy of madame de Pompadour, was far more dismissive in his assessment of Louis, describing him as a king who was 'loved by his people, although he had done nothing for them'. An exaggerated opinion, as one would expect from this avenging court commentator, but one that contained several grains of truth.[3]

The stress of a global war, and the evolution of a more democratic and constitutional age, would impose strains upon the system of mid-eighteenth-century Bourbon absolutism that would have stretched Louis XIV's resources to their limit.

Whether they praise or damn him, most of Louis' contemporary chroniclers agree that the fundamental explanation for Louis XV's troubled personality lay in the circumstances of his childhood. Born on 15 February 1710, the son of Louis de Bourgogne and Marie-Adélaide de Savoie, he was only five years old when, with the death of his all too famous great-grandfather, Louis XIV, the weight of the French crown was placed upon his head. To be expected to imitate the martial actions of Louis XIV was difficult enough, but to have one's adolescence shaped during the licentious period of the duc d'Oréans' Regency (1715–23) did nothing to simplify the problem. It was fortunate in this regard that the royal court was transported from the Regent's Tuileries Palace to the château de Vincennes south of Paris during the period 1715 to 1722. The young king and his entourage would finally decide to return to Louis XIV's Versailles in June 1722, to the great disappointment of the majority of Parisians. In December of the following year, the duc d'Orléans died of a stroke, a consequence of working hard, and playing too hard.

The young Louis XV was well acquainted with death, a fact that would trouble him for the rest of his life. His parents, the duc and duchesse de Bourgogne, had both died of measles, or the dreaded smallpox, during the macabre 'dance of death' that blighted Versailles between April 1711 and March 1712. On 14 April 1711, Louis XIV had lost his son, then, on 12 and 18 February 1812, both his grandson and granddaughter, Louis XV's parents. On 8 March, the body of one of Louis XIV's great-grandsons, the duc de Bretagne, was laid in the royal tomb. All had been bled in an attempt to save their lives, as was the prevailing custom. The young Louis XV's life was probably saved by the determined action of his governess, the duchesse de Ventadour, who refused to allow the court surgeons anywhere near her royal charge. Since Louis XV was just two years of age at the time the tragedy struck his family, the impact of so many deaths was obviously limited, but, over time, the loss of both his parents must have left its mark. It meant, for example, that he was raised by a succession of governors and governesses, some of whom appear to have done their best to transform a troubled child into a psychologically disturbed monarch. The duchesse de Ventadour was the exception who tried to provide a sensitive substitute for Louis' mother during his early years. She appears to have been a woman of some common sense and maternal instinct, and was certainly loved by the young king (he was crowned in 1715) who referred to her as 'Maman'. Michel Antoine thought that Ventadour represented 'his secret garden in a desert without love'.[4] However, it was the custom for governesses to relinquish their duties when their royal charges had reached the age of seven, old enough for a king-in-waiting to be released from a woman's apron strings and transformed into 'a man'. Unwisely, perhaps, the responsibility for effecting this regal transformation was given to the seventy-three-year-old maréchal de Villeroy who expended far too much of his waning energy trying to make the young Louis XV look, and act, like a young Louis XIV. It was de Villeroy who instilled into the impressionable youngster his life-long passion for gaming and hunting.[5]

Over the long term, André Hercule Fleury, bishop of Fréjus, would prove to be the most influential of all Louis XV's tutors, guiding his life from a teenager to a mature adult. Fleury, who was sixty-three on his appointment as Louis' tutor in 1716, would receive his just reward by being raised from the status of a bishop to that of a cardinal and de facto first minister of France. He would dominate the personal life of the king and the political life of France from the 1720s almost until his death in January 1743. On the personal front, he became the father Louis had never known, drumming into the king's consciousness a knowledge of the classics and Christian morality, the central message being that a king whose life did not conform to the ideal of a most Christian monarch would never receive God's blessing. Louis would learn this message by heart, but would never be capable of practising the morality that underpinned it, an example of the double standards that would govern his entire life. Fleury certainly took his duties seriously, but the young Louis was 'lazy, rude, selfish, gluttonous, almost incapable of love and excessively shy'. His reserve when it came to declarations of love is particularly interesting, given his attitude towards sex and love in adult life. Louis would become a master of dissimulation, concealing his private vices behind the mask of a Christian, public monarch.[6]

*   *   *

One of the most influential, if imprudent, chroniclers of our period, Mouffle d'Angerville, provides an intimate and revealing portrait of Louis XV as he entered his adult life. Described as handsome and of above average height, he had 'perfectly formed legs, a noble demeanour, big eyes, with a look that was gentle rather than proud'. His personality was said to be taciturn and withdrawn, indifferent to 'the charms of the fair sex', and exhibiting 'a deep-rooted distaste for public affairs', hardly the most impressive *curriculum vitae* for an absolute monarch.[7] Louis had obviously, and perhaps not surprisingly, developed an aversion to speaking in public from the age of ten. In February 1720, persuaded to attend a meeting of the *Conseil de Régence*, 'he maintained his silence throughout, playing with a kitten'.[8] However, although the kittens would disappear, the '*Silence du roi*' would become a permanent feature of Louis' method of governing, 'unless he was surrounded by his close friends'. Something of a convention among monarchs, court sycophants would interpret the *Silence du roi* as evidence of Louis' capacity for profound thought rather than as proof of any psychological flaw in his character.[9]

From the sudden death of the duc d'Orléans in December 1723 to Louis' bold, if premature, announcement on 16 July 1726 that he would assume the full responsibilities of government, France had the misfortune to be ruled by Louis' cousin, the ambitious duc de Bourbon, and his marginally more gifted young mistress, madame de Prie. The couple did nothing to correct the damage inflicted by Louis' early apprenticeship in the arts and crafts of becoming a king; indeed the period in their care was harmful for

Louis XV, encouraged as he was to indulge himself in hunting, gambling and over-eating, pursuits that did something, at least, to alleviate his increasing morbidity and profound sense of boredom. Meanwhile, the duc de Bourbon and his mistress were making a fortune out of the inventive, over-optimistic policies of the government's finance minister, John Law. One event during these barren years provided the prospect of a cure for Louis XV's psychological problems – his marriage to the daughter of the deposed king of Poland, Marie Leszczynska. A previous, somewhat hare-brained, scheme to marry Louis off for dynastic reasons to the five-year-old daughter of the king of Spain was clumsily aborted, an act that provoked considerable anger at the Spanish court. It is hard to believe, though not untypical of the tactless manner in which these great affairs of state were being conducted during this period, that the duc de Bourbon, with the encouragement of his mistress, had seriously considered marrying Marie Leszczynska himself. He had not been blessed with children, and it was thought that Marie would provide his branch of the Bourbon family with a son and heir. It was not beyond the realms of possibility that Louis, like so many of his relatives, might still succumb to smallpox. It is said that when the incredible news eventually reached Stanislas Leszczynska that his daughter was being asked to marry Louis XV, not the duc de Bourbon, he fainted. Courtiers at Versailles, and the public at large, were equally shocked; their reactions, however, were prompted by disbelief and dismay rather than joy.[10]

The arranged marriage between the fifteen-year-old Louis XV and the twenty-two-year-old Marie Leszczynska was held in Strasbourg cathedral on 15 August 1725; it was followed, three weeks later, by a glittering celebration in the château of Fontainbleau. Early indications suggested that the cynics who considered the union to be simply a *marriage de convenance* would be proved wrong; indeed, the young Louis appeared to be infatuated with his plain, pious wife, and Marie was no less enamoured of her handsome prince. The apparently successful marriage appears to have emboldened the king and strengthened the hand of the duc de Bourbon's enemies, and, on 11 June 1726, the duc, accused of failing to deal with the inflationary and social consequences of the Law affair, was dismissed. Five days later, Louis XV announced in the *conseil d'en haut* (Council of State, referred to as the *conseil d'état* during Louis XV's reign) that he was dismissing his ministers, and that he would govern in the future without a first minister. A new and very problematic page in the history of Bourbon absolutism had been turned: a timid prince had apparently been transformed into a king, created in the mould of Louis XIV. Although Louis did, in theory, assume control of the government, behind the scenes two very influential figures were really pulling the strings of power – Louis' trusted tutor, cardinal Fleury, and Joseph Pâris-Duverney, one of the wealthy Pâris brothers, financiers by appointment to the king. The emergence of Fleury as a major player in the government was illustrated by his promotion to the status of a cardinal, whilst the decree of 15 June 1726, reversing the inflationary policies of John Law, was masterminded by Pâris-Duverney. Bourbon absolutism during the reign of Louis XV may have been founded on the alliance of 'Church and State', but, for long periods, it was financed by the Pâris brothers.[11]

Throughout his reign, Louis XV would always prefer to follow than to lead, not a trait that inspired confidence in a supposed absolute monarch. Louis had always respected, even revered, Fleury who now began his lengthy tenure of power as tutor to the nation, as well as to its king. His first moves were to review the operation of political and economic affairs. On the whole, Fleury chose the king's ministers wisely, as the return to office of one of the great chancellors of Louis XV's long reign, Henri François d'Auguesseau and the appointment of one of its most successful *contrôleur généraux*, Philibert Orry, indicate. Fleury and Orry understood that France was entering a 'golden age' of economic growth, sustained by the uneven development of a modern bureaucracy and the expansion of banking facilities and transport, as well as by the growth of world trade. Fleury ensured that the power of royal mistresses would be restricted to the boudoir, despite the persistent attempts of court favourites to undermine his authority. These efforts were facilitated by Louis' lengthy infatuation with Marie Leszczynska, thus enabling the happy couple to fulfil their marriage vows as decreed by the Catholic Church. This was a new beginning, the 'opportunity of a new life, one that provided him with an erotic antidote to the morbidity that obsessed him'.[12]

It certainly worked in the short term. Marie and Louis produced no fewer than six children during the first seven years of their marriage: twin girls on 4 August 1727, followed by another girl just over a year later. Then, on 4 September 1729, the court was finally able to celebrate the birth of a male child, the Dauphin. Over the next eight years, six more royal offspring would be produced, another boy (the duc d'Anjou) and five more girls. However, by the time the last girl ('Madame le Dernier'!) had been born in 1737, sexual relations between Louis and Marie had apparently ceased. It was rumoured that the queen, now well into her thirties, had resisted the advances of her husband, prompting Louis, still in his twenties, to declare that he would never again suffer such a gross insult to his royal prerogative. Apocryphal or not, the fundamental personality differences between the prim and pious Marie and the increasingly licentious Louis XV slowly but surely drove the couple apart. Marie was described by d'Angerville as 'more of a mother than a wife, and never a lover'. But could this common critique of a wife who fails to transform herself into a passionate mistress in her spare time have been based, not on Marie's 'frigidity', but on her many pregnancies and miscarriages? She is famously said to have declared: 'What a life! Always getting bedded, always getting pregnant, always giving birth.'[13] As the early promise of a happy royal marriage faded, the queen would seek solace in her strong Catholic faith. By the late 1740s, Marie, the Dauphin, aristocratic friends and Jesuit confessors would form the nucleus of the *dévot* party whose exaggerated piety and weakness for *memento mori* (a few ladies-in-waiting would worship in front of lamps framed by human skulls) did little to alleviate Louis XV's morbidity. Louis harboured a positively Faustian fear of death, which was hardly surprising given his increasing tendency to trade in salvation for 'the sins of the flesh', as his Jesuit confessors never failed to remind him. An alternative explanation for Marie's rejection of her husband's sexual advances was her fear of contracting a venereal disease, now that Louis had embarked upon his rather desperate quest for sexual satisfaction that would last almost until his death. The quest can be described as 'desperate' because Louis, a disciple of cardinal Fleury after all, was a deeply religious man, a king who observed the rituals of the Catholic faith. We also have to remember that Louis was living through a period of prolonged and bitter religious conflict between the pro- and anti-papal wings of the French Catholic Church, the Jesuits and the Jansenists, with the former dominating the aisles of Versailles.

* * *

Any discussion of Louis XV's sex life demands a healthy dose of caution and common sense. It was, after all, a career that launched a thousand libellous publications, many of which included accounts of sexual prowess that would have overshadowed those of Casanova, Louis' contemporary: for example, the duc de Castries assures us that Louis made love to his bride no fewer than seven times on their wedding night.[14] Maurice Lever's recent work suggests that Louis XV might have had homosexual tendencies, adding that past historians have preferred to gloss this over for obvious ideological reasons. The sickening fate of Benjamin Deschauffours, who, accused of sodomy and child abduction, was burned alive in the place de Grève on 24 May 1724, may have been used by the court to frighten Louis away from his supposed natural tendencies.[15] It is not within our brief to speculate further on this possibility, although it is necessary to provide a short résumé of Louis' private life so that we might assess its impact upon the management of domestic and foreign policy from the mid-1740s to the mid-1760s, a period that witnessed not only the rise of madame de Pompadour and her protégé, Henri Bertin, but, of greater significance, the decline of France as a world power. What was the popular reaction during the War of the Austrian Succession (1740–48) to Louis' sexual relationships with 'official' mistresses, which included four daughters of the same aristocratic family, as well as madame de Pompadour? What was the cost, in terms of good government and the prestige of the French monarchy, of Louis' subsequent descent into prolonged periods of debauchery, including his patronage of the infamous royal brothel, the 'Deer Park' (*Parc aux cerfs*), during the following decade? And how, and with what consequences, was the success of Henri Bertin's career linked to Louis and Pompadour in a 'royal triumvirate' that made it easier for Louis XV to preside over secret foreign policy initiatives and to satisfy his sexual desires, while Pompadour satisfied her desire for political power and patronage at the highest level?

Louis XV's long career as an adulterer had begun well before Marie Leszczynska had dismissed her husband from the royal bed. He had probably enjoyed several inconsequential affairs between 1732 and 1737, including those with mademoiselle de Charolais and the all too willing young ladies who surrounded her. These were still the days when having aristocratic parents constituted a sure passport to the king's private apartments. Mademoiselle de Charolais, a capricious, witty and spirited character by all accounts, was of unimpeachable aristocratic stock, one of Louis' many cousins no less. She had attracted a string of lovers to her name, and at least one contemporary observer of court life thought that Louis had enjoyed a brief liaison with her.[16] Whatever the truth of this assertion, the coveted position of official mistress to the king was eventually won by the thirty-year-old daughter of a very prestigious aristocratic family, Louise Julie de Nesle, the oldest of the famous, many would have said infamous, five Nesle daughters, four of whom would find their way into the king's bed. Interestingly enough, cardinal Fleury seems to have condoned Louis XV's conduct: there was, after all, nothing unusual about a king having mistresses, while the right mistress might even strengthen Fleury's position at court. Madame de Pompadour would bear this in mind when she was creating a political role for herself during the 1750s. We are dealing here with developments that would affect the governance of France from the time of madame de Pompadour to that of madame du Barry in the early 1770s; we are dealing with the delegation of power by a supposedly 'absolute' monarch. Julian Swann, referring to the relationship between a king, his chief minister, and royal mistresses writes: 'If Louis was sufficiently jealous of his authority to refuse the temptation to appoint a first minister after Fleury's death, he was prepared to abrogate enormous powers of patronage to his mistresses, especially the marquise de Pompadour.'[17] Could these actions do anything to shore up the edifice of Bourbon absolutism?

Louise Julie de Nesle had been born, like the king, in 1710; at sixteen she had married to her cousin, the comte de Mailly. She held one of the most coveted positions at Versailles – lady-in-waiting to the queen. Little wonder, then, that of all Louis' mistresses, including Pompadour, madame de Mailly would be the mistress that the queen hated the most, the woman who had really been the first to separate the king from her affections.[18] Louise was no great beauty, but, apparently, she was very good company: she loved to flaunt her wealth, convinced that diamonds were an aristocratic girl's best friend. For the Goncourt brothers, 'Madame de Mailly's face expressed her personality – ardent, passionate, happy and proud to do everything she could ... to conquer this king of France who was "as handsome as love itself", she did her best to keep Louis XV happy'.[19] There were bacchanalian soirées in the châteaux of Choisy, Rambouillet and Fontainbleau, where Louis could indulge his passion for champagne, gambling and good food. It seems that sexual relations between Mailly and Louis had begun around 1733, although Mailly was not recognised as an 'official' mistress until November 1737. By the late 1730s, however, Louise would be fighting to defend her position against competitors for the king's favour. Her jealousy of rivals, allied to the king's increasing desire for pastures new, would eventually provoke her downfall.

In an attempt to postpone the inevitable, however, Mailly went so far as to join forces with her younger sister, Pauline-Félicité de Nesle. Many courtiers thought that Pauline-Félicité was too ugly to be taken seriously; her husband, Jean-Baptiste Félix Hubert de Vintimille, told courtiers that 'she stank like the devil', but such comments were to be expected since Pauline-Félicité had only married him in 1739 to cover up her relationship with the king.[20] One thing is certain: both her husband and her sister seriously underestimated her abilities and ambitions. More acceptable to the queen than Mailly, Vintimille had spent a great deal of time and thought on what the king really wanted from a *maîtresse en titre*, and how she could best satisfy his, and her own, wishes. There was sex, of course, but that posed no great problems since Louis 'had such a strange attraction for the Nesle blood-line'.[21] Her principal conclusion, and this was to be of the greatest significance for future official mistresses, was that a power vacuum existed between cardinal Fleury's management of his ministers and the king's desire to be involved in running great affairs of state, especially foreign policy. In other words, Vintimille understood that Louis XV wished, periodically, to rule and not just govern the country, and a strong mistress would allow him to create the impression that this was indeed what he was doing. Louis soon became obsessed with Vintimille, the apparent solution to all his problems, much to the consternation of her elder sister, madame de Mailly, who saw her authority over the king evaporate.[22] In September 1741, however, madame de Vintimille died soon after giving birth to a baby boy, 'the spitting image of the king', it was said. Rumours abounded that she had been poisoned, although it is far more likely that the royal surgeons were once again acting as vicars of the Grim Reaper by bleeding their patient after the delivery of her child. Mailly, who genuinely mourned the death of her sister, was given an opportunity of hanging on to power, at least temporarily.

The political situation at court changed radically over the next two years. On 29 January 1743, Louis' long-time tutor and surrogate father, cardinal Fleury, died at the grand old age of eighty-nine. During the last two years of his increasingly feeble grasp on power, the remaining Nesle sisters had protected themselves against their numerous enemies at court by playing one faction off against another. Enter the third of the Nesle brood, Marie-Anne de Mailly-Nesle, better known as madame de Tournelle after the customary *marriage de convenance* at seventeen to the marquis de Tournelle, who obligingly died soon after. In many ways, Tournelle completed the work begun by her predecessor in the king's bed by adopting a more direct approach to the task of endowing Louis XV with the more martial attributes of the Sun King. Tournelle had inherited the best characteristics of the Nesle female line: her complexion was 'dazzling', her carriage 'majestic'. With the help of her increasingly perplexed and sad sister, madame de Mailly, she had been appointed as a lady-in-waiting to the queen on 4 October 1742. She revealed her iron resolve by turning a deaf ear to any suggestions of a *ménage à trois* with her sister, eventually prompting Louis to exile Mailly from Versailles the following month.[23] Although gossip about the king's relationships with madame de Tournelle in particular, and the Nesle sisters in general, was now being disseminated by a horde of songwriters, cartoonists and pamphleteers, Louis responded with one of his many displays of absolutist arrogance – on 21 October 1743, he raised Tournelle to the status of duchesse de Châteauroux, thus promoting her family to the ranks of the peerage. This decision further widened the breach between the monarch and his people, at a time when the press and public opinion were really beginning to make an impact on politics and society, a phenomenon that the court of Versailles, at least under Louis XV, all too often chose to ignore.

There was very little that Louis would not do for his new duchess. In the spring of 1744, he even agreed to march at the head of his troops to fight in the War of the Austrian Succession, distinguishing himself on the battlefield around Metz in Germany. Unfortunately, Louis weakened the impact of this personal crusade for popularity by allowing Châteauroux *and* the fourth Nesle sister, mademoiselle de Lauraguais, to accompany him. Slaying the English and Austrians was popular at home: rumours of yet another *ménage à trois* with the Nesle sisters was not.

Then, in August, Louis was struck down by a serious, undiagnosed illness. The customary bloodletting produced the customary effect: Louis' condition deteriorated. The *dévots* at Versailles, headed by the queen, were convinced that this was a sign of God's displeasure with the king's extra-marital behaviour, a conclusion that was shared by Louis' Jesuit confessors who implored him to get rid of Châteauroux and her sister. Prompted by his priest, it was announced from the king's supposed deathbed that he had 'sought forgiveness from God and his people for the scandal and poor example he had given them'. He now recognised that he was unworthy of the title of 'the Most Christian King and the eldest Son of the Church'. In truth, Louis appeared to care little for popular opinion, but divine retribution was something else – Châteauroux and Lauraguais were sent packing. A few weeks later, Louis made a remarkable recovery, and messengers were sent to Paris to spread the good news that the king had escaped from the jaws of death. The bells of Notre-Dame cathedral rang out in celebration: the 'warrior-king' was no longer referred to as Louis XV, but 'le Bien-Aimé' (the well-beloved'). Louis XV would never again reach such heights of popularity.

The fall from these giddy heights began almost immediately: no sooner had the king recovered than he sought retribution against those priests who had used religious blackmail to separate him from his mistress. On this occasion, the consequences of the king's mood swings reached far beyond the world of the confessional. The battle to rescue the king from the arms of his powerful mistress had been organised by the *dévot* faction, which favoured handing over control of the monarchy to the traditional sword nobility. One must stress the importance of this deeply held desire since it represents one of the sub-texts of Louis

XV's long reign. In *ancien régime* France, it was but a short step from Throne to Altar, and from both to the uncertain ground upon which the traditional aristocracy was waiting to regain power. Michel Antoine tells us that 'the premier chaplain M. de Fitjames, an ambitious and haughty grand seigneur ... and the bishop of Metz, M. de Saint-Simon, were less concerned about the eternal salvation of their master than they were to ensure the supremacy of the clergy over kings, using their ministry as an instrument of humiliating blackmail'.[24] In a few months, Châteauroux, with the assistance of the duc de Richelieu, a powerful, aristocratic courtier, was back in favour; the Jesuit confessor who had counselled Louis to get rid of her was exiled from Versailles to his diocese. However, God, it seemed, was on the side of the *dévôts*: on 8 December 1744, Châteauroux joined the lengthening obituary list of those whom the curse of Versailles had claimed. Her doctors said that she had fallen victim to 'a malign fever'. Some whispered that the old court retainer Maurepas had poisoned her. Louis was plunged back, yet again, into the depths of despair – an early example of bi-polar disease, perhaps – from which Lauraguais failed to rescue him. According to the duc de Richelieu, 'The reign of Lauraguais was neither lengthy nor brilliant, since she rarely caught the mood or the heart of the king.'[25] There was a fifth Nesle sister, madame de Flavecourt, who escaped the capacious royal embrace, thanks to the sterling resistance advanced by her devoted husband. He had had plenty of time to plan his defensive campaign!

Louis XV's relationship with the Nesle sisters was obviously quite extraordinary, but did it have any real impact upon the evolution of Bourbon absolutism during the early years of Louis' reign? The answer must be in the affirmative. In the first place, given our later focus upon the influence of madame de Pompadour, we should note the emergence, or re-emergence, of the *maîtresse-politique*. This was not, of course, a phenomenon peculiar to the reign of Louis XV: the influence exerted over Louis by the duchesse de Châteauroux had prompted contemporaries to compare her with Charles VII's medieval mistress, the legendary Agnes Sorel (1422–50). Comparisons include the accusation that both were poisoned by their enemies at court, and that both wielded far too great a degree of political influence. Sorel has been referred to as the first 'official' royal mistress.[26] Then there was Louis XIV's mistress, madame de Montespan, who had been a patron of artists and sculptors, as well as being an accomplished actor, singer and dancer, whilst madame de Maintenon, with whom Louis XIV eventually contracted a morganatic marriage, had been a great supporter of the Jesuits. However, instructive as these comparisons are, they should not be pushed too far. The world of Châteauroux and Pompadour was not that of Charles VII, or even that of Louis XIV. Secondly, the mid-eighteenth century marked the beginning of a cycle of revolutionary political, economic, social and intellectual change that would lay the foundations of the modern European world. In Britain, 'With the successful distribution of opposition propaganda throughout the nation and with the continuous expansion of the provincial Press a steady diet of Country [political reform] ideology was fed to the middling and lesser property-owners.' In France, 'the secrecy of public affairs which Fleury so prized ... was also becoming a thing of the past. From the summer of 1742, Paris police spies were reporting a city pulsating with stories, rumours, panics, jokes and critiques.' In other words, the emergence of a 'print culture', and the increasing influence of public opinion'were changing the rules of engagement between monarchs and their subjects, and the inability of Louis XV's government to register, and act upon, this change would cost the king dear. Maurice Lever writes that Louis was 'quite indifferent to public opinion, as he was to changes in ideas and morality; he seemed to live in a dream world, founded upon old-fashioned, Romanesque images'. [27] Meanwhile, the governance of France was changing. In the real world, the expansion of the French civil service and the introduction of important legal and administrative reforms were creating a modern, 'parallel government': the existence of *maîtresses-politiques* and the arcane procedures of Louis XV's secret foreign policy initiatives, the *'secret du roi'*, were rapidly becoming an anachronism. From the 1740s, the word 'republic' began to be whispered more frequently *outside* the elitist confines of the salons.

In short, Louis XV's prolonged relationship with the Nesle sisters had encouraged the perpetuation of traditional methods of governing through aristocratic families and court factions, as well as the development of Louis XV's personal and secret diplomacy. Peter Campbell has argued that, until the 1780s, political power in France 'did not operate in a solely bureaucratic way ... the ethic that prevailed was substantially "pre-modern"'.[28] As we shall see in part two of this work, Henri Bertin would become increasingly aware of the divide between 'ancient' and 'modern' France. The 'Grand Design' that he began to develop with Jacob-Nicolas Moreau in the 1760s would seek to shore up the crumbling edifice of Bourbon absolutism by accelerating the creation of a modern administrative system of government, as well as by introducing liberal economic reforms that would accelerate the transformation of the prevailing feudal, socio-economic structures of the French rural economy. Unfortunately, what he would refuse to accept, like so many of his fellow reforming ministers, was the necessity of removing the coping-stone of the Bourbon system – an absolute monarch. Bertin came to believe that if sweeping reforms were necessary, then an absolute monarch, possibly re-branded as a 'philosopher king' or 'enlightened despot' (there were a lot to chose from in mid-eighteenth-century Europe), was the ideal person to undertake them. 'Power to the people' should never replace 'power to the prince': 'parliamentary democracy' was the product of corrupt, British shopkeepers; 'enlightened absolutism' was continental Europe's more efficient analogue. As we shall see in part three of this work, this conviction would fuel Bertin's extraordinary and prolonged interest in the career of the great, *absolute* ruler of China, Kien-long.

The relationship with the Nesle sisters also reveals the extent to which aristocratic factions and family clans were embedded in the structures of Versailles' politics. Under Louis XV, royal mistresses became, more then ever, the essential pawns in the

Versailles chess set: they could, very occasionally, checkmate a king. Towards the end of his career, Fleury had found it increasingly difficult to deal with the strategies of ministers he thought he could trust, and mistresses he knew he could not. The Keeper of the Seals, Germain Louis de Chauvelin, widely thought to be Fleury's successor, had tried to ingratiate himself with Louis XV by providing the genial madame de Mailly, 'with funds from the foreign affairs budget without the knowledge of Fleury'. However, Mailly had also been linked to *les Grands* such as the maréchal-duc de Noailles, whose family had enjoyed favour at court since the days of Louis XIV; de Noailles had married a niece of madame de Maintenon. But all this had not prevented Mailly from supporting the leader of the war party at Versailles, Charles Louis Belle-Isle – a proud, aristocratic 'maréchal-duc' who really did know one end of a musket from the other.[29] Châteauroux's position as mistress would also be sustained by the qualified support she received from the powerful Belle-Isle faction, which encouraged her doomed efforts to remake Louis XV in the image of the Sun King. So many courtiers after Fleury continued to believe that waving aristocratic 'swords of honour' around would provide a way forward for France. It had been the most influential, dissolute, and devious of Versailles' aristocratic plotters, the duc de Richelieu, who had positioned himself at Châteauroux's side during the great crisis of the king's illness at Metz in the summer of 1744. Richelieu could only bask in the glory of being a maréchal, rather than a maréchal-duc at this time, but his influence, buttressed by his prestigious family name, his prowess on the battlefield, and his keen intelligence, was to be felt at Versailles for over forty years, from the days of Mailly, through those of Pompadour, to madame du Barry.[30] Throughout the reign of Louis XV, Richelieu was the undisputed master of making mistresses: he thoroughly deserved his title of *premier gentilhomme de la chambre du roi*.

How did Louis react to the endless machinations of court factions? As we noted above, surrounded by ministers and courtiers who were all too willing to provide him with aristocratic daughters, either to promote their own policies or increase their credit at court, Louis XV had eventually concluded that, if he wished to wield power as a king, as he often did, it was wise to do so in secret, as so many of his predecessors had done; hence the importance attached to the famous *secret du roi*. Official government ministers were obliged to develop foreign policy in the full knowledge that the king, through his private network of police spies and foreign policy agents in Poland, Russia, and, subsequently, Britain, could be undermining their work. Louis XV, like any president of the present Fifth Republic in France, believed that he should play a decisive role in the formulation of foreign policy. From the time of the duchesse de Châteauroux in the early 1740s to the outbreak of the Seven Years' War in 1756, Louis and his cousin, the prince de Conti, would hold private meetings, developing 'a parallel diplomacy to state international strategy ... focused initially around moves to have Conti elected king of Poland'.[31] The French had long treated the Polish throne as a system of outdoor relief for sundry royal princes. Pompadour would be strong enough, at the peak of her power, to outmanoeuvre the king and Conti: Châteauroux might well have done the same, had she lived longer. The essential point is – what kind of government was it that ran *two* foreign policies?

* * *

The court, and the country, had to wait until the spring of 1745 before a uniquely attractive and charming young lady succeeded in rescuing the king from the pit of depression he had dug for himself following the death of Châteauroux. The lady in question had just happened to be sitting in her carriage watching Louis XV hunting in the forest of Sénart. Her maiden name was Jeanne-Antoinette Poisson; her married name, madame d'Etiolles; we know her as madame de Pompadour. At twenty-three years of age, she was twelve years younger than the king, whose path she, and her mother, had been working so hard to cross. When the first rumours of a liaison between Louis XV and the young lady began to echo through the corridors of Versailles, the reaction was that the relationship would be short lived. A royal fling was quite possible, but 'it seemed inconceivable that [the king] should chose a mistress outside the ranks of the aristocracy'.[32] But he did, thus launching the career of one of history's most romantic and iconic figures. Within a relatively short time, madame d'Etiolles would be transformed into a marquise, then a duchess. For recently ennobled families like the Bertins, this romantic liaison between a Bourbon king and a bourgeois mistress suggested that the long apartheid between 'robe' and 'sword' might be ending; for die-hard princes and court aristocrats like the Contis, the Belle-Isles, and the d'Argensons, it was a sign that Louis XV had decided to finish the work of humiliating *les grands* that had been started by his great-grandfather, Louis XIV; for the queen and her pious *dévot* followers, this sordid business was nothing less than a gross insult: the royal children would refer to Pompadour as 'Maman putain' ('mummy whore'). Surely Louis XV knew that any personal relationship that he embarked upon would inevitably be viewed through the distorting prism of class/caste privilege? It was a perilous way to run a great state that was soon to embark upon its life and death struggle with England for supremacy of much of the known world, including North America, the Caribbean, and India.

Nonetheless, even Pompadour's worst enemies at court found it hard to deny that the king's new mistress was something out of the ordinary. Louis' infatuation with her began to percolate through to the general public after a masked ball, held in the Hôtel de Ville on 28 February 1745 to celebrate the marriage of Louis XV's only son, the Dauphin, to the eldest daughter of the king of Spain, Marie-Raphaelle. Paris celebrated the event as only Paris could: at least seven balls were organised in some of the main squares of the capital, from the Bastille to the place Louis-le-Grand (today, the place Vendôme). 'As night fell, rooms were illuminated, wine and meats were distributed, and people joined hands to dance in the streets, mingling with passing Carnival revellers.' What proved to be the most memorable event took place in the Hôtel de Ville, where privileged guests saw Louis XV pick up the handkerchief that madame d'Etiolles had carelessly allowed to slip out of her hands! The adolescent dreams that Jeanne-Antoinette had been encouraged to harbour for so long were about to be transformed into reality.[33]

One of the most reliable descriptions of the king's new mistress – as she soon became – was provided in 1750 by the Austrian ambassador to France, Kaunitz: 'Her eyes are blue, set well apart, her expression charming. Her face is oval with a small mouth, pretty forehead, and an especially nice nose. She has a good complexion ... Her ash-blond hair falls in profusion to her waist ... she is tall rather than short, thin rather than fat; her carriage is noble, her graces touching ... Her figure has something distinguished about it, so uncommon that even other women find in her what they call the air of a nymph.'[34] However, Pompadour's grace and beauty, characteristics that would be periodically renovated for posterity by François Boucher's forgiving brush, were not, by any means, the strongest weapons in her formidable feminine armoury. In the first place, she had been schooled since childhood in the arts and crafts of becoming a king's mistress. Convent-educated, she had been known as 'Reinette' ('Queeny') by some of her fellow-inmates. Her mother, Louise-Madeleine de la Motte, was reputedly more beautiful than her famous daughter, although her loose morals enabled her enemies to dismiss her as nothing better than 'a Palais Royal *putain*'. Pompadour's father, François Poisson, who was a successful supplier of goods to the armed forces, was a much rougher diamond than his wife. His arrest in 1727 for allegedly swindling the royal treasury out of 232,000 *livres* had cast a further shadow over the family name.

To counterbalance these disadvantages, Pompadour's mother had taken great care to secure relationships with people of consequence, such as very wealthy tax farmers and army suppliers; she had allegedly sold her generous favours to the farmer general, Charles-François de Tournehem, as well as to Jean Pâris de Montmartel, youngest of the four Pâris brothers, whose immense wealth had made them one of the most influential financial clans in the history of eighteenth-century France. Jeanne-Antoinette's legal father, François Poisson, had been working for the Pâris brothers when he was arrested. Her biological father could have been any one of the above three, Tournehem, Montmartel or Poisson. Most contemporaries were prepared to put each-way bets (gambling was one of the chief *divertissements* of the court) on Tournehem, given that Jeanne-Antoinette had married his nephew, Charles-Guillaume de Tournehem in March 1741. Through this marriage, Jeanne-Antoinette had not only acquired a small fortune in cash, as well as the estate of Etiolles, but also access to the famous salon of madame Geoffrin. The new madame d'Etiolles was now taught how to add poise, elegance, and good manners to the basic training in the arts that her mother and Tournehem had provided for her. The legendary 'Pompadour' was in the process of being created, a political and socio-cultural confection, by appointment to His Majesty Louis XV. Her charm and intelligence would sustain this artificial creation, but for the rest of her career, she would require the support of strong person-alities in times of crisis. Louis XV obviously did not fall into this category: his failure to provide his famous mistress with solid support in her later years would contribute to her premature death. Royal fairy-tales frequently have short shelf lives.

At the beginning of their relationship, Louis could not have been more obliging. 1745 was to be a memorable year, a year that would bring unexpected military glory for Louis and the much-coveted position of royal mistress for Pompadour. On 11 May, at the battle of Fontenoy near Tournai, the French army, commanded by the competent maréchal de Saxe, defeated an Anglo-Dutch-German army led by the incompetent duke of Cumberland. Happily, Louis XV and the Dauphin were there in person to celebrate one of the few great military victories to be recorded during Louis' long reign. The king's newly appointed 'spin-doctor' (*historiographe du roi*), Voltaire, announced that, 'It is three hundred years since a king of France has done anything as glorious. I am mad with joy', a comment that serves to remind us that only a few leading *philosophes* were opposed to the concept of absolute monarchy.[35] Four days earlier, 'madame d'Etiolles' had separated from her husband; in July, she was given an estate and title of 'marquise de Pompadour'; the following September, she became the king's *maîtresse en titre*. The tireless efforts of her mother, who was to die a few months later, and her influential friends/lovers had not been in vain.

When Louis and the dauphin returned in triumph to Paris on 7 September, the bells of Notre-Dame cathedral again rang out in celebration. A week later, lavish festivities at Versailles were held to recognise the inflated status of the king as 'an arbiter of European politics'. Courtiers and commentators lined up, at last, to compare him with Louis XIV, a comparison that Louis XV considered to be a mixed blessing. He was, after all, not an uncritical supporter of the war party at court; the more pacific approach of his mentor Fleury always remained closer to his heart. As for madame de Pompadour, who shared much of his anti-war sentiment, but who had learned from her predecessor, the duchesse de Châteauroux, that *la gloire* and *la France* were inseparable, it was inevitable that she should have exploited the situation to consolidate her shaky position at court. Her success was quite remarkable: the period from 1745 to 1750 would witness the beginning of her transformation from the position of a mistress to that of the king's closest adviser and chief dispenser of royal patronage. The fact that Louis continued to act as his own 'first minister' helps to explain the complicated political geometry within which the Louis–Pompadour–Bertin triangle would operate during the late 1750s and the early 1760s. Meanwhile, Pompadour's initial task was to reward those who had helped her become the king's mistress. Top of the list were the Pâris brothers: Pâris de Montmartel had supplied the cash to buy the Limousin estate that created 'the marquise de Pompadour'; Philibert Orry, an enemy of the war party and its financiers (the Pâris brothers again) saw the writing on the wall and retired as *contrôleur général*, allowing Pompadour and the Pâris brothers to re-conquer the space they had formerly occupied at court; Charles-François de Tournehem (Pompadour's probable father), was persuaded to pass his office of *fermier-général* to François Poisson, who was almost certainly not her biological father, in return for the far more prestigious position of *directeur général des bâtiments du roi*. When Tournehem died, the post was given to Pompadour's brother, Abel Poisson, who was later to be given the title of marquis de Marigny. Other close friends were also rewarded – her 'chief eunuch' at court, the marquis de Gontaut, had provided a necessary bridge to the court aristocracy and would receive a dukedom for his efforts; the witty, but all too often melancholic, abbé de Bernis would become a close counsellor, ultimately receiving a cardinal's hat in return for services rendered; Voltaire, her principal literary promoter in 1745, would become a *gentilhomme de la chambre du roi*, worth 60,000 *livres* a year; a seat was also found for him in the prestigious *Académie française*. By 1749, Pompadour's tight control of royal patronage would even enable her to secure the 'resignation' of the comte de Maurepas, a long-time servant of the Bourbon monarchy and a favourite of the king. Not all of Pompadour's appointments would prove to be failures by any means but far too many would be made not in the interests of good government, but to secure the position of Pompadour and her *parti*.

By the early 1750s, the first phase of madame de Pompadour's extraordinary career was over. She had moved out of the king's bed to become mistress of much of what she surveyed at Versailles. Châteauroux had girded up the king's loins for war; Pompadour would wage war against the king's notorious feeling of *ennui*. The royal entourage became a travelling circus, pitching its tent each season in luxuriously renovated châteaux that were not too far from Paris, such as Fontainbleau and Rambouillet, as well as in the more intimate mansions such as Crécy in Normandy, purchased for Pompadour by the king in 1746. There was also the small château of La Celle near Versailles where many private suppers and *divertissements* were organised. The duc de Croy, a regular guest and chronicler of the times, recalls an evening there in September 1748. After a splendid meal, enjoyed by a few ministers and favourites, 'a number of musicians entered, all dressed in different apparel and playing a variety of instruments'. Once they were seated, 'madame de Pompadour, representing the Spirit of the Night, rose and sang a few songs in honour of the king'. The musicians, the king and his guests then made their way along two terraces to a clearing 'where M. le duc d'Ayen appeared dressed as the God Pan'. The evening ended with a sail along a small stream in a gondola, followed by dancing and music until dawn broke, heralding the end of yet another 'Romanesque' revelry that sustained a decadent court, led by a king whose boredom threshold was disturbingly low. Regular theatrical performances were also a feature of court life and one of Pompadour's particular passions. She had been trained in the arts of dancing, singing and acting from her childhood. A theatrical company was created at Versailles so that she might flaunt her many talents to an appropriate audience. Its first production on 16 January1747 was both relevant and provocative, given the snobbishness and backbiting of Louis XV's court – Molière's brilliant satire on hypocrisy, *Tartuffe*. Gradually, however, costs began to escalate, and, the following year, theatrical productions were moved to her new, bijou residence of Bellevue. By this time, the king's gifted mistress was already experiencing an occasional spell of the exhaustion that would accelerate her journey to an early grave.[36]

At considerable cost and personal endeavour, the cultural legacy of Pompadour was being fashioned. It was embellished by many of the great artists, architects, painters and sculptors of the day; it popularised the post-Louis XIV rococo style which prioritised the more intimate, the more personal and the more decorative aspects of painting and interior design. Pompadour's favourite painter, François Boucher, became her chief image-maker; architects and sculptors, such as Jacques-Ange Gabriel and Etienne-Maurice Falconet, collaborated in the project. Represented as lover, mistress, friend of the *philosophes*, a French shepherdess or a Turkish sultana, anything that burnished her carefully crafted image would do. This applied to her many residences. Boucher, for example, spent a considerable amount of his time painting the panels of her sumptuous château of Bellevue near Meudon. Bellevue no longer exists, but the lavishly refurbished mansion she purchased from the comte d'Evreux near the Champs-Elysées is used today by the President of the Fifth Republic. To view more tangible evidence of Pompadour's artistic legacy, one should visit the royal porcelain museum at Sèvres, south of Paris, which Pompadour helped to establish. It still houses many of the beautiful *objets d'art* that evoke 'the age of Pompadour'. It would take auction-eers two years to evaluate and organise the sale of all her posses-sions after her death.[37] Whatever the cost, Pompadour and her devotees were convinced that they were adding lustre to the reign of Louis XV and his court, a fact that Louis both recog-nised and appreciated. He, and Pompadour, realised that the cultural legacy of the Sun King, reflected in the glories contained within the château of Versailles itself, was proving to be a more permanent, if not cheaper, monument to his memory than any of his victories on the battlefield.

* * *

The late 1740s and 1750s would complete the transformation of madame de Pompadour from the position of 'first mistress' to that of an ersatz 'first minister'. The duc de Castries thought that for twenty years she was really the queen of France, an inflated proposition.[38] During the early 1750s, possibly 1751, sexual relations between Louis and Pompadour ended.[39] Like Louis himself, Pompadour may well have been afraid of catching a venereal disease; it seems that she had also suffered three miscar-riages. Whatever the reason, Pompadour was now able to devote more time to what she did best – pursuing a cultural and political career. Her role in the dismissal in 1749 of one of the longest serving ministers of Louis' administration, the comte de Maurepas, provides us with evidence of her increasing authority. Maurepas was a man with a wicked tongue, and a pen to match, who had no time for bourgeois royal mistresses who sought to wield political power. He may well have written one of the scandalous verses that Pompadour occasionally found under her table napkin in the mornings:

> This little bourgeois mouse,
> Born in a bawdy house,
> Brings everything down to her level
> And turns the entire court into a hovel.

When Pompadour complained to Maurepas that he did not treat the king's mistresses with the respect they deserved, he replied: 'I treat all of them the same, whatever sort they are'! This insult, prompted by Pompadour's bourgeois origins, proved too much for the king, and Maurepas was forced to resign.[40] As the entire affair indicates, the king was the final arbiter of power at Versailles, keeping himself informed, often by devious routes, of (almost) everything that was going on at court. But should mistresses have been deciding the fate of ministers? Michel Antoine raises this important question, providing us with a sound judgement of Pompadour's authority at this stage of her career. He explains that, although she was not yet in a position to take major policy decisions, she did influence their implementation through her role in choosing those who implemented them. The exercise of patronage was Pompadour's *modus operandi*, although, for Michel Antoine, years during which she was his favourite were also the years when government policy was most uncertain.[41] And this is why Pompadour may still 'abide our question'. Difficult as it is to disrobe her of her intelligence and cultural regalia, one must, in the final analysis, assess her historic importance by examining her political and diplomatic actions during a period of increasing aggression from across the Channel. During the 1750s and early 1760s, France would be governed by a rather unstable king who insisted on pursuing his secret diplomacy, frequently leaving his ex-mistress to fill the post of 'first minister', which he refused to delegate to any of his own ministers. One wonders if William Pitt could ever have achieved as much as he did for Hanoverian Britain under these circumstances.

Many of the limitations on Pompadour's ambition to equal, or even surpass, the influence that the duchesse de Châteauroux had exercised over Louis XV were removed during the early years of the 1750s. The extremely harsh treatment, including imprisonment in the Bastille, meted out against Pompadour's critics during this period certainly reveals her vulnerability, but it also shows Louis' determination to support her. Evidence of Pompadour's increased political stature at this time focuses on three major policy areas – the religious conflict between Jesuits and Jansenists, the related political conflict with the parlements, and her involvement in foreign policy initiatives leading to the outbreak of the Seven Years' War, which we will investigate in the next chapter. There was, however, a very important, concealed, fourth policy, a consequence of the rapidly changing relationship between the king and Pompadour – their 'mutual agreement', designed to control, and manage, Louis' increasingly rather reckless pursuit of sexual pleasure, which conferred even greater authority on the king's ex-mistress. We shall provide a more detailed account of this 'understanding' between Louis and his ex-mistress below, when we address Pompadour's role in Henri Bertin's promotion to *lieutenant général de police de Paris* in 1757.

Given the widely acknowledged instability of government, it is no coincidence that serious religious and political crises occurred during the years immediately preceding, and during, the outbreak of the Seven Years' War that began in 1756. From 1752 to 1754, one of the periodic eruptions between the Jesuit and Jansenist wings of the Catholic Church increased the instability of Louis XV's government, which was already being undermined by British threats to French colonial possessions, especially in North America. In 1713, after almost a century of struggle between the Jesuits and Jansenists, Louis XIV and the papacy had collaborated in the publication of the papal bull, *Unigenitus*, which, it was hoped, would bury Jansenism for good. It contained 101 reasons why loyal Catholics should renounce this 'heretical' doctrine, which was much too 'Calvinist' for followers of the true faith. Far from burying the movement, however, *Unigenitus* gave birth to a second wave of Jansenism that lasted until the abolition of the Jesuit Order in France in 1762. However, 'Post-*Unigenitus* Jansenism … was not about salvation. Its true concerns were political and legalistic, a mask for conflicts more material than spiritual.' In other words, Jansenism was resurrected and reconstructed in the eighteenth century under the influence of a rising tide of incipient nationalism, secularism and political unrest. *Unigenitus*, during the reign of Louis XV, would be denounced as evidence of an unwarranted interference in the affairs of the French nation. This was, historically, a very explosive issue, one that was requisitioned by the thirteen French parlements in the early 1750s to add credibility to their claim that they were defending the 'Gallican Church' (the French variant of Roman Catholicism) against a Jesuit court. This was, at least, a more modest claim than their assertion that they were the true 'guardians of the liberty of the people', a direct challenge to the unreformed Bourbon monarchy. Unfortunately for madame de Pompadour, her appearance upon the political scene had coincided with the appointment in 1746 of Christophe de Beaumont as archbishop of Paris. A die-hard defender of the Jesuits and friend of the queen, he was described by John McManners as a man of 'fanatical intransigence'.[42]

Pompadour's attitude to the pro-Jesuit and anti-war *dévot* party at court had changed perceptibly during the course of 1751, in the first place because 1751 was 'jubilee year', a time when Catholic sinners were encouraged to abjure their sins and make peace with their God, thus assuring them of eternal life. Secondly, Beaumont exploited the mood of heightened religiosity to pursue Jansenist clergy, and the parlement of Paris, over the extremely contentious issue of the *billets de confession*, certificates from Jesuit priests confirming that parishioners on the verge of death had rejected Jansenist heresies. Clergy who swore allegiance to *Unigenitus*, and they represented the great majority of priests, had been instructed by Beaumont to refuse the last sacraments to those suspected of Jansenist sympathies. This was a very difficult issue for Louis XV, a devoted Catholic at heart, but targeted more than ever now by the *dévots*, including the archbishop of Paris, for his loose sexual behaviour. For a time, Louis began to take the salvation of his soul seriously, attending mass and the other offices of the Catholic Church assiduously. Pompadour, realising that this 'religious revival' was a threat to her position at court, and prompted by the king who, given their recent mutual agreement, did not wish to see her exiled, announced that she also wished to make her peace with the Almighty. Pierre de Nolhac records Voltaire's ex-pupil, 'saying her devotions, in her own self-interest ... her pretty little hands holding her Book of Hours [decorated by Boucher of course], in the correct manner during Church services'.[43] Unfortunately, for her enemies at court this public display was not good enough. Louis and Pompadour would have to atone for their inexcusable adultery by separating; Pompadour would have to leave Versailles. The king refused his permission. On the positive side, although the king and Pompadour had not fooled Christophe de Beaumont, nor anyone else for that matter, Pompadour's 'religious conversion', did improve her relationship with the queen and her children, a matter of considerable importance to Louis XV. In any case, the religious fervour released by the year of the jubilee could not be sustained indefinitely. By the spring of 1753, the marquis d'Argenson was convinced that, 'Religious observance is declining in France, not as a result of *"la philosophie anglaise"*, but because people hate their priests, who are going well over the top these days.' Undoubtedly, d'Argenson was referring to Christophe de Beaumont's disproportionate attack on Jansenist clergy.[44]

By this time, the thirteen parlements of France had begun to flex their muscles, transforming a religious drama into a major political crisis. The parlementary crises of the 1750s were very different from those of the early 1730s, reflecting the general advance of the more secular and politicised society we mentioned above. Many magistrates of the parlement of Paris were obviously being influenced by the intellectual revolution associated with the European Enlightenment that was already changing the world that they had known. In February 1752, the government had tried to stop the publication of the first two volumes of the seventeen-volume *Encyclopédie*. Containing anti-clerical articles that shook the foundations of the French Catholic Church to its cellars, Christophe de Beaumont and his supporters discovered that they were now confronted with enemies on all sides. The *Encyclopédie* would make a major contribution, at least among secular, and a few religious, elites towards the de-sacralisation of the monarchy and the de-frocking of the unreconstructed Catholic Church. For example, the Jesuit Order would be banned in France by the early 1760s. Magistrates in the parlements, already well-versed in law and history, drew inspiration from these intellectual winds of change, citing, in particular, two works of political theory: Montesquieu's famous *Esprit des lois*, published in 1748, which misconstrued the true nature of the British constitution, but provided French *parlementaires* with equally misguided parallels between British and French 'constitutional democracy'; and the far less famous, but more populist, *Historical Letters on the Functions of the Parlement* by Louis-Adrien le Paige, published in 1753–4. Servants of the crown now began to unearth and consult dusty charters from the Middle Ages in order to prove that the monarchy, not the parlements, had liberated the people from the shackles of medieval feudalism. This movement to adopt an *historical*, rather than a religious, validation of monarchical power would provide Bertin's friend and colleague, Jacob-Nicolas Moreau, with the first building blocks of their future 'Grand Design'.[45] Meanwhile, relations between the parlements and the crown became increasingly complex. Julian Swann refers to 'a gradual process of what we might call the "politicisation" of judicial officers', with the parlement itself becoming a forum 'for the intrigues of the court'.[46]

Following another quarrel over the refusal of the sacraments to a dying priest, the parlement of Paris issued a decree on 18 April 1752 prohibiting the use of *billets de confession*. Louis denounced the decree and said that everyone should take a vow of silence about *Unigenitus*. As in Fleury's time, this pious wish only produced a great deal of rowdy discussion. Finally, in December, the parlement decided it would try to impeach the archbishop of Paris, Beaumont having made more noise than anyone else on the issue. When this failed, the parlement drew up its *Grandes Remonstrances*, a scarcely veiled attempt to claim co-responsibility with the crown in governing the country. Not surprisingly, Louis and Pompadour rejected the idea out of hand, and, in May 1753, members of the Paris parlement were exiled to various parts of the country. They were not allowed to return to their benches until September of the following year, by which time rumours of the impending war against Britain had begun to drown out those of priests giving, or not giving, the last rites to dying Parisians.

The evolving crisis between the parlement, the monarchy, and the Church had placed madame de Pompadour, and Louis, in a most difficult predicament: Pompadour's survival at court now depended, more than ever, upon her ability to serve the king in a political/diplomatic capacity. Moving too far in the direction of the *philosophes* and the Jansenists had always presented some danger for her; supporting the parlements would have been even more dangerous. Both Louis and Pompadour were convinced that if the cause of Bourbon absolutism was to survive then supporting the alliance of Throne and Altar was a categorical imperative; that is why she had moved, temporarily, in the direction of the *dévot* party. By October 1755, the marquis d'Argenson was convinced that Pompadour's health was being adversely affected by her practice of 'getting up in the middle of the night to pray, then attending mass every day'. Three months later, he wrote 'Pompadour was acting as the first minister'.[47] However, Christophe de Beaumont's rigid intransigence was making it almost impossible to strike up a compromise with the parlements. Perhaps a successful war would restore the authority of the monarchy over the parlements?

* * *

Before embarking upon our investigation of the relationship between the Seven Years' War and the further decline of Bourbon absolutism, we must return to our account of Louis XV's private life following the end of his sexual relationship with madame de Pompadour. From the standpoint of her ability to survive as Louis' ersatz first minister, the unofficial position that she undoubtedly held by the outbreak of war in 1756 , Pompadour's mutual agreement with Louis is of crucial importance in our assessment of the instability of the Bourbon government. In the first place, the agreement operated at a critical time in European history, making it far more difficult to confront and overcome the momentous internal and external challenges the government faced, in particular the war between England and France, the parlementary challenge, from a vocal minority of the magistrates, to the concept of absolutist government, and the expansion of a more vocal and critical 'public sphere'. Under these pressures, Pompadour's deal with Louis XV would weaken her authority and street credibility, precipitating her death in 1764.

By the middle of the 1750s, Louis' appetite for sexual satisfaction had grown more pronounced. Only forty-five in 1755, the various excesses in which he indulged made him look older than he was. It is also evident that Pompadour had become an accomplice in the management of Louis XV's extra-curricular activities. It is difficult to separate hard facts from libellous accusations when dealing with Louis XV's personal conduct; the accusations of contemporary courtiers and chroniclers have to be weighed against a background of vicious personal and factional intrigue. One must distinguish between superfluous prurience and the impact of Louis' behaviour upon the governance of France. According to the the duc de Castries, the king developed a distinct preference for young girls as he grew older, preferably virgins, who might protect him against sexually transmitted diseases.[48] The majority of these girls appear to have been occasional partners, often ignorant of the fact that their partner for the night would not be the 'Polish seigneur' they were introduced to, but the king of France: Louis wished to be at least as secretive about his private life as he was about his participation in foreign policy. Obviously, Louis had no interest in publicising his 'private affairs' and Pompadour accepted this clandestine procedure 'on the understanding that these girls would be no threat to her. "It is his heart I want! All these little girls with no education will not take it from me. I would not be so calm, if I saw some pretty woman of the court or the capital trying to conquer it"'.[49] What did place extra stress on Pompadour's nervous and highly-strung constitution, however, was the emergence of the occasional *maîtresse en titre*, chosen by her enemies at court to fill the position she had decided to vacate. In 1752, the marquis d'Argenson and his mistress, the comtesse d'Estrades, had hatched a plot with the future duc de Choiseul to place the latter's cousin, madame Charlotte-Rosalie de Romanet, in the king's bed. The liaison was short-lived, due to Choiseul's Machiavellian manoeuvres and the indiscretion of madame d'Estrades who was overheard describing Pompadour as 'la vieille coquette' once too often. The cautionary tale of madame d'Estrades' dismissal for insulting Pompadour prescribed the limits within which court intriguers were obliged to operate. Nonetheless, Louis would pursue his dual policy of maintaining 'official mistresses' at court as well as being provided with his young girls, who were usually transported to his private apartments from a house, purchased for Louis XV, near the château of Versailles. In return for her understanding, and complicity, Pompadour would be given a far greater participatory role in government, unique in character, determined, in part, by Louis XV's unique, secretive method of ruling, but one that allowed her, over time, to appropriate many of the functions of a 'first minister'. On the political front, the practice of government was becoming even more dysfunctional.[50]

Realpolitik had replaced romance, an extremely important key to an understanding of the mind and career of madame de Pompadour. Her oft- declared love for the king had become inseparable from her ambition to find a niche in history. In the pursuit of this goal, Pompadour could rely upon the advice of her intimate, inner circle of supporters, some of whom she could actually trust; Louis would draw upon the culture of deviance and sexual licence that prevailed at Versailles. Erica-Marie Benabou, a respected authority on the history of eighteenth-century Parisian sex, described Louis XV as an *'amateur suprême'* in the art of illicit sex.[51] His most valued tutor in this art was cardinal Richelieu's great-nephew, Louis François Armand du Plessis, duc de Richelieu, a *maréchal de France* and, as *premier gentilhomme de la chambre du roi*, one of the king's closest confidants. Richelieu was a renowned *roué* and worldly-wise cynic, the Don Juan of Versailles. He was assisted in his efforts to secure attractive young ladies for the king by the ever-faithful comte de Saint-Florentin, Louis XV's longest serving minister, who would be rewarded for his loyalty with a dukedom in 1770. Appointed secretary of state in 1725, and still serving Louis when he died in 1774, Saint-Florentin's brief included the management of the king's household and religious affairs, as well as responsibility for certain royal affairs in the provinces. One of his many illegitimate sons, the comte de Langeac, would became the lover of one of Louis XV's most troublesome ex-mistresses, mademoiselle Tiercelin de la Colleterie. Like his colleague, Henri Bertin, Saint-Florentin was a robe noble, totally dedicated to the service of the monarchy, which was just as well since the duchesse de Châteauroux had once bracketed him with a clutch of ministers who were 'so mediocre that it was hardly worth the bother of speaking to them'![52]

Two of Louis XV's *premier valets de chambre*, François Gabriel Bachelier and Dominique Guillaume Le Bel, were responsible for choosing many of the king's sexual partners. Bachelier, 'a large and imposing figure' had played an important role in securing the services of the Mailly sisters in the early 1730s. There was no shortage of girls as ambitious, aristocratic mothers and avaricious owners of some of the high-class brothels in Paris (madame Dhosmont's establishment was well known to the police) competed for the honour of providing Louis XV with mistresses, *grandes et petites*. Bachelier's successor as Louis XV's first *valet de chambre*, Dominque Le Bel, was described by madame de Campan as 'Louis XV's minister et confidante de ses plaisirs secrets'. From his apprenticeship in the 1730s to his death in 1768, Le Bel not only acted as the principal procurer of young girls, but he also played a key role in many of the plots and scandals that rocked the court of Versailles during this rather tarnished 'golden age' of court decadence. Madame de Pompadour herself had been brought to the attention of the king as a result of her mother's ambitious plans, implemented through the intermediary of Le Bel, who had allegedly been one of her lovers, and the assistance of her cousin, Binet de Marchais, *premier valet de chambre du dauphin*. One should not be misled by the description that the word 'valet' conjures up when applied to Bachelier and Le Bel: both were men of considerable wealth and social standing. Bachelier's father had served Louis XIV: the family owned the small château of La Celle, situated just a few miles from Versailles, that Bachelier *fils* sold to Pompadour in 1748 for no less than 260,000 *livres*. Le Bel may not have been quite as wealthy as the Bacheliers, but his appointment as Bachelier's successor upon the latter's death in 1754 obviously increased both his income and his influence.[53]

These 'superintendants of the king's pleasures' were very important members of the discreet team that ran the infamous house, or houses, near the château of Versailles, known to posterity as the Deer Park. This was the institution that did most to bring Louis XV's personal reputation into disrepute, the institution that housed his 'young girls'. The land comprising the Deer Park had originally been the site of a seventeenth-century royal game park. It was close enough to ferry young girls between their residence and the château of Versailles, but far enough away to ensure a certain degree of anonymity and security. By the 1750s, residential buildings had been built on the park land and the king's estate agents may have commandeered a few during the early 1750s. The *hôtel particulière* eventually designated for the king's mistresses, was no. 4 Rue de Saint-Médéric. It was eventually purchased on behalf of the king on 25 November 1755 and remained in royal hands until 1771, although it may not have been used very much after death of Pompadour in 1764, and was only used intermittently during the mid and late1750s.[54] Louis XVI would have had no use for it. Among the first inmates of this house in the rue Saint-Médéric at the beginning of 1753 were mademoiselle Trusson, the daughter of a clerk in the Foreign Office, who had performed as a singer in Pompadour's private theatre, and a daughter of a president of the parlement of Toulouse, mademoiselle Niquet. Mademoiselle Niquet was married off in 1753 to a former *fermier-général*, which established the practice of providing marriage partners and generous dowries to those women who had served their time in the Deer Park.[55]

As time passed, Louis began to express a preference for young girls from less elevated social circles. The most famous of all these 'putains', as the marquis d'Argenson was wont to call all the king's mistresses, was Marie-Louise O'Murphy, commonly referred to as 'Louison'. According to police reports, she was the fourteen-year-old daughter of street traders, whose older sisters were reputed to have had some experience of walking the streets.[56] It is ironic, but revealing, that the great painter, François Boucher, whose many portraits did so much to immortalise the face and fashionable attire of madame de Pompadour, should also have left us a famously erotic painting of Louison (or a young girl generally accepted to be Louison) whom the king sought to enthrone as his official mistress. Was Boucher making the point that had struck so many of Louis XV's subjects – the moral collapse of 'le Bien-aimé'? It may not have been interpreted in this way by court elites and sycophants. There is, for example, the puzzling 'oriental' portrait of Pompadour, dressed as a sultan's wife. Colin Jones suggests that the portrait 'stressed the marquise's dominant position over the other women in the king's life'.[57] Pompadour certainly had good reason to assert her authority over her competitors, but, if this was all Pompadour saw in such portraits, then she may not have been quite as intelligent as her many admirers suggest. There was, of course, a necessary complicity in Pompadour's actions: her career depended upon it. There was also the contemporary craze in France for all things 'oriental', Louis and Pompadour may have thought that some 'eastern magic' might rub off on them if they associated themselves with successful Turkish and Chinese forms of authoritarian rule, and *'galanterie'*. This is by no means a fanciful suggestion, as we shall learn in part three of this study, which focuses upon Henri Bertin's fascination with the great Chinese Emperor, Kien-long.

Louis' affair with Marie-Louise O'Murphy is important for several reasons. In the first place, there was the king's infatuation with a young and uneducated girl. It was reported that he showered her with gifts, expensive jewellery and a luxuriously appointed apartment in Versailles. There was even loose talk of elevating Louison to the position of an official mistress, much to the disgust of the queen: in the quaint circumstances of Versailles' royal etiquette, 'mistresses' might be acceptable, so long as they stayed within the boudoir, but 'official mistresses' constituted an insult to the queen and often a threat to the king's ministers. Secondly, the scandal over the king's behaviour was now attracting national and international attention, at a time when the undeclared war between England and France, which at this stage was being fought mainly in the colonial sphere, was threatening to upset traditional alliances between the Great Powers. A report from the papal nuncio on 22 October 1753 stated that, 'There is every indication that Pompadour's reign is over ... it is generally believed that the favourite has taken the decision to leave before she is pushed out.' As for Louison, she was being kept away from the public, probably in a house situated in the Deer Park, 'due to the fact that she may be pregnant.'[58] As usual, popular rumour exaggerated the real danger posed by Louison, but she managed to retain the affections of the king beyond her second pregnancy (the first appears to have ended in a miscarriage) in the summer of 1754. One thing is certain, the entire affair must have been a nightmare for Pompadour. The spectacle of a fourteen-year-old girl, a pawn in the hands of Pompadour's enemies, giving orders to ministers and poking fun at the king's 'first minister', could only have provoked laughter and incredulity amongst monarchy and diplomats throughout Europe. Eventually, however, even Louis was obliged to confront the ludicrous position in which his infatuation had placed him, and his country. In November 1755, Louison was given the huge sum of 200,000 *livres* as a dowry and married off to an army officer from the Auvergne, M. de Beaufranchet d'Ayat. There was an interesting, and revealing, conclusion to these extraordinary events – the contract for the purchase of the rue Médéric house in the Deer Park was signed on the very same day that Louison signed her marriage contract. Pompadour had apparently decided that there was a time and place for everything, and the place for the king's future *petites maîtresses* was in the rue Médéric, not the corridors of power in Versailles.[59]

Marie-Louise O'Murphy was not the last of Louis' conquests to aspire to the elevated position of 'official mistress'. One candidate merits a few words – the bourgeois beauty, Anne Couppier de Romans who produced a son that Louis, uncharacteristically, would recognise. Romans would remain the king's mistress from 1759 to 1764. Alongside these young ladies, the parade of anonymous girls in the Deer Park appears to have continued, at least until the death of Pompadour in 1764. Michel Antoine, a well-informed and reliable source, concludes that Louis' 'participation in this merry-go-round ... infringed, in a disgraceful fashion, the moral laws associated with a Most Christian King'.[60] Antoine's charge cannot easily be dismissed. 'Morality' would become a key component of Henri Bertin and Jacob-Nicolas Moreau's 'Grand Design', which engaged with the argument that Louis XV was bringing disgrace upon the monarchy at a time when religious morality was a hot topic of conversation, widely discussed between *philosophes*, Jesuits and Jansenists. A pamphlet published as late as 1790 would refer to the Deer Park as the place where 'a horde of victims, eventually thrown back into society, carried with them the corruption, taste for debauchery, and all those vices with which they had obviously been infected by conducting their infamous acts in this abominable place'.[61] This accusation is clearly an example of Revolutionary rhetoric, but there can be absolutely no doubt that the Deer Park did cast a permanent shadow over Louis XV's reputation. It has obscured his achievements as a monarch, especially his very important, if irregular, support for reforming ministers, such as Trudaine, Machault and Henri Bertin, as well as the artistic and cultural legacy of his reign, which is all to often associated, exclusively, with madame de Pompadour. Nonetheless, Louis' actions unquestionably helped to undermine the foundations of the Bourbon monarchy, at the very time that the institution itself was being criticised by the parlements, and when the French armed services were gearing up for the most serious conflict between England and France since the days of Louis XIV. A king, weakened physically, and psychologically, by his constant excesses, subject to periods of debilitating *ennui*, surrounded by close advisers such as the prince de Conti, whose constant pressure for Pompadour's dismissal harmed both the king and his ex-mistress, was hardly in a position to lead France to a famous victory.[62]

Almost a century after Louis' death, the Goncourt brothers provided a defence of Louis XV's obsessive and immoral behaviour, based, in part, upon the decline and fall of an aristocratic society. They argued that, although western civilisation had reached its apogee in France during the course of the eighteenth century, it contained the seeds of its own destruction. From this general, and patriotic, proposition, they went on to argue that Louis XV's personal behaviour reflected the social and cultural malaise of the mid-eighteenth century: 'When a civilisation has reached the most expansive stage of its existence; when a society is experiencing the full flowering of an exquisite state of corruption ... a strange disease afflicts humanity. It takes the form a boring and infinite weariness ... This strange disease was the great moral sickness of the eighteenth century.' The Goncourts concluded that 'Louis XV's life provides us with the most notable example of a man seized by ennui; he was also its most notable victim'. The Goncourts' 'moral sickness' was given literary and theatrical representation with Choderlos de Laclos' *Liaisons dangereuses*, the most infamous, and corrosive, novel of the eighteenth century. In 1782, Madame de Riccoboni, a contemporary novelist, would describe Laclos' anti-heroine, Madame de Merteuil, as 'an aberrant monster ... providing strangers with a revolting vision of the morals of this nation'. Whether one accepts the Goncourts' somewhat specious socio-cultural theorising or not, their diagnosis of Louis XV's personal dilemma is illuminating. He did, after all, operate within the context of a court riddled with hypocrisy and debauchery, and a society whose foundations were being shaken by powerful political, socio-economic and intellectual changes.[63]

As for madame de Pompadour, the Goncourts thought that she had the genius, the patience and the determination, if not to make Louis XV forget his condition completely, then to find ways of easing and alleviating it by keeping him amused. Difficult again to reject this analysis out of hand: Pompadour's entire career was indeed based upon her efforts to relieve Louis' *ennui*, but at what cost? Long before the calamity of the Seven Years' War, Pompadour had begun to exert a negative influence over the governance of France through the important, if indirect, role she played in the creation and maintenance of the Deer Park, and her subsequent control of government policy, primarily by appointing ministers and generals whose chief attribute was their willingness to pursue policies devised by a distracted king and his increasingly distraught ex-mistress. Pompadour claimed that she was serving the best interests of the monarchy. However, by 1756, the gap between the personal interests of the monarch and those of the nation had widened alarmingly. Fifteen years earlier, the duchesse de Châteauroux had tried, with a modicum of success, to make a warrior-king out of Louis XV; Pompadour was content to see him in the boudoir, not on the battlefield. What impact did this make upon public opinion? Michel Antoine concludes that Louis XV did not worry too much about this: 'His mistake was that he completely failed to realise that if he left himself open to malicious gossip and slander, the monarchy, not just his own personal reputation, would be placed in jeopardy.'[64] This was the historic legacy of Louis XV's actions.

The mystery is how Pompadour managed to survive for so long the many 'slings and arrows of outrageous fortune' that assailed her. In June 1754, for example, she had been shattered by the loss of her beloved daughter, Alexandrine, whom she had once thought of as a possible wife for the boy produced by Louis and the duchesse de Châteauroux, as well as by the death of her 'official' father, François Poisson. On the eve of the official outbreak of the Seven Years' War in 1756, the abbé de Bernis, a somewhat unreliable protégé of Pompadour, again found her in very low spirits, disgusted with the intrigues of the court, thinking, yet again, of relinquishing her several burdens. Louis XV, to no-one's surprise, refused to agree to her resignation. Bernis' advice was to 'make the king happy, given the state of France, the financial crisis, universal insubordination, and the loss of the king's authority'.[65] It was an impossible task, even for the gifted and devoted madame de Pompadour.

One had to try, however. An open declaration of war, as opposed to the covert war that had been waged for years against the hated English, had become an increasingly popular project among many of Louis XV's courtiers, who believed that they had little choice in the matter. Maybe this resort to arms would unite the nation. Those who supported the idea were to be bitterly disappointed, and the ailing Pompadour, who was to play a major role in the prelude to and progress of the war, would die, a nervous wreck, shortly after the Seven Years' War ended in 1763. Louis would live for another decade, but his personal failings, together with the nation's reactions to the disastrous outcome of the war, meant that a major re-evaluation of Bourbon absolutism would have to be undertaken if the system were to survive. Richard Bonney is right to observe that French absolutism was something of a 'moveable feast', changing in accordance with time, circumstance, and the personality of the monarch.[66] Throughout its lifespan, however, there can be no doubt that a king's personal reputation *did* matter, at least in the eighteenth century. The peers of the realm had made this clear even to the great Louis XIV when he had legitimised two of his illegitimate sons. The decision was annulled in 1717–18, much to the pleasure of the peers who expressed their belief that, 'Even if the king enjoys absolute power, his acts must still conform to the rules he agreed to during his coronation, as well as to the Christian French tradition.' The peers were not prepared to defend *'un intérêt égoiste'*.[67] One of the fault-lines undermining the Bourbon monarchy throughout the second half of the eighteenth century would be the alienation of the *noblesse de l'épée* from the monarchy and the failure of the monarchy to pursue the most realistic alternative strategy – a new partnership with the *noblesse de robe* and the landed and commercial bourgeoisie. The disaster of the Seven Years' War would offer the opportunity for *radical* change. As we shall see in part two of this work, once the war had ended, Henri Bertin, along with his life-long friend, Nicolas Moreau, would devote their attention to the realisation of a reform programme, which, at the very least, would recognise the 'rise of the bourgeoisie'.[68]

Notes

1 Jean-François Chiappe, *Louis XV* (Paris, 1996), pp.15–16.

2 Jonathan Dull, *The French Navy and the Seven Years' War* (London, 2005), p.xii and p.22.

3 Albert Meyrac, *Louis XV, ses maîtresses, le Parc aux Cerfs, d'après le journal-mémoires de d'Argenson, les chansons du temps et les mémoires du duc de Richelieu* (Paris, 1914), p.12.

4 Antoine, *Louis XV*, p.28.

5 Jean-Christian Petitfils, *Le Régent* (Paris, 1986), pp.607–10.

6 Peter Campbell, *Power and Politics in Old Régime France, 1720–1745* (London, 1996), pp.45–50; Antoine, *Louis XV*, pp.89–95; Comte Fleury, *Louis XV intime et les Petites maîtresses* (Paris, 1933), p.44.

7 Albert Meyrac, *Vie privée de Louis XV* (Paris, 1921), p.49. Meyrac's study is based upon Mouffle d'Angerville's, *Vie privée de Louis XV, ou principaux événements, particularités et anecdotes de son règne* (London, 1781). D'Angerville co-authored the seven volume *Mémoires de Bachaumont*, published in Amsterdam between 1774 and 1776. Many

historians who have taken an interest in the seamier side of Louis XV's private life have mined this work.

8 Fleury, *Louis XV intime*, p.15.
9 Fleury, *Louis XV intime*, p.20.
10 Antoine, *Louis XV*, pp.150–8.
11 Lewis, *France, 1715–1804*, pp.28–33.
12 Maurice Lever, *Louis XV, libertin malgré lui* (Paris, 2002), p.46.
13 Mouffle d'Angerville, *Vie privée de Louis XV*, pp.82–3.
14 Castries, *La Pompadour* (Paris, 1824). Castries, like many chroniclers of Louis XV's private life, relies for some of his anecdotes on Madame d'Hausset's *Mémoires* (Paris, 1824). Other frequently mined sources are Mouffle d'Angerville's *Vie privée de Louis XV*, Edmond and Jules Goncourt's *Les maîtresses de Louis xv et autres portraits de femmes* (Paris, 2003), which first appeared in 1860, and Pierre de Nolhac's *Louis XV et Madame de Pompadour* (Paris, 1928).
15 Lever, *Louis XV*, p.18 and pp.57–8.
16 Antoine, *Louis XV*, p.485.
17 Julian Swann, *Politics and the Parlement of Paris under Louis XV, 1754–74* (Cambridge, 1995), p.53.
18 Mouffle d'Angerville, *Vie privée de Louis XV*, p.145, n.1.
19 Goncourt, *Les maîtresses de Louis XV*, p.57.
20 Lever, *Louis XV*, p.57; Fleury, *Louis XV intime*, pp.57–8.
21 Antoine, *Louis XV*, p.489.
22 Goncourt, *Les maîtresses de Louis XV*, pp.91–101.
23 Antoine, *Louis XV*, pp.488–90. It seems that madame de Tournelle was well versed in these matters. Jacques Dumaine informs us that she had had three lovers before the king. J. Dumaine, *Louis XV et le Parc-aux-Cerfs* (Paris, n.d.), p.14.
24 Antoine, *Louis XV*, pp.374–5; Castries, *La Pompadour*, pp.32–4.
25 Mouffle d'Angerville, *Vie privée de Louis XV*, p.137, n.2
26 Colin Jones, *Madame de Pompadour: Images of a Mistress* (London, 2002), p.34. Sorel's body was exhumed in September 2004. High levels of mercury were found in specimens of her hair and skin, according to an enquiry conducted by the *conseil de l'Indre et Loire*.
27 Harry T. Dickinson, *Liberty and Property. Political Ideology in Eighteenth-Century Britain* (London, 1979), p.192; Colin Jones, *The Great Nation: France from Louis XV to Napoleon* (London, 2002), p.123, Lewis, *France 1715–1804*, chap. six; Lever, *Louis XV*, p.127.
28 Campbell, *Power and Politics*, p.9.
29 Fleury, *Louis XV*, p.67; Campbell, *Power and Politics*, p.157.
30 Antoine, *Louis XV*, pp.374–5.
31 Jones, *The Great Nation*, pp.239–40.

32 Antoine, *Louis XV*, p.496.

33 De Nolhac, *Louis XV et madame de Pompadour*, pp.9–13.

34 Christine Algrant, *Madame de Pompadour, Mistress of France* (London, 2003), p.108. Many famous portraits of Pompadour have been captured by Jones, *Madame de Pompadour*.

35 Algrant, *Madame de Pompadour*, p.41.

36 Castries, *La Pompadour*, pp.86–94; De Nolhac, *Louis XV et Madame de Pompadour*, chap. 4.

37 Jones, *Madame de Pompadour*, pp.82–5.

38 See the marquis de Castries' final judgement, *La Pompadour*, pp.324–5.

39 De Nolhac states that sexual relations ended around the beginning of 1752, although there was 'une longue négligence' before the final break, *Louis XV et madame de Pompadour*, p.274.

40 Mouffle d'Angerville, *Vie privée de Louis XV*, pp.227–8.

41 Antoine, *Louis XV*, pp.498–501.

42 William Doyle, *Jansenism* (London, 2000), p.2 and pp.71–4; John McManners, *Church and Society in Eighteenth-Century France* (Oxford, 1999), 2 vols, Vol.I: *The Clerical Establishment and its Social Ramifications*, p.187; Swann, *Politics and the Parlement of Paris*, p.27.

43 De Nolhac, *Louis XV et Madame de Pompadour*, p.290.

44 D'Argenson, *Journal*, vol.8, p.35.

45 We have adopted the term 'Grand Design' to describe Jacob-Nicholas Moreau's massive historical archive, which laid the foundation for his ideological attack on the parlements and the *philosophes* (referred to by Keith Baker as 'this grand strategy' (see Baker, *Inventing the French Revolution* (Cambridge, 1990), p.74), as well as Henri Bertin's subsequent contribution as a reforming secretary of state after 1763, together with his quite remarkable 'Enlightenment' correspondence with French Jesuit missionary/mandarins in Peking, which would continue until the outbreak of the Revolution of 1789. Moreau and Bertin would work together for over thirty years, transforming a 'strategy' into a 'Grand Design'.

46 Swann, *Politics and the Parlement of Paris*, p.75; Keith Baker, 'Memory and Practice', in Baker, *Inventing the French Revolution*, pp.31–58.

47 D'Argenson, *Journal*, vol.9, p.196 and p.175.

48 Castries, *La Pompadour*, p.134.

49 Algrant, *Madame de Pompadour*, p.150.

50 Antoine, *Louis XV*, pp.502–4; Fleury, *Louis XV intime*, pp.91–6.

51 E-M. Benabou, *La Prostitution et la police des moeurs au XVIIIe siècle* (Paris, 1987), p.400.

52 Fleury, *Louis XV intime*, pp.191–7; Goncourt, *Les maîtresses de Louis XV*, pp.83–4.

53 Guy de Batut (ed.), *Louis XV* (Paris, 1933), p.199; Goncourt, *Les maîtresses de Louis XV*, p. 283.
54 Madame d'Hausset, *Mémoires*, pp.64–6; Dumaine, *Louis XV et le Parc-aux-Cerfs*, chap. 4; Fleury, *Louis XV intime*, p.51.
55 Antoine, *Louis XV*, pp.503–10.
56 Benabou, *La prostitution*, pp. 402–3.
57 Jones, *Madame de Pompadour*, p.111. Jones is almost certainly right to assume that these portraits acknowledged the king's 'new sexual arrangements'.
58 Goncourt, *Les maîtresses de Louis XV*, p.301, n.1.
59 Fleury, *Louis XV intime*, pp.120–5.
60 Antoine, *Louis XV*, p.506.
61 L.-G. Bourdon, *Le Parc au cerf, ou l'origine de l'affreux déficit, par un zélé patriote* (1790), pp.6–7.
62 Antoine, *Louis XV*, pp.615–17.
63 Goncourt, *Les maîtresses de Louis XV*, pp.251–3; Lewis, *France 1715–1804*, pp.210–11.
64 Antoine confirms the important role played by madame de Pompadour in the creation of the Deer Park. He writes that she was 'the superintendant of the king's pleasures', the all too willing assistant of Richelieu, Bachelier and Le Bel: *Louis XV*, pp.501–2.
65 Batut, ed., *Louis XV*, pp.106–10.
66 Richard Bonney, 'Absolutism: What's in a Name?', *French History* , vol.1 (1987), pp. 93–117.
67 J.P. Labatut, 'La revendication du pouvoir noble en France aux XVIIe et XVIIIe siècles', *Fédération historique du Sud-Ouest. Actes du colloque franco-britannique, 27–30 septembre 1976* (Bordeaux, 1979).
68 G. Lewis, 'Rising Tides. The Rise of the Bourgeoisie and the Fall of the Bourbon Monarchy' in *Socialist History*, vol.33 (*Origins of the French Revolution*), pp.1–21.

Chapter Three

The Seven Years' War and the Advent of the 'Grand Design'

1759, according to Frank McLynn, was 'the year Britain became master of the world'.[1] An exaggeration perhaps, and one that would certainly have annoyed the great Chinese Emperor, Kienlong, who preferred to believe that foreign powers were satellites that revolved around his 'Celestial Empire'. Nonetheless, the Seven Years' War (1756–63) did record permanent shifts in the balance of world power, as well as significant changes in the relative strengths of British constitutional monarchy and French absolutism: victory would immeasurably strengthen the constitutional Hanoverian monarchy in Britain; defeat would seriously weaken the absolutist Bourbon monarchy in France, increasing the pressure for the radical reform that would provide the stimulus for Bertin and Moreau's 'Grand Design'.

The mutual agreement that had been arranged between Louis XV and Pompadour in the early 1750s had enabled Louis to regularise his complicated sex life, leaving Pompadour to satisfy her growing ambition for the exercise of real political power. One of the consequences of this sexual and political *ballet-à-deux*, however, would lead to a further disintegration of the already unstable, faction-ridden system of government, led by an insecure monarch. The fundamental reasons for the increasing instability of government were Louis XV's secretive methods of wielding his supposed absolute power, together with

Pompadour's questionable exercise of patronage and political power, legitimised only by her position as the king's ex-mistress. By 1756, 'Pompadour's protégés', most of whom were too inexperienced, or too incompetent, to deal with the national and international crises of the late 1750s, had begun to appear centre-stage. Meanwhile, behind the scenes, influential courtiers such as the duc de Richelieu worked to undermine Pompadour's authority by finding nubile mistresses for Louis XV's bed: Pompadour desperately needed ministers to protect her increasingly vulnerable position at court. Among the favoured few we find Henri Bertin, a loyal protégé, prepared, first as *lieutenant général de Paris* from 1757–9, to track down Louis and Pompadour's enemies, and then, as *contrôleur général des finances* from 1759–63, to assist Pompadour in her continual battle to shore up Louis XV's insecure, absolutist defence against the critical attacks of the parlement de Paris. Bertin would become Pompadour's indispensable accomplice, the third member of the royal triumvirate – Louis–Pompadour–Bertin – that would operate at Versailles from 1757 to 1764.

Bertin's complicity in the more questionable activities of his monarch is easier to understand when we recall that if Louis and Pompadour desperately wished to mask the truth, and cost, of the Deer Park, as well as the purchase of stately homes, Bertin also had something to hide, his own 'family skeleton' in the Bastille, his elder brother, the marquis de Fratteaux. It was hardly surprising, then, that Bertin found himself being pushed rapidly, sometimes rather unwillingly, up the very greasy pole of Versailles politics. His difficulty was that, although intelligent, and, like Pompadour, committed to the defence of Bourbon absolutism, Bertin was more of an administrator than a statesman or diplomat. On the way to the top, he would have to deal with the ambitious duc de Choiseul, whose influence would increase during the Seven Years' War in direct proportion to the waning authority of Louis and Pompadour. Choiseul was jealous of Bertin's influence and contemptuous of his ability, likening him to 'a glass of corked wine', a comment that reveals something of

Choiseul's character, but more about the caste snobbery of the aristocratic *vrai noble*. He would exhibit a similar contempt for the abbé de Bernis, ambassador to Vienna, and foreign minister during the 1750s. All this was very typical of Versailles politics after the dismissals of two effective ministers, Machault and the comte d'Argenson, in 1757, an event that marked a new phase in the divisive struggle of 'sword' versus 'robe', exacerbated by the behaviour of a king who, all too often, allowed an ex-mistress to speak on his behalf. Jonathan Dull argues that, 'Louis' dislike of confrontation of any kind and his weak self-confidence, so dangerous in a war leader, already had undermined the functioning of his government.'[2]

The massive strain imposed by the several crushing defeats suffered by France during the Seven Years' War would further undermine the antiquated structures of Louis XV's government. Since the end of the War of the Austrian Succession in 1748, a 'phoney war' had been waged intermittently between the French and the British. Fought primarily on the high seas, Britain had seized the opportunity to expand and improve her navy (60 per cent of the money earmarked for the armed forces in Britain during the 1750s was spent on the navy), a prescient move that the French, for a variety of reasons, failed to imitate. It was obvious to the French Navy minister, the comte de Maurepas, that if France were to compete with 'perfidious Albion', the cost and direction of foreign policy should be re-assessed to deal with the expanding colonial conflict.[3] But, France's controversial treaties with Austria would move French forces towards central Europe, not Canada. Many of the increasingly powerful cabals of aristocratic courtiers of Versailles preferred fighting on land rather than the high seas, refusing to accept the emerging consensus that the long-term future belonged to those countries that had access to the markets, goods and raw materials required by emerging consumer and industrial societies – the coffees, teas, and spices, the cotton plantations, the sugar and the millions of impoverished slaves who died so that the European rich might live to re-build their castles and estates. 'Globalisation', as a world trading phenomenon, had been launched with the creation of the British East Indies Company in 1598. Its French counterpart, the *Compagnie des Indes*, would be launched a century later.[4] Behind the 'Diplomatic Revolution' of 1756 that would reverse centuries of hostility between France and Austria lay a revolution in the global economic system. William Pitt the Elder, with the backing of the City of London, realised this, but, unlike the British, the French had always been a continental as well as a maritime nation. This, in essence, would be one major reason for France's disastrous defeat in the Seven Years' War, her colonial losses weighing more heavily than those suffered on the Continent.

Given her adventurous, but unpopular, decision to link her foreign policy with Austria, for so long the dominant military power on the continent, France could not afford to ignore the reactions of the Prussian king, Frederick II. Frederick was determined to hold on to, or, if circumstances allowed, expand the boundaries of Prussia, while George II was equally determined to defend his vulnerable Hanoverian possessions. Austria and Russia were even more apprehensive of the expansionist designs of Frederick II, the former determined to secure the return of the industrial province of Silesia that Frederick had seized in 1741.[5] Prompted by the rapidly changing situation on the Continent, serious diplomatic negotiations between another of Pompadour's protégés, the abbé de Bernis, and the Austrian ambassador, the comte de Starhemberg, had begun in September 1755. Bernis' brief was to attempt the almost impossible – keep Prussia and Russia on board despite Maria Theresa's determination to regain the lost province of Silesia. François-Joachim de Pierre, the future cardinal de Bernis, would play a leading role in the diplomatic and political drama of the Seven Years' War. An intelligent, if over-emotional, man, a *bon viveur* and sometime poet, his correspondance with the comte de Stainville (promoted to the rank of 'duc de Choiseul' after 1758) and Pompadour would reveal a man who knew that French foreign and domestic policies were little short of disastrous, but was inclined to push the panic-button all too often. His repeated warnings of impending disaster would have earned praise from the Greek mythological prophet of doom, Cassandra.[6] In Bernis' defence, it has to be admitted that the situation was extremely complicated: Austria and Russia were old allies and Frederick was worried about the possible encirclement of his expanding state by their respective armies, which led directly to another diplomatic shock – the Convention of Westminster between Prussia and Britain, concluded in March 1756. By the terms of this cynical (so far as the Austrians and the French were concerned) agreement, Britain would help to defend the Prussian state against a possible Russian threat, whilst Prussia would help to defend George II's possessions in Germany. Three of the greatest continental powers, France, Austria and Russia, were now lining up against Britain and Prussia.[7]

The first Treaty of Versailles (1 May 1756) between France and Austria was defensive in nature, an attempt to square the circle created by the diplomatic dance of the main European powers. France, realising, somewhat belatedly, the financial and logistical implications of her maritime war with Britain, could not possibly ignore the threat posed by the central and eastern powers. With the support of Louis XV, whose genuinely held Catholic beliefs predisposed him towards alliances with Catholic states, Pompadour and her increasing number of hand-picked ministers gambled that if France and Austria joined hands to threaten George II's prized possession of Hanover, then Britain might be constrained from attacking French possessions in the Caribbean, North America and India. Even the omniscient Voltaire, who appreciated the difficulty of fighting on land and the high seas, was persuaded that the 'Diplomatic Revolution' with Austria was a wise move, but then Voltaire was never keen on colonies. He argued that Maria-Theresa's Austria no longer posed a major threat to France (or Britain) given the disintegration of Charles V's over-mighty Habsburg Empire, and what appeared to be the end of the Low Countries as one of the main theatres of European wars. There was some truth in this, but it was Prussia that kept Maria Theresa awake at night: the loss of the potentially rich province of Silesia to Frederick the Great during the War of the Austrian Succession still rankled. For his part, Frederick was under no illusion about Maria Theresa's determination to regain the province, and, as usual, he got his retaliation in first. On 28 August 1756, he marched his army into the kingdom of Saxony as a first step towards the invasion of Bohemia, a vital Austrian possession. On 16 October, Dresden, the capital of Saxony, fell to the Prussians, and Frederick's troops marched on towards Prague to confront the main Austrian armies. France was immediately drawn into the conflict. Russia, more worried now about the expansionist (Frederick preferred the adjective 'defensive'!) threat from Prussia, predictably fell in line with Austria and France. The 'phoney war' had ended, and the best laid plans of Pompadour and Maria Theresa had already been subverted. As an interesting aside, it is extraordinary, given the paternalist culture of the eighteenth century, that three formidable women, Catherine the Great of Russia, Maria Theresa of Austria and madame de Pompadour of France, were leading the struggle to reshape the European continent.

* * *

At first the fortunes of war swung against Britain and its Prussian ally. The British possession of Minorca (a relatively short sail away from Gibraltar) had fallen at the end of June 1756 to a French invasion force led by the duc de Richelieu, or 'my little Minorquin' as Pompadour now called him. By the summer of 1757, the Prussian advance into Austrian territory had been halted after the rout of Frederick's army at the battle of Kollin on the river Elbe. George II's incompetent son, the duke of Cumberland, following a distinctly poor campaign to protect Hanover, was pressurised into signing, on 8 September 1757, the Convention of Kloster-Seven with the French, an agreement that was little more than an abject surrender, which explains George II's decision to force his son to resign as commander of British forces in Germany. In contrast, Pompadour's stock at Versailles rose to new heights, giving her almost a free hand in appointing ministers and generals. However, events would prove that, although her determination and courage were unquestioned, her political judgement was distinctly shaky. In just a couple of months, as the expectation of victory dissolved into the fear of defeat, the marquise would be facing renewed attacks, especially from those critics who had never forgiven her for the 'treachery' of the Treaty of Versailles. They reminded her that France was being drawn into fighting for Austrian interests in eastern Europe during a period when Britain had sunk, or seized, over 300 French merchant ships on the high seas, capturing around 6,000 men. The dilemma that weakened French governments, from Louis XIV to general de Gaulle – should France retain her Great Power status by accepting the fact that she was, fundamentally, a continental power, or should she also defend her imperial possessions – was never posed more acutely than during the 'reign' of madame de Pompadour.

The decision to sign the Second Treaty of Versailles on 1 May 1757 suggests that Louis and Pompadour did not fully appreciate the nature of this dilemma, or, if they did, it was now too late to rectify the situation they had helped to create. By the terms of this new treaty, France agreed to supply over 100,000 men to help Austria defend its territories, together with a subsidy of 30 million *livres*. France was already providing subsidies to the Russians and the Swedes: this new agreement would place a massive strain on French finances. The parlements, scenting a government in distress, were in no mood to assist by agreeing to extra taxes. Critics then, as now, find it difficult to explain why France sacrificed so much to help Maria Theresa gain revenge over Prussia.[8] However, as time passed, French leaders would begin to realise that their foreign policy should be focused more on Pitt's London than Maria Theresa's Vienna, but French aristo-cratic officers would still prefer to die on the 'Retreat from Moscow' under Napoleon, than on the high seas. Under Louis XV, French foreign policy would be determined by geography and all too often by the cultural traditions of an aristocratic military class. At the peak of the crisis in the late 1750s, the comte de Belle-Isle, one of France's top generals, would hesitate to take a ministerial post that he considered to be beneath him.

From the autumn of 1757, however, the tide of war began to flow rapidly against the French, undermining the influence that Pompadour and her protégés wielded on the battlefield, and, therefore, at court. Debilitated by tuberculosis and depression, exhausted by the repeated blood-letting imposed upon her delicate frame by the scalpels of her surgeons, Pompadour's responsibility for the debacle of the Seven Years' War now began to weigh more heavily upon her shoulders. On 5 November 1757, at the battle of Rossbach, the Prussian army inflicted one of the most serious defeats ever experienced by the French army: a more humiliating defeat, according to Voltaire, than those of Agincourt and Crécy. But greater humiliation was to follow: another crushing defeat by Frederick II over France's Austrian allies at the battle of Leuthen on 5 December, followed by the retreat of French forces from George II's German possessions and the rout of the French army at Krefeld on 23 June 1758. If the opening two years of the war had been difficult, 1759 was to prove disastrous. As all British schoolchildren used to learn, general Wolfe's victory over the marquis de Montcalm at the battle of Quebec (12–13 September) made it possible for Britain, not France, to seize control of the vast territory of what we now know as Canada. Two years earlier, at the battle of Plassey (23 June 1757), 'Clive of India' had virtually sealed the fate of French influence in India. What British schoolchildren are rarely told is that long before Horatio Nelson became one of our most celebrated cult figures, admiral Sir Edward Hawke had won one of the great naval victories in world history at the battle of Quiberon Bay on 21–22 November 1759. Fought in a raging gale, Quiberon has rightly been described as a stunning achievement.[9] Like the far more famous battle of Trafalgar in 1805, it dashed hopes of a French landing on British shores. For Louis and Pompadour, there really was little choice now but to engage in serious peace negotiations. An important page in the history of the world, and an important corner in Pompadour's career, had been turned.

* * *

In this chapter, which focuses upon the scale and consequences of the defeat suffered by France in just seven years, we will assess the responsibility carried by Louis XV and Pompadour for the debacle of the Seven Years' War, and assess the supportive role played by Henri Bertin, first as *lieutenant général de police de Paris* in 1757, then as *contrôleur général des finances* from 1759 to 1763. As *contrôleur général*, one of Bertin's main briefs would be the resolution of the financial crises caused by military defeats, without agreeing to one of the principal demands of the Paris parlement – an opportunity to audit the collection of state taxes, as well as the private expenditures of Louis XV and Pompadour. This bitter struggle, evoking memories of the battle between Charles I and his parliaments in the mid-seventeenth century, would have serious repercussions for the operation of France's political and constitutional system. We have noted that, from the outset, many commentators described the conflict between Britain and France as 'Pompadour's War'. At the beginning of 1756, the capricious court chronicler, the marquis d'Argenson, had claimed that Pompadour was now 'in charge and acting as First Minister'; in February of that year, he wrote that she was still 'pretending to work for peace between France and England'.[10] However, the part she played in the dismissal of two very experienced ministers in February 1757, Machault d'Arnouville and the comte d'Argenson, illustrates not only the power she had acquired by this date, but also the lack of judgement she often revealed in the exercise of that power. The former had been foolish enough to suggest that Pompadour should leave the court following Damiens' abortive attempt on the king's life on 5 January; as for the latter, one of Louis' particular favourites, Pompadour had always disliked and distrusted the d'Argenson clan, especially the comte's brother, the marquis d'Argenson, whose journal leaves us in no doubt of his contempt for her. With the departure of these two influential court figures, Pompadour's personal room for manoeuvre appears to have been considerably enlarged, but at the cost of responsible, stable government. The dismissal of Machault and d'Argenson marked a significant turning point in the political and administrative history of Louis XV's reign.

Pompadour lacked the vision to replace these competent ministers with talented and effective successors; all too often she chose courtiers whose principal qualifications for government posts in the administration or armed forces were that they had stood by her in the past. The replacements as ministers of finance and the army, the marquis de Paulmy and Peyrenc de Moras, have been described as 'nonentities, and only moderate nonentities to boot'.[11] As for the army, a major military crisis was hardly the best time to install her cronies at the head of the French armies. In the spring of 1758, the comte de Clermont, a Bourbon-Condé prince of the blood, and another Pompadour favourite, took over command of French troops in western Germany from the duc de Richelieu. Clermont has been accused of being 'an even greater disaster than his philandering predecessor'. The following summer, the prince de Soubise (who had led French troops at the disaster of Rossbach) was given command in western Germany. In Frank McLynn's opinion, Soubise was yet another 'nonentity', 'timid and indecisive as a commander, possessing no military talent and owing everything to his being a favourite of Madame de Pompadour'.[12] Oiling the wheels of the creaking military machine Pompadour and her ministers had created was Pâris-Duverney, a member of the powerful Pâris family of brothers who had acted as financial puppet-masters of the state since the fall of John Law in the 1720s. Pompadour had written to Pâris-Duverney just before the prince de Soubise had engaged the Prussians at Rossbach in November 1757 begging him to assist the French army. The intimate, cajoling tone of her letter was again typical: 'If you promise me this [a massive loan], I will have no more worries and will look forward to a happy outcome. You are quite perceptive, my Blockhead; you know me, see how grateful I shall be.'[13]

There was someone else who had reason to be even more grateful to Pompadour than Pâris-Duverney, and that was Henri Bertin. From his vantage point as *intendant* of the Lyonnais, he must have registered the increasing popular discontent with

Pompadour as the tide of defeat began to engulf the French army and navy in 1758. There was the comte de Clermont's defeat, on 23 June, at the battle of Krefeld, near Dusseldorf, followed by the loss of Louisbourg on Cape Breton island, strategically important for the defence of Canada and for the protection of valuable French fishing rights off Newfoundland, a few weeks later. One consequence of these disasters would be the dismissal of the abbé de Bernis, Pompadour's choice as minister of foreign affairs. Having lost any hope of victory following the crushing defeat of the French army at Rossbach the previous year, he had decided to transmit his pessimistic assessment of the situation in a remarkable letter to Pompadour, which contained accusations that were being repeated on the boulevards and in the salons and coffee houses of Paris and the provinces: 'Canada lost, Louisbourg in the hands of the English, above all the treasury empty, not a *écu* to be squeezed out of Montmartel [one of Pompadour's very wealthy mentors], no clothing for the troops, no boots for the cavalry, a navy without sailors; finally, Vienna, as insatiable as ever, withdrawing from engagements it can no longer honour, anarchy taking hold of the royal council with each minister looking after his own interests without a thought for the general good.'[14]

It was a fairly comprehensive charge-sheet, and many of its claims were repeated in a letter that Bernis despatched to the French ambassador to Vienna, the comte de Stainville, whose elevation to the peerage as the duc de Choiseul in August 1758 marked the rise to power of the only French politician able to match the vision and audacity of William Pitt in London. In this letter, Bernis, possibly aware of the fact that Pompadour and Choiseul might be plotting against him, but anxious to retain some power at court, suggested that Pompadour's position had become extremely vulnerable: 'Paris detests her, accusing her of being responsible for everything that has happened'; as for Louis XV, Bernis 'wished that he would put into practice what he thought was right'. He ended his jeremiad with these typically over-dramatised, but very prophetic, words: 'I see ahead a hideous revolution in the political world'. For Bernis, the only possible solution would be the creation of a 'triumvirate', composed of Pompadour, Choiseul, and, of course, Bernis himself, a trio powerful enough, in his estimation, to force Louis XV to spend more time on his royal duties than on his mistresses and the hunt.[15]

This was *precisely* the reasoning behind the creation, the previous year, of what we have referred to as the Louis–Pompadour–Bertin 'royal triumvirate'. Bernis' memoirs make it quite clear that, along with Choiseul, whose bargaining skills as a courtier made Bernis appear incompetent, he did not believe that this royal trio could deal effectively with the nature and scale of the crisis undermining Louis XV's authority. The obvious flaw in his argument was the fact that Louis, who depended upon Bertin's integrity, was not part of Bernis' triumvirate. A ministerial triumvirate without Louis XV, who, for all his moral and leadership faults, still thought of himself as an *absolute* monarch, and occasionally acted like one, was a political concept that Bertin and Moreau would support in their 'Grand' Design, which would undermine the project from its inception. There was also the fact that Pompadour was not weak enough, yet, to allow a charismatic and ambitious aristocrat like Choiseul to threaten her own position. Hence her move to dismiss Bernis on 6 October 1758, replacing him with no less a figure than the rising star at Versailles, the duc de Choiseul, a potential enemy who had to be brought onside. Bernis' correspondence makes it painfully clear that Pompadour and Louis XV had become heartily sick of Bernis' prophecies of doom, and that Choiseul, who was to deny Bernis any further role in the government, was instrumental in Bernis' disgrace. The naïve and all too honest abbé de Bernis would be rewarded for his pains with a cardinal's hat on 9 October 1758, thus realising at least one of his ambitions – to follow in the steps, somewhat belatedly, of his hero, cardinal Fleury.[16]

* * *

By the end of 1758, with criticism from the public and her many enemies reaching unprecedented heights, Pompadour felt that she had to construct a more effective shield against her enemies.

An inner defence ring already existed, composed of the *directeur du cabinet de la poste* and the far more influential *lieutenant général de police de Paris*, a quasi-minister of the crown. The former vetted the private mail of courtiers before passing on the more salacious and informative missives to Louis and Pompadour via the *lieutenant général*, thus enabling them to keep some sort of check on court intrigues and gossip. It is hardly surprising that Pompadour's enemies should have described both Robert Janel (*directeur de la poste*) and Nicolas Berryer (*lieutenant général de police*) as untrustworthy and sinister figures. The marquis d'Argenson thought that 'This Janel ... is a great nave and traitor; he has already deceived two or three ministers under whom he has served, but who would make use of these evil, treacherous and perverse souls?' As for Nicolas René Berryer, *lieutenant général* from1747 to 1757, he was the 'loyal servant who has tracked down [Pompadour's] enemies, spreading misinformation and doubt about those who might seek to dislodge her'. Police reports for the period also contain revealing information on the activities of the marquis de Paulmy, Louis XV and Pompadour's choice as minister for war after Paulmy's uncle, the comte d'Argenson, was forced out in 1757. Erica-Marie Benabou suggests that Paulmy's willingness to obey Louis and Pompadour's orders explains why the police filed reports of his athletic sexual exploits in the higher-class whorehouses of Paris, somewhat ambiguously, under 'no action'.[17] It would have been rather difficult for Pompadour to complain anyway, given the royal frolics of Louis XV in his Deer Park. It was a very different story in the crowded and stinking streets of the poorer *faubourgs* of Paris where no minister of the crown had a reputation lower than Berryer's. His house had been besieged by a mob in May 1750 as a result of his hardline approach to the problem of ridding Paris of a disturbing influx of beggars, the consequence of two poor harvests. Poor children were rounded up by the police, and rumours began to circulate that they were being transported to the icy colonies of New France (Canada). Many of the rioters believed the somewhat ludicrous, but widespread, rumour that a royal prince was suffering from leprosy, and had been advised by the court doctor to bathe in children's blood. Berryer's stock amongst the poorer inhabitants of Paris never really recovered, dragging the reputation of Pompadour down with it.

What Pompadour wanted as the misfortunes of war continued to sap her confidence was a few more loyal and devoted favourites around her. To achieve this objective, Pompadour's 'eyes and ears', Nicolas Berryer, had already been given a seat on the prestigious internal affairs committee (*comité des dépêches*) in October 1757. His replacement as *lieutenant général de la police de Paris* was someone with a much safer pair of hands, someone, in fact, who owed his entire career to Pompadour's patronage – Henri Bertin. His official nomination as *lieutenant général* had been announced on 5 November 1757. It was, from Bertin's standpoint, an excellent career move. Viewed against the broader canvas of French politics and policing during the reign of Louis XV, it also marked the beginning of the 'royal triumvirate' – Louis, Pompadour and Bertin. Control over the police chief of Paris was absolutely vital to the success of the triumvirate, especially in the delicate matter of the king's private life. Arlette Farge, one of the best-informed historians of the police service in Paris, tells us that as *lieutenant général de la police de Paris*, Bertin could exercise 'une influence secrète et prodigieuse'.[18] The post, which was first created in 1667, had gradually assumed ministerial status, although this was never formalised, despite the fact that the administrative and supervisory responsibilities of a *lieutenant général de police* for the capital were numerous and exceedingly onerous. Apart from the obvious duties of policing Paris, which included the supervision of military garrisons, public morals and hygiene, illicit assemblies and the University of Paris, Bertin was also responsible for certain religious matters. As if this were not enough, there was the immense task of overseeing the provisioning of a capital city whose population had increased from 510,000 inhabitants in 1700 to 576,000 in 1750. Finally, there was the close, and sometimes stormy, relationship that a *lieutenant général* had to maintain with two of the most powerful institutions in Paris – the Châtelet, where the *lieutenant général* held his own police court, and the Paris parlement. Bertin, a born administrator, would add several cubits to his stature during his short, but valuable, experience as the police chief of Paris.

Police resources to defend public order in the great city of Paris appear to have been pitifully small: in late 1757, they consisted of only 105 mounted officers and 566 men on foot. This force was supported, however, by 3,000 or so semi-military *Gardes françaises*. In the last resort, *ancien régime* governments were forced to rely upon the army. In some districts, there were probably as many spies and informers (*mouchards*) as policemen operating in Paris. That lonely sentinel and contemporary recorder of Parisian life, Sébastien Mercier, tells us that, 'The security of Paris at night is assured by ... three hundred *mouchards* [government spies] ... As soon as two people strike up an intimate conversation, a third is sure to be seen hanging around to overhear what they are saying.'[19] No doubt illicit sex was frequently the topic for discussion whenever two or three Parisians did get together, which offers one reason for the expansion of the 'moral brigade' (*police des moeurs*) on the orders of Bertin's predecessor, Berryer. The early 1750s was a period in which attacks against 'cynical displays' of debauchery and immorality became more common. Moralists and reformers pressed the authorities to 'extinguish' the fires of unchecked, immoral behaviour. One police report estimated in 1762 that around 25,000 prostitutes were plying their trade in the capital: thirty years later, the publications of Louis-Sébastien Mercier and Rétif de la Bretonne would still be focusing upon the dangerous social consequences of the spread of prostitution and pornography in the city.

Between the 1740s and the famous ordinance of the *lieutenant général de police*, Lenoir, in 1778, the Parisian authorities would introduce a raft of measures to deal with what was deemed to be 'public immorality'. Berryer had created separate departments for dealing with prostitutes and 'sodomites' as early as 1747. There was, of course, one law for the court of Versailles, and another for the general public; whilst court aristocrats could cavort, under surveillance, without much fear of being arrested, a handful of lower class homosexuals were actually burned at the stake, including two working-class men of 18 and 25 who had been arrested in the street in 1750. There were obviously hierarchical circles of sin – the king had his Deer Park, the aristocracy their private parties in town mansions, the bourgeoisie their more discreet apartments and brothels, and the labouring poor, their cheap inns, dark alleys and fields.[20] Did all this matter to the king and his ability to take control of a government in crisis? Indeed it did. One of the pressing problems for Louis XV by the early 1760s, for example, was how to finance his increasingly expensive private life, including the maintenance costs of the illegitimate children it produced. Discontent amongst the general public had prompted the magistrates of the parlement of Paris to ask from which pocket Louis XV was taking the money to finance his 'personal expenses'. While French soldiers and sailors continued to die in Europe and the colonies to rescue something from the disaster of the war with Britain, the government was pressing the parlements to levy higher taxes to cover the massive national debt. What were Louis and Pompadour doing to economise? By the late 1750s, the parlements would be seeking answers to this awkward question.

Another relevant question would be whether Bertin was complicit in the disreputable behaviour of Louis XV and Pompadour. Again, the answer has to be that he was. Arrangements had already been made for Louis to acquire a private income from the collection of indirect taxes. A share of the revenues from several tax collection offices had been bought over some years on the king's behalf, and the proceeds placed in a special royal purse. But these royal ruses, which, if made known to the general public, would not exactly have endeared Louis to his people, did not produce enough cash to cover the rising costs of Louis' private life.[21] An opportunity to replenish the royal purse occurred in March 1762, when the comte d'Eu, brother of the prince de Dombes and a relative of Louis XV, agreed to exchange the principality of Dombes (situated near Trévoux along the river Saône) for crown land in Normandy. Henri Bertin was the minister who assumed the responsibility of drawing up the contract relating to the purchase of the principality, copies of which were sent to the parlements of Paris and Rouen, as well as to the royal tax and accounting offices (*chambre des comptes*) in the capital. However, instead of treating the income from his new acquisition as part of the royal domain, Bertin, acting on Louis' instructions, created a *'département spécial'*, specifically designed to assist with the costs of the Deer Park, as well as those relating to royal ex-mistresses and illegitimate children. Princes of the blood, who had expected to receive a share of the proceeds from the sale of the principality of Dombes, as well as the magistrates of the Paris parlement who were constantly pressing for greater financial transparency on the part of the king, were outraged at this diversion of income from part of the royal domain to a private account created to pay for Louis' sex life. They had every right to be aggrieved as a more detailed examination of the accounts relating to the principality reveals.

The comte d'Eu had signed a ten-year lease in 1755 with a Parisian bourgeois, Joseph Rat, giving the latter an annual sum of 172,000 *livres* for the right to collect the income deriving from the principality of Dombes. On the expiration of this lease in 1765, Henri Bertin would appoint an expert, Joseph Imbert, to make an inventory of all the 'rights, impositions, and revenues of the principality', which led to an increase in Joseph Rat's lease from 172,000 to 200,000 *livres* a year, that sum to be deposited in Louis XV's *département spécial*. Louis XV would eventually acquire an average annual income of *c.*250,000 *livres* a year between the signing of the new lease with Rat on 1 January 1766 to Louis' death in 1774. Every leaseholder during this period would have to sign an agreement stating that the details of their contract with the king would not be passed to the parlements or the *chambre des comptes*. Furthermore, royal control of seigneurial courts on the principality of Dombes ensured that no appeals against their decisions would be passed to a higher court, other than the king's council in Versailles. For example, when the inhabitants of the parish of Garneras lost a case against their local seigneur over the payment of 990 *livres* for the renovation of the parish church, they were denied the right to appeal and asked to pay a total of 2,602 *livres* to cover legal fees, as well as the cost of renovating the church. At the end of the day, poor peasants were helping to finance not only the lifestyles of their seigneurs, but also the disreputable private lifestyle of their sovereign.[22]

Documentary evidence in the *archives nationales* confirms Jacques Dumaine's contention that Henri Bertin played the key role in managing the secret income of Louis XV, allocating funds to pay pensions to discarded mistresses and providing money for the education and upkeep of Louis' illegitimate children. Dumaine argues that the accounting problems associated with managing these delicate matters became so complex that Bertin had to hire an assistant, a notary by the name of Lage de Chaillon, who was charged with the responsibility for the actual payment of pensions to mistresses and the maintenance of 'the little fawns' from the Deer Park. The nineteenth-century novelist, Eugène Le Roy, wrote that 'Louis gave him [Bertin] the responsibility of looking after the girls in the *Parc aux Cerfs* who were either pregnant or who had ceased to please the king, as well as that of arranging the marriage of illegitimate offspring who had been raised in the Convent of the Presentation. These girls and their daughters appear to have been treated sympathetically.'[23] Henri Bertin's unfailing loyalty to Louis XV, or to be more precise, the Bourbon monarchy, which, as we saw in Chapter One, had been so generous to the Bertin family, would be rewarded with further honours, including the office of *contrôleur général des finances* (1759–63), and the even more prestigious position of secretary of state (1763–80).

It appears that Bernis had been right to question the motivation behind the creation of the Louis–Pompadour–Bertin triumvirate. If he believed, as an increasing number of courtiers at Versailles did, that Bertin had been chosen, primarily, to protect the best interests of the king and his ex-mistress, rather than those of the nation, then the evidence again suggests that he was thinking along the right lines. When challenged on this issue, Bertin would almost certainly have borrowed Voltaire's description of him: 'Bertin, who in his king, always saw his country.'[24] Pompadour had also always acted on the principle that the monarchy was the sovereign power in France, not this relatively new, and dangerous, political concept of 'the nation'. This goes to the heart of the matter – the court and the country were not speaking the same political language, or to be more precise, the meaning attached to the old political terminology no longer represented, after the 1740s, what an increasing percentage of the people thought it should. The word 'sovereign', for example, was no longer coterminous with the king; it was increasingly being employed to describe 'the power of the people', especially when news of the crushing naval defeat of Quiberon Bay on 20 November 1759 circulated around country. The court would continue to employ the old lexicon of Bourbon absolutism, with diminishing effect, while Louis XV would continue to use the ailing Pompadour as one of his distorting mirrors until she died of tuberculosis, aggravated by exhaustion – the 'prime minister' who never was! By this time, Choiseul had become the de facto 'prime minister' that France desperately needed.

* * *

If only Pompadour had received more support from Louis XV, the man to whom she had devoted her entire life. Throughout the period of the Seven Years' War, however, Louis continued to exercise what he regarded as the two most important attributes of his royal privileges – sex and secrecy. Pompadour lived in continual fear, not of Louis' 'little girls' who grazed in the king's Deer Park, but the well-born mistresses her enemies introduced to the court, hoping that one of them would destroy her influence over the king. The prince de Conti thought that Marie-Anne Louise Adélaide, marquise de Coislin, would make an excellent candidate. In the first place, she was a relative of the infamous

Nesle sisters whom Louis had found so attractive in the 1740s. Also, Coislin was a striking lady with the personal confidence and poise one could expect from someone of her aristocratic pedigree. She had no qualms about using her superior social status to discomfort Pompadour, whom she described as 'a bourgeois dressed up as a duchess'. The most striking, and relevant, fact about this royal liaison was that it had occurred during one of the government's worst wartime crises. The summer and autumn of 1757 had been a period of continuing conflict, linked to the costs of war on three continents, between the Paris parlement and the crown. On 5 November, the French army had suffered its worst defeat of the decade at the battle of Rossbach, during a period in which Pompadour, coincidently or not, had been forced to endure one of her many serious bouts of ill health. Fortunately, for Pompadour, Coislin's reign proved to be relatively short: she demanded too much from a king who had too many female admirers.

However, the Coislin affair was followed by a far greater threat to Pompadour's position: the king's relationship with Mademoiselle Anne Couppier de Romans, 'a young and pretty girl from the provinces with whom the King was as infatuated as he could be'.[25] Once again, Louis humiliated Pompadour by continuing his affair with mademoiselle Romans for several years. On 13 January 1762, Romans presented the king with a son who was given the rare privilege of being 'recognised' if not legitimated (none of Louis XV's illegitimate offspring received official recognition). Little wonder that Pompadour was often on the point of settling for a quiet life during these years, toying with the idea of leaving the court with a handsome pay-off and, possibly, another little château as a retirement home. One might accept that the peculiar, but widely accepted, moral codes of eighteenth-century (Christian) monarchs should not be scrutinised through twenty-first century lenses (although it should be noted that Louis XV's behaviour was widely and roundly condemned at the time, and not only by his Jesuit confessors), but one surely has to conclude that if Louis' behaviour does not merit the extreme condemnation of contemporaries such as the crusading lawyer, Mouffle d'Angerville, it did nothing but harm to Pompadour, his ministers, and his country during one of the most critical periods in the history of Bourbon absolutism.[26]

The mutual agreement between Louis and Pompadour had failed to alter Louis' vacillating, obsessive and secretive approach to governing. As for Pompadour, it has been alleged that when the threat to her position from madame de Coislin became all too apparent, she arranged for a 'pretty young girl' to be installed in the Deer Park, with the aim of getting Louis to forget about Coislin.[27] One could, of course, argue that a *maîtresse en titre* other than Pompadour (too obsessed by her devotion to Louis XV), might have given Louis better advice, a duchesse de Châteauroux, perhaps? But it is difficult to believe that anyone could have altered Louis' *modus operandi* by the end of the 1750s. Even under Châteauroux's tutelage in the 1740s, Louis had maintained the fiction that he was in complete charge of foreign policy. The attempt upon his life by François Damiens on 5 January 1757 only served, understandably, to increase his congenital lack of self-confidence, as well as his profound distrust of anyone who was not a member of his inner circle.

Until 1756, Louis had used the prince de Conti (or perhaps vice versa) to conduct his secret foreign policy. It was focused primarily on Poland and sought, above all, to make Conti king of that country. Pompadour's 'secret diplomacy' did not quite run on parallel lines, and Conti eventually resigned from his semi-official position to lead the attack on Pompadour in the Paris parlement. As for Louis (whose wife, it is worth remembering, was Polish), he continued to meddle in Polish and Russian affairs, appointing the comte de Broglie as Conti's replacement. In May 1758, de Broglie, temporarily tired of sorting out Louis' foreign intrigues, gave up his position and joined the comte de Clermont's army in Germany. He returned in March 1759 as Louis' roving ambassador and, along with his brother, the duc de Broglie, and the baron de Breteuil, based in St Petersburg, worked to undermine the official foreign policy and peace talks conducted by Pompadour and the duc de Choiseul. Was this the way to run foreign policy in a country facing defeat abroad, and economic disaster at home? It is possible that Louis began to ask himself this question, given that on 18 February 1762, the two de Broglie brothers were exiled to their estates. Unfortunately for his country, the move did little in the long run to stop Louis pursuing his own fantasies about what France should really be doing abroad.[28] By the late 1750s, 'the chance for crying "Vive le Roi!" for *le Bien Aimé* was still there, but few found it worthwhile to make the effort'. Many Parisians had sympathised with the reasons Damiens gave for his attempted assassination of the king in January 1757– higher taxes, a collapse of national confidence, and the refusal of the archbishop of Paris, Christophe de Beaumont, to confer the sacraments on dying people who had not received a certificate from their priests attesting that they were *bona fide* Catholics. Even the parlement of Paris had issued public statements which expressed some sympathy for Damiens' criticisms, although this did not prevent the parlement from supporting the brutal manner in which Damiens died – his body burned and broken before being torn, then hacked, apart by four horses and their handlers.[29]

Finally, there were the immense costs involved in keeping the king's official, and unofficial, mistresses, in the grand style to which quite a few had been accustomed. Mouffle d'Angerville believed that the first of the Nesle sisters to become Louis XV's mistress, in the 1730s, Louise-Julie, had received 40,000 *livres* a year in *rentes*, a town house in the rue Saint-Thomas du Louvre, and the settlement of all her debts, which, if true, amounted to a staggering 763,000 *livres*. The next Nesle in line, Pauline-Felicité, had apparently been given a gift of 200,000 *livres*. The third and most beloved, Anne-Marie, had not only received the income from the duchy of Châteauroux, amounting to 85,000 *livres* a year, but also a monthly income of 150,000 *livres*, plus diamonds worth 500,000 *livres*. The diamonds alone would have kept a skilled Parisian craftsman and his family in comparative luxury for their entire lives. We established in our preceding chapter that the

106

sixteen-year old Marie-Louise O'Murphy was given a dowry of 200,000 *livres* when she was married off in 1757 to a noble officer (who, somewhat ironically, was killed at the battle of Rossbach!). The papal nuncio had recorded on 22 October 1753 that 'Morfi' had recently been taken to Fontainebleau 'where an apartment had been prepared; she had received diamonds and magnificent dresses'.[30] Subsequent mistresses did not, apparently, receive such generous bounties. Mlle. Tiercelin, who succeeded Mlle. Romans, in 1763, was even obliged to spend a short time in the Bastille for making too many financial demands upon the king.

The immense cost of the Seven Years' War, together with the profligacy and incompetence of the court, was bringing the country to its knees, and Louis XV could not escape the consequences. The cost of providing for the king's private life was constantly being raised in scurrilous news-sheets, which tended to focus more on the cost of keeping Louis XV's 'young girls' in the Deer Park than on his court mistresses, although it was not always easy to separate these two categories. Mouffle d'Angerville estimated that the cost of the Park, excluding the cost of caring for illegitimate children, 'was not a *sou* less than one milliard livres', but one of the editors of his work, Albert Meyrac (writing in 1921), thought that this wonderfully round figure constituted a gross exaggeration. We are indeed in the realm of statistical fantasy when dealing with most critics of Louis' private affairs, if only because Louis and Pompadour did everything they could to hide the truth, although, when Henri Bertin became *contrôleur général*, there would be some attempt to create a modicum of order out of the financial chaos. Meyrac, admitting the difficulty of unravelling the king's financial affairs, concluded that 'we must put the cost of running the king's "little house" (4 rue Médéric) at a few hundred thousand livres', which might be somewhere nearer the truth.[31]

As for Louis' illegitimate children, the spotlight that had fallen upon Louis' private life led to an improvement in their situation after 1760, which serves as a reminder that Louis XV was the first French monarch to endure the continual intrusion of the modern press. According to Tim Blanning, 'it was the Jansenist dispute of the 1750s which marked the turning-point in French publishing, as periodicals moved from the tedium of celebratory journalism to the reporting of current affairs'.[32] Estimates of the number of Louis XV's illegitimate children vary from eight to over 30: two of them, the marquis de Luc and the abbé de Bourbon, were special cases, the only two children to receive some de facto legitimation from Louis XV. Unsurprisingly, they were the sons of the two women for whom Louis appears to have harboured real affection: the duchesse de Châteauroux and Anne Couppier, better known as mademoiselle de Romans. The marquis de Luc, Châteauroux's son, who was raised by the man Châteauroux had been obliged to marry, obviously enjoyed the benefits of the largesse Louis had bestowed upon his favourite mistress. The second son, the abbé de Bourbon, received all the benefits of the original settlement made by Louis when he left Mademoiselle de Romans, together with those derived from her subsequent marriage to the marquis de Cavanac in 1772. The only other child to be favoured was, again unsurprisingly, the daughter of Louis and Marie-Louise O'Murphy who received the very modest annual *rente* of 84 *livres* on a capital sum of 1,200 *livres*. If the memoirs of madame Hausset, housekeeper of the Park, are to be believed (there is some doubt that they should be), each one of the king's remaining illegitimate offspring was given an annuity of 12,000 *livres*.[33] If these acts of generosity did something to mitigate the reckless-ness of Louis XV's behaviour, it did little or nothing to restore his reputation as a self-styled 'Christian king', as his frequent bouts of depression and remorse suggest.

The legendary extravagance of Pompadour would exacerbate the problems of the royal triumvirate. If we compare the value of the châteaux built or renovated by madame de Pompadour, together with the cost of the estates, pensions and jewellery she received from Louis, then the expenditure of previous mistresses pales into insignificance. The architectural jewel in her property portfolio was the château of Bellevue near Saint Cloud. Furnished with exquisite taste and commanding wonderful views of the

Seine, south-west of Paris, it cost the taxpayer around two and a half million *livres* to complete. Louis' open-ended drafts on the royal treasury paid some of the costs: what was good for the king was also good for Pompadour, which is why the parlement of Paris wanted to put a stop to all this lack of financial transparency. Pompadour always fought, tooth and nail, to thwart the plans of the parlement. Mouffle d'Angerville, who died in 1794, having provided a stack of 'evidence' for Revolutionary pamphleteers, was uncompromising: it was Pompadour who had forced Louis to throw discretion to the wind in order to satisfy her 'mania for new building projects'. Between them, they allegedly spent 'fantastically enormous sums of money' to build, furnish, and maintain châteaux and town mansions: 'Every *contrôleur général* was obliged to find the money to fulfil the king's every fantasy.' Albert Meyrac, less prone to flights of fancy, agrees that Madame de Pompadour was extravagant – she 'showed no awareness of how her prodigality would be perceived by the nation's tax payers [spending] at least two million livres a year'. More recently, Colin Jones has presented the best possible case for the defence. Yes, Pompadour was extravagant, but he asks us to remember that, through her support of the building programme undertaken by the royal department of public works, headed for a time by her brother, the marquis de Vandières, it has to be said, her tireless patronage of architects, designers, sculptors, and painters, her support for the foundation of the *Ecole militaire* (1751) and the world-famous porcelain factory, the *Manufacture royale de Sèvres*, she promoted the artistic and cultural revolution of the mid-eighteenth century. In other words, madame de Pompadour was the acceptable face of Bourbon profligacy.[34]

* * *

Given, on the one hand, Bertin's intimate knowledge of Louis XV's private life, and, on the other, Louis and Pompadour's lengthy involvement in the imprisonment of his elder brother, the marquis de Fratteaux, it is obvious that Louis and Pompadour needed Bertin almost as much as Bertin needed them. His complicity in the more questionable behaviour of Louis XV and Pompadour, tried and tested by his appointment as *lieutenant général de police* from 1757 to 1759, had strengthened the bonds of the royal triumvirate, with Bertin as the junior partner. He was duly rewarded in November 1759 with promotion to one of the great offices of state, *contrôleur général des finances de France*: what better choice could Louis and Pompadour make to conceal their lavish spending from the prying eyes of the parlements, and the nation, than the nation's finance minister? Bertin knew that the post was a poisoned chalice if ever there was one: Louis-Joseph Boullogne, appointed to the office on 25 August 1757 had been replaced in March 1759 by Etienne de Silhouette, who had only lasted until Bertin's arrival in November of the same year. On the positive side, however, Bertin had considerable administrative and financial experience: 'Bertin's long career in the service of both Louis XV and his successor symbolised all that was best about the administrative monarchy.'[35] He was also given an assurance that Pompadour would stand shoulder to shoulder with her long-time favourite. Georges Bussière tells us that there should 'be no doubt about the matter – [it was Pompadour] who was … the principal instrument in [Bertin's] promotion as the supreme head of the country's finances'. Voltaire would describe Bertin as 'le médecin malgré lui', referring to his initial reluctance to accept the post. Pompadour's correspondence also records her 'perfect agreement' with Bertin over the business of finding a new governor of the Bastille, an agreement that led to the appointment of Bertin's brother-in-law, the comte de Jumilhac, as governor on 27 May 1761. For Bertin's incarcerated elder brother, the marquis de Fratteaux, this must have been a particularly bitter pill to swallow.[36]

At this stage, we must return, briefly, to Bertin's predecessor as *contrôleur général*, Etienne de Silhouette, in order to discover the origins of the 'Grand Design'. Silhouette was a reforming minister who had tried to implement a fiscal policy that threatened to check the profligacy of the crown and reduce the incomes of the privileged classes, too radical an approach to secure the agreement of the Paris parlement. However, Bertin would learn lessons from Silhouette's struggle with the parlement, as well as from his association with the physiocrats. These were years during which, confronted with the possible collapse of the monarchy, Bertin's profile as a reformer was being shaped. The most striking debt he owed to Silhouette was his appointment of Jacob-Nicolas Moreau, co-founder of the 'Grand Design', as an *avocat des finances* in 1759. Moreau, already a government propagandist for the Seven Years' War, had been pressing for the government to 'act more directly, by taking the offensive in the ideological battle' between the crown and the parliaments, allowing him, and like-minded colleagues, 'to put back before the eyes of the nation the ancient records that cry out against the pretensions of the parlements'. He argued that the practice of placing the records of royal legislation in the hands of the parlements gave them far too much power, since ministers, few of whom kept their own departmental records, had insufficient access to this treasury of royal legislation. In Moreau's opinion, the government should create its own royal library, a *dépôt de législation* that would provide the ammunition for an 'ideological counteroffensive' against the parlements.

This counteroffensive was clearly a response to the growth of national consciousness that we have identified above in relation to the advent of a more educated, democratic society. According to Moreau, the crown had to recognise that, over recent decades, the parlements had managed to transform the law 'into a kind of contract between the people and the sovereign, with the parlements claiming to act as representatives of the nation'. To save Bourbon absolutism, the crown had to contest, and reject, this claim. Moreau's project did not simply represent another chapter in the increasing conflict between the crown and its critics; it marked the inauguration of his 'Grand Strategy', to weaken the authority of the parlements and their supporters. Silhouette also encouraged Bertin's interest in the study of Chinese politics, an interest that would continue for over thirty years to exert a powerful influence on the reforming Enlightenment agenda of what would evolve, together with Moreau's ever-expanding *dépôt de legislation*, into Bertin and Moreau's 'Grand Design' to save the monarchy.[37]

* * *

With a staff of around 150 officials, a *contrôleur général*'s brief covered an extraordinary range of responsibilities, including direct and indirect taxation, industry, internal and external trade, grain prices, customs and excise and financial matters relating to the armed forces, as well as control of privileged trading companies such as the *Compagnie des Indes*. Bertin would hold onto his job for four years, no mean feat when one considers that between 1754 and 1759 no fewer than six *contrôleurs généraux* had come and gone. We should also remember that Bertin assumed office in 1759, the year, according to Frank McLynn, 'when Britain became master of the world'.

During the early 1750s, per capita taxation had already risen to almost ten *livres*, which did not represent a significant increase from the figure recorded during the two previous decades. By 1761, however, per capita taxation had increased to 13.17 *livres*. By the end of the war in 1763, French taxpayers would be complaining loudly about what proved to be the highest level of taxation levied before 1789. Although incomplete records and the 'creative bookkeeping' of *ancien régime* governments make reliable statistical analysis difficult, some general conclusions have been reached. In the first place, it is clear that taxation in France did increase significantly during the course of the Seven Years' War: direct taxation almost doubled between 1756 and 1760, rising from 94 to 174 million *livres*. Even before the outbreak of war in 1756, the French believed that they were being asked to carry far too heavy a tax burden, especially when compared with the British. In fact, the French were being treated relatively leniently; during the 1760s, tax levels in Britain were often twenty-five per cent higher than those in France. Secondly, Britain's historic victory over the French would be financed by relying upon the support of a strong parliament and fairly cheap loans from the city of London, together with rather heavy taxation on consumer goods. In France, Bertin would have to deal with the unenviable legacy of a massive war debt, the frequent obstruction of the parlement of Paris and its twelve provincial counterparts, and a public that was losing its faith in the king. Bertin (and Pompadour) concluded that, on the fiscal front, he 'had no other option but to raise existing taxes and have recourse to the so-called extraordinary revenues', i.e. further borrowing, amounting to 700–800 million *livres* at high rates of interest. As for rising discontent with the entire political and economic system, that would have to be placed on the agenda of the 'Grand Design'. He and his new colleague, Jacob-Nicolas Moreau, knew that French fiscal policy was fundamentally flawed by inefficient collection and social discrimination. Taxes were levied inequitably upon the main social classes – peasants, bourgeois and nobles – whilst the extremely wealthy Catholic Church only paid, periodically, what it considered to be a 'free gift' (*don gratuit*).[38]

Fiscal inequality, related to the Catholic Church's refusal to pay anything like its fair share of taxation, was a matter of national concern. The *contrôleur général*, Machault, had done his best in 1749 to convince Louis that the Church should be asked to make a realistic contribution to new taxes such as the *vingtième* (an occasional tax amounting to one-twentieth of a taxpayer's income), but the king refused to support his minister, understandable only if one were living in the past. The majority of the privileged nobility and bourgeoisie were included in the tax rolls for the *taille* (the basic government tax since 1439), but what they paid depended largely on where they lived and their place in the social hierarchy: whoever they were and wherever they lived, in terms of percentages related to income, it was usually the peasantry that shouldered the main fiscal burden. Nonetheless, discontent on the part of the privileged orders increased as the government tried to recruit them into the ranks of the nation's taxpayers. Machault's 'extraordinary' tax, the *vingtième*, had aroused widespread resentment, especially, but not exclusively, amongst the clergy. Michael Kwass has suggested that 'By levying universal taxes, the monarchy created a new type of royal subject: the privileged taxpayer, who, while remaining at least partially exempt from the *taille*, nonetheless made direct tax contributions to the crown.' Kwass concludes that this was a step in the right direction, but adds that, 'The birth of this new social being heralded neither the coming of fiscal equity nor a resolution of the monarchy's chronic financial crises; commoners continued to bear the lion's share of the direct tax burden, and the monarchy continued to operate on the edge of bankruptcy.'[39] The failure to tax, equitably, the huge wealth of the Church and the privileged orders represents a major structural fault in the edifice of Bourbon absolutism. The political consequences were to prove very costly, and, despite his best endeavours towards the end of his term in office as *contrôleur général*, Henri Bertin had to admit his failure to defeat the well-entrenched opposition to radical fiscal reform.

Throughout the period of the Seven Years' War, the thirteen parlements of the realm frequently proved to be the most powerful institutional obstacle to government initiatives, especially in matters relating to religion and taxation. Their opposition was not only founded upon their traditional, legal role as 'the keepers of the laws and customs of the kingdom', but also as an historical institution with a duty to act as a political and constitutional check upon Bourbon absolutism. The confidence and political clout of the parlements had been increasing since the death of Louis XIV in 1715; their claim to be the natural 'guardians of the nation' had become more attractive as public opinion, strengthened by the growth of a popular press, had emerged as an important factor in political life. Julian Swann argues that, 'after 1750, if not 1715, there was a gradual process of what we might call the "politicisation" of judicial affairs. In other words, the parlement of Paris came to serve as a useful forum for the intrigues of the court'.[40] There were claims that ministers of the crown were bribing magistrates. Increasingly confident of their influence, fuelled by the evolution of a more informed and politicised 'public sphere', the parlement of Paris had tried, with some success, to unite all the twelve provincial parlements under its own umbrella – the so-called *union des classes* (the word *'classe'* in the *Encyclopédie* refers to a specific 'convocation' or 'assembly'). Supporters of Bourbon absolutism, like Bertin and Moreau, described these moves as disturbing evidence that the parlements were transforming themselves into a 'national' institution or a 'Senate', along the lines of the English parliament. The bloody collapse of Stuart absolutism in mid-seventeenth-century Britain was never far from the minds of Louis XV and madame de Pompadour, and their fears were not without cause: the last of the absolute Bourbon monarchs, Louis XVI, would be executed in Paris in January 1793: the last of Louis XV's mistresses, madame du Barry, would suffer the same fate at the end of the same year. From this angle of vision, Bertin and Moreau's 'Grand Design' would prove to be a failed attempt to avoid history repeating itself.

The greatest success by the parlement of Paris during the period of the Seven Years' War would be achieved in the religious sphere, with the assistance of the liberal and pragmatic duc de Choiseul. During the early 1730s, and again during the 1750s, religious conflict between Jansenists and Jesuits inside the Catholic Church had frequently soured relationships between the crown and the parlements, the latter usually supporting the Gallican, 'nationalist' line of the Jansenists against the Roman Catholic 'ultramontane' stance of the Jesuits. On 4 September 1754, the parlement of Paris had returned to the capital after a fifteen-month exile imposed by the government following its attacks on the Jesuit archbishop of Paris, cardinal Beaumont. Just two days earlier, Louis XV had introduced a 'law of silence' on religious issues, but neither Beaumont, still refusing to give parishioners suspected of Jansenist sympathies the holy sacraments, nor the influential Jansenist minority in the parlement were capable of remaining silent for long.[41] However, Beaumont's single-minded, anti-Jansenist campaign would prove to be his 'last hurrah' for the Jesuit cause. Humiliating defeats during the Seven Years' War would energise nationalist sentiment, which, in turn, would strengthen the campaign to abolish the Jesuit Order in France – not exactly the outcome that Louis XV and Pompadour had expected. For Pompadour, it was not the Jesuits but the parlements, eager to exploit every opportunity of weakening the crown, that were acting treacherously. For Choiseul, the immediate problem was to prevent the parlements from blocking post-war economic and fiscal reforms: if this meant throwing the 'papal' Jesuit Order, which had never been popular with the influential Jansenist group in the Paris parlement, to the parlementary wolves, then it was certainly a price worth paying. By 1764, the Jesuit Order would be outlawed in France.

When Pompadour's protégé, Henri Bertin, assumed office as *contrôleur général* in December 1759, the military situation already bordered on the desperate, and this only served to aggravate the strained relationship between the crown and the parlements. In 1756, the government had introduced a second *vingtième* that was to last until the end of the war (Machault's first *vingtième*, introduced in 1749, having been transformed into a permanent tax), but proceeds from this tax had proved totally inadequate to meet the national deficit. During the summer of 1759, Silhouette had tried to introduce a third *vingtième*, as well as a tax on a wide range of consumer goods and the suspension of treasury payments on government funds. There was even talk of introducing a land register which would provide the foundation for the levy of a single ten per cent tax on property. The parlement of Paris, bolstered by the presence of the peers and princes who had recently been allowed to participate in its deliberations, was distinctly unimpressed. Proposed new taxes, especially those relating to the *vingtièmes* and *capitation* (a poll tax, first levied in 1695 to pay for Louis XIV's wars) would be levied on the privileged as well as the poor, and this was a bridge too far for many for many sections of the nobility and the clergy to cross, one that threatened the 'natural order' of social privilege. The parlement preferred to keep the spotlight on the personal profligacy of the court, spearheaded by Louis and Pompadour, as well as the millions wasted on subsidies to keep the discredited Austrian alliance afloat. Silhouette's programme had to be imposed upon the parlement through a *lit de justice* (the forcible registration of a royal edict by the king in parlement) held on 20 September 1759, but this did little to quell widespread discontent, and, in November, Silhouette was dismissed in favour of the more pliant Henri Bertin. By this time, revolt on the part of the Paris parlement had spread to the *Cour des aides* and some of the provincial parlements, notably the parlement of Rouen, which decreed that 'a law had to be accepted, and the right to see that it is accepted belongs to the nation'.[42] The provincial parlements were following the audacious example of the Paris parlement.

Bertin, counselled by Pompadour, worked hard and long to win over the court's critics to some, at least, of Silhouette's proposals. To Bertin's regret, the idea of a land registry (*cadastre*) and a single tax was temporarily dropped; in return, the parlement of Paris accepted the need for a third *vingtième*, although its duration was reduced from three years to two. Bertin's revision of Silhouette's programme was finally registered in March 1760, but this was by no means the beginning of the end of the struggle between the parlement and the government; it was not even the end of the beginning. When, in June 1761, Bertin sought permission to prolong the levy of the second and third *vingtièmes*, it was only granted through the imposition of another *lit de justice* held on 21 July 1761.[43] By this time, Choiseul, having secured the friendship of the king, as well as the offices of war minister and foreign minister, was beginning to act as de facto first minister, relegating Pompadour, increasingly weak in body and spirit, to an inferior position. Government policy was now passing into the hands of a man who could be compared with his British counterpart William Pitt, without provoking hollow laughter. Having eased the relationship between the parlements and the crown, Choiseul also negotiated a *pacte de famille* in August 1761 with the Bourbon king, Charles III, which would enable Spain to join the war against England at the beginning of the following year. However, this was 'too little, too late' to swing the fortunes of war in France's direction, but it would do something to help Louis and Choiseul secure an acceptable peace treaty. A new era in French and world politics was beginning to dawn.

*   *   *

It is our contention that Frank McLynn is right to conclude that, 'Once Louis XV had decided to be his own Prime Minister, and especially when Madame de Pompadour became his principal advisor, political anarchy began.' That 'anarchy' had certainly been promoted, as McLynn points out, by the return of aristocratic, often inept, ministers.[44] Michel Antoine entitled Chapter XVI of his classic biography of Louis XV, which covers this period, 'Monarchie ou Anarchie'. The foundations of Bourbon absolutism in the mid-eighteenth century had already been shaken by many convulsions – military, economic, social and intellectual – but its street credibility and international standing was unquestionably further damaged by the actions of Pompadour and Bertin, both of whom had placed loyal service to their monarch above their duty to the country. They refused to accept that Louis XIV's dictum, 'L'Etat c'est moi', had become increasingly anachronistic as the influence of Enlightenment ideas developed. Choiseul was intelligent and pragmatic enough to realise this; Henri Bertin and Jacob-Nicolas Moreau would also come to realise that radical reform was a 'categorical imperative', although they would always refuse to sacrifice the cause of Bourbon *absolutism* at the altar of *constitutional* government.

The personal and intimate correspondence between Bertin and Pompadour reveals the pressure under which they both laboured. We have already noted that Louis chose to fall passionately in love with his young black-haired beauty, Anne Couppier Romans, during a period of acute crisis for France. Despite her failing health, Pompadour worked tirelessly throughout the period of Louis' obsession with Romans and their son, to provide the king with intelligible accounts of internal and external affairs. Let us take the example of the ongoing struggle with the parlement of Paris. In the summer of 1761, Pompadour received an important missive from Bertin concerning the unhelpful reaction of the president of the parlement, Mathieu-François Molé, to his proposed tax policies. Pompadour was anxious to reassure her protégé, writing that the king had gone hunting over an hour ago, but before his departure, she explained, she had begged Louis 'to tell Molé that it was his job, and no-one else's, to ensure that the government's plans were implemented'. Pompadour added that 'M. de Choiseul has also left for the hunt', but, seeking, possibly, to undermine the authority of her most powerful rival, with whom she was obliged to work, Pompadour added that 'he no longer has anything to say on the matter'. In an attempt to soothe Bertin's obviously ruffled feathers, Pompadour ended her letter with a wish that he 'would do everything he could to get some peace and quiet'. The royal triumvirate was clearly not operating as efficiently as it had done in the late 1750s. In a subsequent letter to her favourite, again focusing on the 'unpatriotic' behaviour of the Paris parlement, Pompadour told Bertin that the king had now read recent correspondence and was, unlike Choiseul who was now on speaking terms with Voltaire, 'horrified' at the parlement's attitude. She concluded: 'I must keep quiet, which does not mean that I do not think about these matters. But I am just [the king's] parrot', a revealing comment, one that reflects Pompadour's declining influence. The courageous marquise, however, was still a parrot that was strategically placed on Louis' shoulder, as this reply to another of Bertin's letters indicates: 'I write this letter to inform you that the issue you raised has been settled, save for the king's assent which I expect he will not refuse.'[45]

Pompadour's method of dealing with the damaging collisions between the crown and the parlements was to employ the full arsenal of her diminishing charms and occasionally naive diplomatic skills to win over important *parlementaires*, only to discover, all too often, that Louis, advised by the duc de Choiseul, had cut the ground from under her feet. Choiseul was obviously courting Louis' friendship, confident that he was the 'first minister-in-waiting'. He had already found ministerial and ecclesiastical positions for members of his family, and secured the appointment of his friend, Jean Joseph de Laborde, as court banker. The foundations for his future domination of French politics in the 1760s had been well and truly laid.[46] In the meantime, Pompadour and Bertin, worried about the prospect of an ignominious peace with Britain, were sending out signals intended to convince enemies at home and abroad that France's financial situation was not half as bad as they thought. We have noted that Bertin's first provocative move to solve the financial crisis he had inherited was to levy a third *vingtième*, as well as doubling the *capitation* on those who did not pay the *taille*. In round figures, he expected that these measures would bring in 36 million *livres* in additional taxation for 1760–61.

Neither Prussia nor England was fooled by these rather desperate moves, and the war continued to drain the French treasury. Influenced by success on the battlefield as well as on the high seas, credit from Holland, Switzerland and Germany was now being diverted to Britain, which was also deep in debt, but, still credit-worthy. In France, emergency measures had to be taken to ensure that the French army and their subsidised allies were being paid enough to keep them in the field. Pompadour managed to convince the wealthy *receveur général des finances*, Beaujon, from La Rochelle to loan them a million *livres*, a drop in the ocean really, given that France's loans for the entire war were somewhere between 700 and 800 million *livres*. Bertin assured Beaujon that he needed this relatively small sum just to tide him over until revenue from his new taxes started flowing into the treasury. More significant in terms of power politics was the information that the court banker, Pâris de Montmartel, probably Pompadour's real father, was being moved aside to make room for Choiseul's protégé, Laborde. But none of this really provided a long-term solution to France's financial problems. Indeed, more loans, when added to those that had been contracted at increasingly high rates of interest since the 1740s, simply increased the heavy burden of debt repayment that had helped to create the financial crisis in the first place, a burden that, together with the cost of supporting the Americans in their fight for independence from Britain in the late 1770s, would contribute to the collapse of absolute monarchy in 1789.[47]

By the summer of 1760, the government was being forced to defend itself on all fronts. The Paris parlement, employing the 'union des classes' with the twelve provincial parlements, was still threatening to metamorphose into a national opposition movement to the crown. Pompadour worked tirelessly to stiffen Louis XV's resolve with the result that the duc D'Aiguillon, *commandant-en-chef* of Brittany, one of the most recalcitrant provinces, was forced to withdraw his support for the parlement of Rennes, which registered the new taxes on 22 August 1760. These relatively minor royal victories, however, which did little to tackle fundamental issues, came at a price: Pompadour was literally working herself to death. At the end of one of her letters to D'Aiguillon, expressing her pleasure that something, at least, had been achieved, she wrote: 'Bonsoir M. de Cavendish [her pet name for D'Aiguillon]. All this is too much for a weak and convalescent mind.'[48]

The government's failure to borrow abroad at acceptable rates of interest, together with its failure to secure immediate support from the parlements, meant that the crisis dragged on until an uneasy compromise between the crown and parlements was reached on16 June 1761. It was agreed that, in return for a more sympathetic response to government policy from the parlements, the government would delay the introduction of Bertin's third *vingtième* and the doubling of the *capitation* until the end of 1763. But how was Bertin to make ends meet in the interim? On 3 July, Pompadour, painfully reaching the end of her tether, told Bertin that '... peace, at home and abroad, is too serious a matter for me to suffer the intrigues that endanger both'. She asked if she could see Bertin the following Monday to discuss the entire situation, adding that 'You are obviously as angry as I am. This is why I am convinced that we should meet.'[49] Pompadour knew that Bertin wanted to introduce radical changes to France's taxation system, founded on the idea, supported by Silhouette and encouraged by many physiocrats, of a new land tax to be levied on all classes of society. It was obvious that before a single *livre* was levied, the government would have had to undertake a massive survey of all landowners, and that, for the great majority of the privileged orders, this procedure would have meant the beginning of the end of (feudal) civilisation as they knew it.

As if struggling to save a war-torn nation from financial collapse was not enough, there were other issues, far more delicate and personal issues that did nothing to cure Pompadour's spasms of nervous collapse. There was the constant criticism of her lavish expenditure on purchasing châteaux and the chic accessories with which to furnish them; the cost of all those works of art and expensive jewellery; the 'gifts' of priceless Sèvres porcelain pottery. The Paris parlement, growing more audacious with every successful act of resistance, pressed for greater financial transparency on several matters, including expenses relating to the cost of Louis' mistresses and his extra-curricular activity in the Deer Park. Henri Bertin, called upon to solve the apparently unsolvable (the threat of national bank-ruptcy), was occasionally driven to consider the possibility of resignation. On one occasion, Pompadour had to admonish 'My [*sic*] *contrôleur général*' for not adopting a sufficiently hard line against the parlements: 'I am indignant, to say the least, about the stance you have adopted with these plebeians [the *robe* nobility of the parlements]. It is not worthy of a *contrôleur général* of the king of France.'[50] Perhaps, given the decline of Pompadour's authority, Bertin had been trimming his sails in order to accommodate the pro-parlement stance of the duc de Choiseul. As we saw above, Choiseul's decision to sacrifice the Jesuits can be explained, in part, by the necessity of keeping the parlement of Paris onside as he pressed for higher taxes and more war loans.[51] The problem was that the parlement, supported now by the prince de Conti, was continually raising the stakes. It sought the right to supervise all royal 'private' expenses that were paid by the treasury on receipt of nothing more than a note signed by the king (the '*bons du roi*'), pointing out that these 'extraordinary expenses' had risen from 17 million to 117 million over the past 20 years. Pompadour exploded with rage. She told Bertin that she did not think much of the parlement's 'little proposition that we should account for our expenses … I am surprised that you had the patience not to spit in their faces'. On 7 July 1761, Choiseul told Bertin that he would take responsibility for the king's extraordinary expenses: the triumvirate of Louis XV, Pompadour and Bertin had collapsed. Louis told Choiseul not to worry too much, explaining that 'the thefts in my household are enormous, but it is impossible to prevent them'.[52] Pompadour agreed, naturally; she told Bertin that the attitude of the parlement completely justified her contempt for the magistrates of the parlement, adding, 'You see how wrong you were to be honest with them. I can't say it often enough: they have to be managed with an iron fist.' This, as Bertin realised, was easier said than done. He knew that court expenses would have to be reduced, if only to reassure the parlements and the public.[53]

Much of the debate between the court factions at Versailles and the parlements was shadow boxing. What was really at stake was the integrity of Bourbon absolutism; its capacity to retain something of what Louis XIV had bequeathed to his more pliant and pacifist successor at a time when traditional aristocratic values were unravelling. Most commentators agree that it was the duc de Choiseul's political and diplomatic skills during the early 1760s that enabled Louis XV, also anxious to pluck something positive from the jaws of defeat, to secure both a fairly reasonable external peace with France's enemies, leading to an internal compromise with the parlements. Neither the Treaty of Paris, signed on 10 February 1763, nor the Treaty of Hubersburg, signed five days earlier, significantly diminished French power and influence on the Continent: the real loss was to its reputation as a global power, a loss that Colin Jones describes as 'huge and humiliating'.[54] Although France retained control of its sugar-producing islands in the Caribbean, it lost virtually all its North American and Canadian possessions, apart from the islands of Saint Pierre and Miquelon, and the rich fishing grounds off New Foundland, as well as many of its possessions in India. France's hazy dream of founding an African empire would have to wait for another century.

The balance of world power between France and Britain had changed, irrevocably. Internally, the balance of power between the crown and the parlements had swung away from the French monarchy: both institutions were now claiming to represent 'the nation', and now the government would have to tackle the problem of meeting the crippling financial and political costs of a humiliating defeat. From late 1762, Bertin and Moreau, an economic adviser in the treasury at this time, had been conducting a major overhaul of the county's finances. The fruits of their labour were presented to the king's council following the Treaty of Paris. Bertin was prepared to make concessions to his critics including the suppression of the wartime third *vingtième*, but, in return, he wanted to revive the idea of a single land tax (favoured by his reforming predecessors, Machault and Silhouette) founded upon a new register of land ownership (the *cadastre*). The *capitation* tax would also be doubled and measures would be taken to reduce the massive national debt by imitating England's successful 'sinking fund'. There could be no doubt that Bertin's programme would have hit the privileged rich far harder than the impoverished poor, and, in consequence, it had to be imposed by *lits de justice,* held on 3 May and 31 May 1763. The stubborn resistance of the parlements, in Paris and the provinces, was a reflection of their evolution as a major institutional threat to Bourbon absolutism; critics of the government were also reflecting the popular perception of a discredited and corrupt monarchy. The parlement of Paris repeatedly raised the issue of government profligacy and wanted to supervise the royal books: the *cadastre* may, just may, have been acceptable, but how exactly was it to be implemented? As in the dark days of Charles I of England, the parlements had the government by the neck, and although the evidence of Pompadour's private correspondence with Bertin makes it perfectly clear that they both wanted to relieve the pressure, Choiseul, clearly bent on adopting a liberal and constitutional approach to solve the national crisis, did not. It seems that Choiseul, now a great hunting companion of the king, convinced Louis to dismiss Bertin by the end of 1763 in favour of the magistrate in the Paris parlement who had led the resistance to the crown, Clément Charles L'Averdy. Julian Swann emphasises the major significance of Bertin's dismissal: 'In effect. Bertin was the first to confront a problem that would hound successive *contrôleur généraux* for the next two decades and eventually topple the *ancien régime*.'[55] However, Bertin's departure did not mean the end of his personal campaign to save the monarchy from this 'final solution': in fact, as a result of Louis and Pompadour's gratitude to him for all his efforts on their behalf, his career as a reforming minister had just begun.

What had ended was the influence of the Louis XV, Pompadour and Bertin triumvirate. In less than a year, Pompadour would be lying in her early grave. Madame de Pompadour was the most famous casualty of the Seven Years' War. She had received a visit at the beginning of 1764 from Madame de Geoffrin's daughter, the marquise de Ferté-Imbault, who tells us that their conversation revolved around the state of the country, her health and Louis XV's latest sexual conquests. Even at death's door (she died on 15 April 1764), sexual politics and matters of state were still interchangeable.[56] For Pompadour, however, it was time to spend more time putting her own affairs in order and preparing her last will and testament. Although raised in a bourgeois household, she exhibited a keen interest in her feudal privileges, as befitted someone who had reached the giddy heights of a king's mistress and counsellor. Her debt to her loyal, long-time favourite, Henri Bertin, for helping her settle some of her private affairs is reflected in the closing remarks of one of her letters: 'It gives me the greatest pleasure to tell you once again that no-one is more conscious than I of the debt I owe you.'[57] That debt was paid after Bertin was dismissed as *contrôleur général*, when, to the chagrin of the triumphalist Choiseul and his supporters, he was rewarded with the prestigious post of 'secretary of state'. This gift was the last act of gratitude from the monarch and his famous mistress to the minister who had faithfully, and confidentially, managed the private affairs of Louis XV, as well as the all too public conflict between Pompadour and the parlements.

On 15 April 1764, Pompadour lost her lengthy battle with the Grim Reaper. She exhibited on her deathbed the same courage and fortitude that had characterised her entire career. As her confessor was about to leave the room, she is said to have whispered: 'One moment, Monsieur le curé, we shall go out together.' Pompadour was buried in the Capuchin church situated in the place Vendôme, alongside her mother and beloved daughter, Alexandrine, for whom, in happier times, she had planned a royal wedding to one of Louis XV's sons. Louis XV, to whom she had devoted her entire adult life, visited Pompadour shortly before she died. He wrote to his son-in-law of 'A relationship of almost twenty years, and a solid friendship. But God is the master...' The attitude of most ordinary Frenchmen and women was summed up in the epitaph coined by one wit:

> Here lies one who was twenty years a virgin,
> Seven years a whore and eight years a pimp.[58]

This cruel, reductive aphorism provides a useful corrective to the many sycophantic accounts of Pompadour's life. She had, after all, mortgaged any claim to moral superiority by her sanction of, and participation in, Louis XV's grossly immoral behaviour. Nonetheless, Pompadour, for all her faults, was an intelligent woman, a promoter of *haute culture* and a supporter of many Enlightenment values; also a survivor of the political and immoral snake-pit into which the court of Versailles could so often transform itself. Her death would mark the beginning of a new phase in Bertin's career and a new historicist approach to the task of saving the Bourbon monarchy. Bertin, together with the man who would remain his close friend for almost thirty years,

Jacob-Nicolas Moreau, would now direct their careers, and devote what spare time they had, the first as secretary of state, the second as royal bibliographer, to their 'Grand Design' to prevent the collapse of Bourbon absolutism. The success they achieved would dictate the course of their private lives; their failure to save the political system they served, and sought to reform, would influence the evolution of French politics until, and into, the Revolution of 1789.

Notes

1. Frank McLynn, *1789, the Year Britain Became Master of the World* (London, 2004), p.389.
2. J. Dull, *The French Navy and the Seven Years' War* (London, 2005), pp.21–2.
3. André Picciola, *Le Comte de Maurepas: Versailles et l'Europe à la fin de l'Ancien Régime* (Paris, 1999), pp.301–10.
4. Eric Williams writes that 'Europe's superiority ... can be directly explained by her exploitation of the European economy by the regular profits from these plantations and slaves'. Cited by Fernand Braudel, *Civilisation and Capitalism, 15th-18th Century*, vol.3, p.42.
5. Jeremy Black, *From Louis XIV to Napoleon: The Fate of a Grat Power* (London, 1999), pp.85–6.
6. See, for example, Bernis, *Mémoires et lettres de François-Joachim de Pierre, Cardinal de Bernis (1715–1758)*, 2 vols (Paris, 1878), Bernis to comte de Stainville, 20 Aug. 1758, vol.1, p.266.
7. Black, *From Louis XIV to Napoleon*, pp.107–9.
8. Jones, *The Great Nation*, p.238.
9. McLynn, *1759*, pp.375–81; Dull, *The French Navy*, pp.161–2.
10. D'Argenson, *Journal*, vol.8, 17 Jan. and 13 Feb. 1756.
11. Jones, *The Great Nation*, p.235; Swann, *Politics and the Parlement of Paris*, pp.142–53.
12. McLynn, *1759*, pp.260–3.
13. Algrant, *Madame de Pompadour*, p.226.
14. Castries, *La Pompadour*, p.259.
15. Bernis, *Mémoires et lettres*, vol. 2, pp.247–8.
16. Bernis, *Mémoires et lettres*, vol. 2, pp.255–75, and, for Bernis' sycophancy towards Louis XV, pp.352–7.
17. Algrant, *Madame de Pompadour*, p.183; Benabou, *La prostitution*, pp.171–2.

18 Arlette Farge, *Vivre dans la rue à Paris au XVIIIe siècle* (Paris, 1992), pp.200–2; Suzanne Pillorget, *Claude-Henri Feydeau de Marville, Lieutenant général de la police de Paris, 1740–47* (Paris, n.d.), pp.104–39.

19 S. Mercier, *Paris Le Jour, Paris La Nuit* (Paris, 1990), pp.61–6.

20 Benabou, *La prostitution*, p.26 and pp.180–3.

21 Antoine, *Louis XV*, pp.842–3.

22 A.N., E 2784/2, *arrêtes du conseil*, 1 Jan. 1765; *procès-verbaux* of cases coming before seigneurial courts, 28 Oct. 1763; 30 Oct. 1766, and 1 Aug. 1768.

23 Dumaine, *Louis XV et le Parc-aux-Cerfs*, pp.29–30; Chevé, *La noblesse du Périgord*, pp.138–9.

24 Chevé, *La noblesse du Périgord*, p.139.

25 Algrant, *Madame de Pompadour*, pp.232–9 and pp.260–2; Antoine, *Louis XV*, pp.825–47.

26 Mouffle D'Angerville, *Vie privée de Louis XV*, pp.284–7 and p.318, n.1.

27 Algrant, *Madame de Pompadour*, p.233.

28 Antoine, *Louis XV*, pp.809–11.

29 Jones, *The Great Nation*, pp.226–31.

30 D'Angerville, *Vie privée de Louis XV*, pp.143–4; Castries, *La Pompadour*, pp.26–8; Goncourt, *Les maîtresses de Louis XV*, pp.131–6; Dumaine, *Louis XV*, pp.30–4; Antoine, *Louis XV*, pp.504–5.

31 D'Angerville, *Vie privée de Louis XV*, pp.284–7.

32 Tim Blanning, *The Culture of Power and the Power of Culture: Old Regime Europe 1660–1789* (Oxford, 2002), p.157.

33 Dumaine, *Louis XV et le Parc-aux-Cerfs*, p.29; Antoine, *Louis XV*, pp.842–4.

34 D'Angerville, *Vie privée de Louis XV*, pp.234–5; Jones, *Madame de Pompadour*, pp.100–8; Goncourt, *Les maîtresses de Louis XV*, pp.282–90. See also the duc de Castries, who, on the basis of an estimate written by Pompadour herself, suggests that her total expenditure amounted to 36 million *livres*, the equivalent of around 720 million francs in 1983: *La Pompadour*, pp.326–8.

35 Swann, *Politics and the Parlement of Paris*, pp.182–91.

36 Bussière, 'Etude sur Henri Bertin', *BSHAP*, vol.35 (1908), pp.274–7.

37 Baker, *Inventing the French Revolution*, pp.59–65.

38 James Riley, *The Seven Years War and the Old Regime in France: the Economic and Financial Toll* (Princeton, 1986); Joel Félix, *Finances et politique au siècle des Lumières: le ministère L'Averdy, 1763–1768* (Paris, 1999), pp.33–69; Peter Mathias and Patrick O'Brien, 'Taxation in Britain and France, 1715–1810: A Comparison of the Social and Economic Incidence of Taxes Collected for the Central Governments', *Journal of Economic History*, vol.5 (1976), pp.601–50.

39 Michael Kwass, 'A Welfare State for the Privileged?', in Mark Ormrod, Margaret Bonney and Richard Bonney (eds), *Crises, Revolutions and Self-Sustained Growth: Essays in European Fiscal History* (Stamford, 1999), p.376.

40 Swann, *Politics and the Parlement of Paris*, pp.75–6.

41 Swann, *Politics and the Parlement of Paris*, pp.88–90.

42 Bussière, '*Etude sur Henri Bertin*', *BSHAP*, vol.35 (1908), pp.286.

43 J. Félix, 'The Financial Origins of the French Revolution', in P. Campbell (ed.), *The Origins of the French Revolution*, pp.44–8.

44 McLynn, *1759*, pp.69–70.

45 B.N., *nouvelles acquisitions*, vol.6498, fol.244 and fol.248; Bussière, '*Etude sur Henri Bertin*', *BSHAP*, vol.35 (1908), p.292.

46 Antoine, *Louis XV*, pp.752–3.

47 Tim Le Goff, 'How to Finance an Eighteenth-Century War', in Mark Ormrod *et al.*, *Crises, Revolutions and Self-Sustained Growth*, pp.396–400.

48 Bussière, '*Etude sur Henri Bertin*', *BSHAP*, vol.35 (1908), p.281.

49 B.N., *nouvelles acquisitions*, vol.6498, fol.242, n.d.

50 B.N., *nouvelles acquisitions*, vol.6498, fol.246, n.d.

51 Antoine, *Louis XV*, p.802.

52 Algrant, *Madame de Pompadour*, pp.261–2; Bussière, '*Etude sur Henri Bertin*', *BSHAP*, vol.35 (1908), pp.291–4.

53 B.N., *nouvelles acquisitions*, vol.6498, fol.238, n.d.

54 Jones, *The Great Nation*, p.244; Dull, *The French Navy*, pp.236–44.

55 Swann, *Politics and the Parlement of Paris*, p.219; David Hudson, 'The Parlementary Crisis of 1763 in France and its Consequences', *Canadian Journal of History*, vol.7 (1972), pp.97–117; Félix, *Finances et politique*, pp.69–79.

56 Jones, *Madame de Pompadour*, p.150.

57 B.N., *nouvelles acquisitions*, op. cit., fol.256.

58 Algrant, *Madame de Pompadour*, pp.286–90.

Part Two
Bertin's *'Petit Ministère'*: Enlightenment Constrained

Chapter Four

Economic Reform, Public Reaction and the 'Grand Design'

Henri Bertin must have left his post as *contrôleur général* with mixed feelings: in the first place, he was someone who had never courted controversy, had never coveted a post that inevitably attracted a certain amount of invective and personal abuse; secondly, he was disappointed that so many of his reform projects, particularly the introduction of a fiscal system based upon a new land survey, had fallen by the wayside. Descended from a recently ennobled robe family, and a protégé of the much-vilified 'bourgeois' marquise de Pompadour, he was frequently snubbed by *les Grands* at Versailles, occasionally by the duc de Choiseul, who would dominate the French political scene during the 1760s. After 1763, however, Bertin's position at court was considerably strengthened by his appointment as secretary of state, a reward that was founded, in large measure, upon the fact that he knew more than, or at least as much as, anyone else at Versailles about Louis XV's private life, apart from his protector, the comte de Saint-Florentin. Significantly, Bertin and Saint-Florentin, both entirely dedicated to the service and the protection of Louis XV, would be the only secretaries of state left in the government when Choiseul was dismissed in 1770. Louis was always aware of Bertin's vulnerable position as a provincial robe noble surrounded by aristocratic courtiers, which is why he decided to elevate him to the rank of *ministre d'état* in November

1762, thus allowing Bertin to become a member of the highest royal council, the *conseil d'état*, which dealt specifically with foreign policy and appeals from lower royal courts. As a minister of state, he would retain much of his authority even after his dismissal as secretary of state in 1780; indeed, his deliverance from many of his responsibilities as a bespoke secretary of state would give him more time to devote to the 'Grand Design', which by the 1780s would attract the support of Louis XVI.

However, an attempt to endow Bertin with full noble status failed as a result of the royal genealogist's rigid application of the new regulations on ennoblement that had been introduced in 1760, a reminder that there was an unwritten constitution curtailing the actions of Bourbon monarchs – they were 'absolute', not 'despotic', as government propagandists like Jacob-Nicolas Moreau repeatedly pointed out. Nonetheless, Louis and Pompadour chose to ignore the slight on their favoured minister by appointing Bertin to the ennobling post of *Grand Trésorier de l'Ordre du Saint-Esprit*. At a private royal ceremony held on 26 December 1762, Bertin acquired the *de jure* status of a fully-fledged noble, although many sword nobles would continue to question Bertin's status as a true *gentilhomme*. When, a year later, Choiseul, eager to placate the Paris parlement, managed to persuade Louis XV that Bertin should be dismissed as *contrôleur général*, Bertin immediately became the target of court satirists. One publication asked readers to imagine a scene in madame de Pompadour's parlour the day after Christ's birth. Among the 'great and the good', gathered to pay homage to the infant Jesus, we find Henri-Léonard Bertin:

> Feeling rather ill at ease,
> Bertin said as he entered:
> 'Give me a chair please,
> So that I may nurse this child,
> I am a freelance minister just taking the air
> And, to pass the time
> I offer you Seigneur
> My *petit ministère*'.

Such disparaging portrayals of Bertin's *'petit ministère'* would hang like an albatross around his neck for the rest of his career, as did the accusation that the minister had left his elder brother, the marquis de Fratteaux, to rot in the Bastille.[1]

The few historians who have studied aspects of Bertin's career have been far more generous in their evaluation of his work. Keith Baker has described him as 'one of the crown's most enlightened and innovative ministers'.[2] Bertin's actual brief as secretary of state appears to have been constructed as a result of a compromise between the crown and Bertin himself. Louis and Pompadour were understandably determined to hang on to a loyal and trusted minister who was privy to the innermost secrets of the pact they had made in the early 1750s. However, the duc de Richelieu suggested, with some justification, that Louis XV's gift had more to do with royal sex than the regulation of government policy. He ridiculed the notion that Bertin had a 'department' to administer, suggesting that his first duty was 'the responsibility for the supervision of the king's pleasures, the premises that housed his *sultanes*, the marriages of those whom the king had got tired of, the money paid to those who were prepared to marry these women, and the fate of the king's [illegitimate] children'.[3] The truth was far more complex. Bertin was given an opportunity to construct a unique department of state that would be abolished with his political disgrace in 1780. It was tailor-made to provide him with an opportunity of continuing some of the work he had carried out as *contrôleur général*, as well as enabling him to pursue many of the economic and intellectual interests he had developed during his ministerial career. It has to be admitted, however, that Bertin's bespoke department was a revealing example of the unsystematic system of absolute government under Louis XV, one that was often targeted at protecting the best interests of an absolute monarch rather than those of the country at large.

To understand fully the nature of Bertin's role in government, we need to divide his many responsibilities into two sections: the first covers the more formal responsibilities of a minister of the crown, especially those dealing with the reform of agriculture and mining; the second concerns his *'Correspondance littéraire'* – an ambiguous description of his contribution to the renovation of the Bourbon monarchy, often with tools borrowed from the Enlightenment. We noted in our previous chapter that his colleague, Jacob-Nicolas Moreau, journalist, propagandist and pamphleteer, had been given a job in the ministry of finance on 30 October 1759. Baker informs us that Moreau's tireless campaign against the political pretensions of the French parlements required 'a constant search for historical documents; an interminable process of argument, criticism, and response; and an obsessive historiographical effort that was never ended, but simply interrupted and rendered null, by the events of the Revolution'.[4] As was the case with so many other Enlightenment projects, historical research would be used to validate the proposed 'new model monarchy', conceived in the aftermath of the Seven Years' War. In addition to his supervision of, and support for, Moreau's work, described as the *Travaux littéraire*, Bertin would also embark, under the description of the *Correspondance littéraire*, upon his quite remarkable thirty-year correspondence with a small colony of French Jesuit priests living in Peking, responsible for both the dangerous work of Christian proselytising and service as 'mandarins' to the Emperor Kien-long. In the latter capacity, the priests acted as literary and linguistic experts, philosophers, medical researchers, mathematicians and astronomers. As we shall discover in Chapter Six, the letters between these priests and Bertin would not only make a major contribution to the 'Grand Design', but also provide an important chapter in the history of the 'global Enlightenment'.[5]

* * *

The Seven Years' War had transformed France's place in, and acquaintance with, the wider world, and the duc de Choiseul was aware of the necessity for radical socio-economic *and* constitutional change. He welcomed the opinions of the intellectuals, journalists, and politicians who were currently colonising those increasingly public spaces that had once belonged to the monarchy. During the 1750s, around forty works dealing with economic affairs had been published, as opposed to seventy-three during the 1760s, and sixty-one during the 1770s. Quesnay's very influential *Physiocratie* would reach the bookshops in 1767. Harnessing the prevailing winds of economic liberalism, France would benefit from 'an unprecedented period of growth, and, although it would be an exaggeration to use the term "economic miracle", it might not be stretching things too far to describe the most successful years of Choiseul's reign as the "Sept Glorieuses"'.[6] These were years that witnessed the foundation, or expansion, of those trading colonies that survived the defeat by England, as well as the creation of a few new possessions, a consequence of the expansion of national and world trade following the peace treaty of 1763. The profits from this trade during the second half of the eighteenth century would boost the population and wealth of commercial and industrial centres in both France and Britain. Massive fortunes would be made by the entrepreneurial and privileged few; thousands of châteaux, manor and town houses would be built or renovated.

Choiseul was also radical in his approach to constitutional and religious affairs. To the dismay of many of Louis XV's supporters, he courted the magistrates of the parlements, outlawing the Jesuit Order in France in order to gain their favour. Some of these magistrates had encouraged the idea that the parlements were now 'the guardians of the people', 'representatives of the nation', two steps too far for supporters of the monarchy. Bertin and Moreau's 'Grand Design' would be surprisingly liberal in its approach to socio-economic reform, including the introduction of a more flexible caste/class system, but far less enthusiastic about any constitutional change that would threaten the absolute powers of a Bourbon monarch. The dismissal of Choiseul in 1770, followed by Maupeou's 'despotic' coup the following year would reveal the dislocation between progressive socio-economic change and an antiquated political system that, having failed the nation in the Seven Years' War, was now in very poor condition to implement the radical reform programmes that were a 'categorical imperative' if Bourbon absolutism was to survive. Throughout the period covered by this study, including the early years of the Revolution of 1789, this dislocation between socio-economic liberalism and political conservatism would erode the foundations of Bourbon absolutism, leading Louis XVI, despite a few radical moves in the direction of economic and political reform, to the steps of the guillotine in 1792.

Any assessment of Bertin's work during the 1760s, then, has to be made by placing it within the context of an expanding world economy, political and economic changes within France, and a society that was beginning to pose a serious challenge to the concept of Bourbon absolutism. French colonial trade had increased by 119 per cent between 1730 and 1740, and by 71 per cent between 1740 and 1745. Between 1765 and 1776, it would increase by 80 per cent, faster than any other sector of the economy. Whilst agricultural and industrial exports rose fivefold between the late 1750s and 1770, colonial trade increased tenfold. The production of coal would rise from 50–75,000 tonnes in the 1700s to 600,000 tonnes by 1790; iron production was far less impressive, reaching around 65,000 tonnes by the early 1770s. Denis Woronoff suggests that the take-off in the French cotton industry, which he dates to around 1760, constituted 'the ultimate expression of the élan that ran through the eighteenth century'. Two major characteristics define patterns of growth in the agricultural sector, the first, that there was no 'agricultural revolution' *à l'anglaise* – France would remain a net importer of grain; the second that rich farmers producing for expanding urban markets would find it easier to buy out small subsistence farmers. At Lapeyrouse near Toulouse, large farms (over 100 hectares) had accounted for less than 15 per cent of the land in the 1680s, a percentage that would double by the 1780s. Jean-Marc Moriceau's magisterial study, *Les fermiers de l'Ile de France XVe-XVIIIe siècle*, concludes that the rich 'gentlemen farmers', who had risen to the top during the slow transformation of this rich grain-producing region between the 1650s and the 1750s, would lead the technical transformation of agriculture over the next century. This was the 'quiet revolution' that would produce the leaders of Bertin's *sociétés d'agriculture* in the 1760s.[7]

All this was accompanied by what Daniel Roche identifies as a 'biological push' in France during the eighteenth century. From 1700 to 1789, the population appears to have increased by one-third, from 21.5 to 28.6 million inhabitants; life expectancy is said to have increased from 20 to 29.6 years. However, this was not what many contemporary influential savants believed. The Rousseauesque debate over the virtues of the simple country life was linked to a widespread belief that science, industry and urbanisation were dehumanising and depleting France's population. It is difficult, for example, to understand fully the emphasis placed by most physiocrats on the importance of land as the ultimate source of all wealth without appreciating the perceived impact of demographic decline. Daniel Roche has highlighted the importance of the Enlightenment endeavour to establish a 'link between natural phenomena and social realities, the connection with space, the constraints of the economy and social behaviour'.[8] Bertin was intelligent and informed enough to realise that he was living though an unsettling period of profound change. He had been finance minister in an administration that had begun to pioneer 'free market' reforms, challenging the Colbertian legacy of regulated mercantilist economics that had survived the reign of Louis XIV. He had benefited from the pioneering work of Vincent de Gournay, whose work as an official in the *Bureau de Commerce* during the 1750s laid the foundations for the subsequent free-market reforms associated with Choiseul's 'Seven glorious years'.[9] A decree of 7 September 1762 had opened up the countryside to free trade by authorising 'the inhabitants of the countryside, as well as those in places which have no guilds, to spin every kind of material, to manufacture every kind of material, and to finish articles in accordance with government regulations'. This encouraged the expansion of France's massive 'proto-industrial' (emerging industrial) sector, which had long-term consequences for the future structures of French society and the precise brand of capitalism that would triumph in France. On 25 May 1763, internal freedom of the grain trade had been introduced, followed the following year by some relaxation of the rules governing the export of grain. Such radical free market policies were bound to foment rebellion in poorer urban and rural communities, as well as among the swelling ranks of proto-industrial workers. This was why, throughout his period in government, Bertin would urge caution to those colleagues, such as his more famous disciple Jacques Turgot, who, influenced by Adam Smith, sought to go much farther, much quicker. In both the political and the socio-economic sphere, Bertin would always be a cautious reformer.

Bertin's sometime pupil, Jacques Turgot, responsible for a raft of radical projects during the mid-1770s, would have appreciated the significance of the remarks made by the Scottish economic theorist, Sir John Steuart, which argued that in France 'Trade and industry are in vogue; and their establishment is occasioning a wonderful fermentation with the remaining fierceness of the feudal constitution.' But 'fermentation' was the *mot juste* that troubled Bertin, who was aware that radical economic change could unleash the kind of social rebellion that had pockmarked the history of the Bourbon monarchy from its inception. Steuart brilliantly, and presciently, explained the dilemma with which Bertin and Jacob-Nicolas Moreau would be confronted until the Revolution of 1789 realised their worst fears: 'In countries where the government is vested in the hands of the great lords, as is the case in all aristocracies, as was the case under the feudal government, and is still the case in many countries in Europe, where trade and industry are nonetheless daily gaining ground, the statesman who sets the new system of political economy on foot, may depend upon it, that either his attempt will fail, or the constitution of the government will change.'[10] This accurately sums up the fate that would befall Turgot's radical reforms in the mid-1770s, as well as the eventual failure of Bertin and Moreau's 'Grand Design'. The attempt to pour new, bourgeois liberal wine into old monarchic and aristocratic bottles was doomed to fail.

*   *   *

Agriculture and industry were the two areas of (shared) responsibility that would consume most of Henri Bertin's time as secretary of state until his dismissal from government in 1780. His contribution to the slow transformation of France's rural economy during the 1760s and 1770s has been documented by André Bourde's masterly three-volume study, *Agronomie et agronomes en France au XVIIIe siècle*, in which Henri Bertin is described as someone who 'was, in several different domains, an initiator and a pioneer'. He concedes, however, that Bertin's capacity for implementing major reforms would always be limited by the fact that he was obliged to share his responsibilities, *inter alia*, with the finance department (*contrôle général*), which is why Bourde describes Bertin as 'a kind of minister of agriculture and transport, but adding, reassuringly, that 'it was in Bertin's office that the great problems relating to agriculture were discussed'.[11] As for transport, Bertin's strong suit would be his friendship, founded during his intendancy in the Lyonnais, with Daniel-Charles Trudaine, a collaborator of Vincent de Gournay. Between 1750 and 1775, Trudaine and his son, Trudaine de Montigny, would transform the commercial and transport map of France, beginning with the construction of 25,000 kilometres of roads that facilitated schemes to open up trade and industry to outside competition.

The tireless efforts of the Trudaines did indeed improve commercial links between Paris and the historic Atlantic and Mediterranean ports such as Nantes, Bordeaux and Marseilles. However, France remained a nation that, when compared with England, contained vast stretches of countryside in which an impoverished, increasingly proto-industrialised, peasantry, speaking little or no French (especially in the south and west), would continue to pursue medieval methods of farming well into the nineteenth century. In 1735, France had been an agrarian country with 20 million inhabitants living in the countryside and just four million living in large cities and towns. Although her population would rise to some 28 million by 1789, the ratio of the rural to the urban population would not change significantly, whereas, in England, the urban population would rise from one-tenth of the national total to one-quarter during the course of the eighteenth century. This population shift constituted the bedrock of England's 'agricultural revolution'. The fact that there was no comparable transformation of the countryside in France deter-mined, in part, the degree of social immobility we find when comparing French with English society. There was a rigidity in the French political and social system, which prompted David Parker to conclude that 'the relative autonomy of French political and ideological superstructures can fairly well be delineated by the unsuccessful attempts of the state to go beyond the limits of the social and economic structure of which it was part. It proved unable to restructure French society in order to compete with the capitalist countries to the north'.[12] Bertin, as we have seen, was aware of the problem and, during his brief spell as *contrôleur général*, had re-floated Silhouette's plan for the introduction of a single tax, founded upon a new land register, payable by all property-owners irrespective of their class, or caste, status. The venture delighted his many physiocratic friends at the same time that it dismayed most of the magistrates in the Paris parlement, as well as most of the great aristocratic landowners at the court of Versailles. The fears engendered by Bertin's *cadastre* undoubtedly contributed to his 'resignation' as *contrôleur général* in 1763.

Nonetheless, in his new apparition as secretary of state without a coherent portfolio, Bertin could reflect on the rising support for agricultural reform that had been evident before the outbreak of the Seven Years' War, much of it inspired by what had been happening in Britain, which had supplied the doctrine and the example. In 1750, Duhamel du Monceau had published his *Traité de la culture des terres*, which sought to adapt many British reforms to French conditions. In 1962, he produced his theoretical and practical manual for the 'New Agriculture'. His work was supple-mented by the researches of his more famous colleagues in the *Académie des sciences*, the naturalist Buffon and the chemist

Lavoisier. Everything pertaining to nature and farming, from the conservation of forests and the care of animals to the cultivation of the potato, became a matter of concern and interest to academicians in Paris and noble 'gentlemen farmers' such as the marquis de Turbilly in the provinces, as well as to many enterprising village farmers, a prime example of the operation of Enlightenment applied science.

But how could the good news concerning the 'New Agriculture', which was being discussed in the plush salons of Paris, be disseminated among poor subsistence farmers in the provinces? Jean-Marc Moriceau, whose study of farming in the productive region of the Ile-de-France contains many examples of rural entrepreneurship, provides us with the answer. Moriceau identifies three types of *agents de diffusion*. First, and foremost, administrators, 'ministers such as Bertin [as secretary of state], whose activities reached far beyond the limits imposed upon him at the *contrôle général* (1759–63), partly because he retained the services of an active, economical, and influential secretariat until 1780; everything was discussed in his offices until he was dismissed by Necker [in 1780]'. 'The second type of agent consisted of aristocrats such as the Rochefoucaulds, and "gentlemen farmers" such as Turbilly, as well as systematisers like Duhamel and Lavoisier. Finally, there were the bourgeois and noble landowners, and educated farmers. The latter are the least known but, without doubt, the most numerous.'[13] Unlike his far more famous disciple, Jacques Turgot, Henri Bertin was more comfortable in the company of *agronomes*, occasionally referred to as 'technocrats', than in the company of the physiocrats. What separated these two schools of economists? André Bourde explains: *Agronomes* 'were less methodical, and, above all, less systematic than the physiocrats; ... they were more flexible in their analyses of society and human beings'.[14] This admirably suited the character and temperament of Henri Bertin.

On the other hand, Jacques Turgot's analysis of the evolution of a modern economy recalls some of the ideas of Adam Smith and Karl Marx, apart, of course, from Turgot's physiocratic mantra of land as the original source of all wealth. His insistence on the progressive and transformative potential of capitalism and his sociological analyses of 'class' struggles obviously impressed Marx, who described Turgot as 'that radical bourgeois minister who initiated the French Revolution', praise that would have horrified Henri Bertin![15] Bertin preferred to walk on safer ground, although some of the tenets of physiocratic doctrine, when combined with the advantages of Chinese authoritarian political and social policies, would influence his thinking throughout his later career, as we shall see in Chapter Six. It is interesting to observe how Peking, not Paris, became the focal point of his midnight reveries on political and social control as the contradictions between his political and socio-economic ideas became more glaring during the late 1770s and 1780s. It was a desperate call, but he seemed to believe that Peking just might resolve the dilemma that could not be resolved in Paris. The conclusions drawn from his reveries would be incorporated into the 'Grand Design', especially those that offered a solution to the central problem of protecting the concept of absolutism from any possible constitutional change. He accepted, rather than embraced, liberalism; the only 'ism' that he and Moreau would ever truly embrace was Bourbon absolutism. Fortunately, under Louis XV, the concept of 'absolutism' was flexible (or incoherent) enough to allow periodic flirtations with liberal policies, even if its supporters appeared to be walking with one leg in a splint.

The fundamental operational difference between Turgot and Bertin is evident in the latter's approach to the creation and establishment of agricultural societies during the 1760s, an achievement that revealed Bertin's commitment to cautious radical reform as well as to the continuity that links his reforms as *contrôleur général* to those introduced during his time as secretary of state. Bertin's original scheme included the creation of an agricultural society in every *généralité* (main fiscal and administrative unit) in the kingdom. On 1 March 1761, responding to initiatives taken by provinces such as Brittany, the government had announced the foundation of the first agricultural society in Paris;

its jurisdiction would ultimately cover the towns of Meaux (Ile-de-France), Beauvais (Picardy) and Sens (Yonne). The rules and regulations that governed the procedures of this founding society would serve as a model for all subsequent societies.

Lyon, France's second city, enthusiastically followed the capital's lead, using the occasion to praise Bertin, its erstwhile intendant, in the process: 'Our secretary has informed us that M. Bertin, during his period in charge of the treasury, constantly supported agriculture, which must always be regarded as the principal and most dependable source of this country's wealth; he always sought to encourage farmers and improve their methods of production. He has now persuaded the king to establish, under his surveillance, societies whose members, applying themselves with equal measures of zeal and intelligence, are obliged to communicate their thoughts to, and share their discoveries with, the general public.'[16] These zealous and intelligent individuals, guided by the old physiocrats and the new intendant of the Lyonnais, decided that their main bureau would be opened in Lyon, with four subsidiary offices in the towns of Montbrison, Saint-Etienne, Roanne and Villefranche. Originally, the Lyon bureau consisted of twenty members; the subsidiaries were composed of ten. Provision was made for the appointment of associate members. Once the intendant had succeeded in organising the ground rules for a society, Bertin's office would be informed and arrangements made for the government to give its legal blessing. By 1763, planning for the creation of fifteen societies had begun.

From the beginning, Bertin had benefited from the advice and encouragement of ministers such as Trudaine, and 'improvers' such as the marquis de Turbilly (the French 'Turnip Townsend'). His early protector at court had been the influential duc de Noailles, a *grand seigneur*, agronomist and botanist. Turbilly actively encouraged the formation of societies in Tours, near his own estates, as well as in Angers and Le Mans. He, too, was lavish in his praise of Henri Bertin: 'people will associate you, monsieur, with the renovation of agriculture in France, where it will be remembered that this remarkable event occurred during your ministry, whose memory will forever be cherished'.[17]

French men and women did indeed experience something of a 'psycho-socio-economic' sea-change in their lives during this period. We must note that, between the publications of the *Encyclopédie* in the early fifties, through the shattering experience of the Seven Years' War, to the implementation of Choiseul's 'liberal revolution' in the 1760s, the state did try to improve the lives of rich and poor alike, especially in rural areas. The great Voltaire had experienced something of a Damascene conversion in the late 1750s as he worked hard to improve his estates in Ferney and Tournay: 'he began to feel that the problem of evil was not some large and dramatic catastrophe in a far-away country but was here and now in the everyday sufferings of the poor and downtrodden; moreover, he realised that he now had a personal responsibility for trying to alleviate it on his own estates'. Enlightenment reform signalled a significant shift from state control to self-help, from regulation to the free market, and the 'sage of Ferney' was one of those opinion-makers who welcomed the change. The recognition that government intervention might mitigate the worst features of human poverty constitutes an important advance in popular consciousness during the eighteenth century, even if the 'free market' solutions on offer were welcomed more by the rich than the poor. Voltaire summed up what he thought was happening in the country in one of his many poetic 'epistles':

> In a desolate canton an inhabitant grows rich;
> Turbilli [*sic*], in the Anjou, imitates and applauds him;
> Bertin, who, in his king always sees his country,
> Offers a helping hand for his labours;
> Trudaine, who knows full well that farming
> Is the driving force behind the nation's wealth,
> And, that when it comes to supporting the state, we owe as much
> To Cérès' scythe as to Bellone's sabre.[18]

146

More agricultural societies would be founded in the 1760s and 1770s – one in Aix in 1765 and another in Perpignan, as late as 1779. Nonetheless, that acute, if biased, English observer of French agriculture, Arthur Young, who visited the Parisian Agricultural Society in 1789, was distinctly unimpressed: 'The secretary reads the titles of papers presented, and gives some little account of them, but they are not read unless particularly interesting.' Young tried to press the case of the introduction of turnips, 'But that they conceive to be an object of impossible attainment; they have done so much, and the government so much more, and all in vain, that they consider it as a hopeless object. I did not tell them that all hitherto done has been absolute folly; and that the right way to begin, was to undo every thing.'[19] Now, Young had a sharp tongue (he launched similar attacks upon English agricultural societies), but his dismissive comments at least provide us with an observation point from which to assess the strength and composition of the opposition to Bertin's radical political and socio-economic reforms.

In the first place, there was, to put it mildly, if not exactly a 'black hole', then certainly a distinct absence of collective responsibility at the centre of Louis XV's government, if we include in our definition of government a collection of ministers with well-defined and demarcated responsibilities. The machinery of *ancien régime* government was not easily adapted to the massive problems of late eighteenth-century civil and military affairs. The very term 'government' had not entered the lexicon of political life until the 1720s. Government offices were scattered over Paris and Versailles: it was not until 1759 and 1762 that purpose-built offices were constructed to house the staff of the secretaries of state for war and foreign affairs.

Bertin's new post was cobbled together in 1763 after a discussion between Louis XV, Pompadour, Bertin and other secretaries of state who fought to defend their own territory. Bertin was given a staff of just twenty-five to cover the many diverse responsibilities attached to his office; the secretary of state for the Navy could draw upon the experience of eight senior and sixty-two junior clerks. During his period as *contrôleur général*, Bertin had been in charge of thirty-four senior secretaries, with his junior ministers each employing one, two or three dozen junior clerks. The unique influence and authority of the *contrôle général*, with its *intendant des finances* exerting an influence over a wide range of departments, was to prove a constant thorn in Bertin's side throughout his time as *le petit ministre* (1763–80). After Bertin's resignation as *contrôleur général* in 1763, the *intendant des finances*, whose name weighed as heavily as the responsibilities he held – Henry François-de-Paule Lefèvre d'Ormesson – would retain control over many important, and contentious, agricultural issues, including irrigation, land-clearance, pasturing rights (*parcours*) and division of common lands.[20] This is why much of the praise for the limited success of the agricultural reform movement that was implemented between the 1750s and the 1780s is often attributed to Bertin's successor as *contrôleur général*, Clément L'Averdy. The attribution is hardly credible: Bertin had worked hard, albeit in vain, to create a separate and co-ordinated department of agriculture during his time as *contrôleur général*, setting up a *comité d'agriculture* within the department as early as January 1761.

Although his plans were never fully realised, tribute should nonetheless be paid to Bertin for his commitment to the task of creating agricultural societies. He had made it crystal clear from the outset that the societies 'would devote their work entirely to agricultural affairs and all that related to them, without becoming involved in other matters'. This, as we shall see, was an ultimately unsuccessful attempt to distinguish the new agricultural societies from the traditional royal academies. Many towns, Tours, d'Alençon, Bourges, Poitiers, for example, welcomed, at first, Bertin's scheme for the creation of agricultural societies. They could draw upon what Georges Bussière describes as 'ready-made' agricultural associations, but these clubs and associations had a history and were rooted in local soil. Bertin was a 'centraliser'; throughout his period as *contrôleur général*, he had been forced to confront the increasing decentralising authority of the parlements. He made it plain that his new societies should not make proposals 'that were incompatible with the actual requirements of the state'. However, the problems he faced with the creation of agricultural societies could not be divorced from the legacy of bitterness and distrust bequeathed by his largely unsuccessful attempts to introduce a new land register and bring the parlements to heel over fiscal reform. Partly as a result of Choiseul's new policy of appeasing the Paris parlement, Bertin had been replaced on 13 December 1763 by one of his antagonists in the parlement, the young Jansenist magistrate, Clément L'Averdy. With Choiseul eager to gain the support of the parlements, and L'Averdy determined to retain a significant measure of control over agricultural affairs as the new *contrôleur général*, Bertin, *'le petit ministre'* was never really master in his own ministerial house, certainly not so far as agricultural affairs were concerned.[21] Some of the most recalcitrant provincial parlements, Rouen, Toulouse, Grenoble, and Bordeaux, fortified by closer ties with the Paris parlement (the *union des classes*), were determined to defend the 'historic rights and privileges' of their provinces. To Bertin's chagrin, his own provincial parlement at Bordeaux proved to be the hardest nut to crack, focusing their opposition upon the authority and powers, especially voting rights, that had been granted to the *intendant* in Bertin's plans for the creation of his new societies. He tried in vain to reassure his critics: 'it was never the intention that the authority vested in the intendant, by order of the king, should be exploited in an abusive manner; rather the idea was that it should offer another way of giving these societies the support that their zeal gives them every right to expect from His Majesty'.[22] However, fears of 'ministerial despotism' walked the battlements of most eighteenth-century parlements, and everyone knew that the *intendant* was the main instrument of government ministers seeking to impose their authority over provincial institutions. This proved to be the most acute problem facing reformers throughout France, and, indeed, in other comparable countries. 'When will the state get off my back?' is not a *cri de coeur* peculiar to the twenty-first century.

The marquis de Turbilly and Bertin tried hard to smooth ruffled feathers by separating the work of agricultural societies from that of the royal academies. These academies, many of which had been founded in the seventeenth century, continued to flourish in the eighteenth: Peter Jones has described the phenomenon as 'a notable thickening of the circuits of intellectual discussion in the 1760s and 1770s'.[23] Bertin was eager to distinguish the work of his societies, which was intended to be more practical than theoretical, more popular than elitist, from that of the literary, philosophical or scientific academies. After all, these were the days when Antoine Parmentier was propagandising the virtues of the humble potato. Enlightenment applied science was being offered to ordinary citizens, introducing the virtues of rationalisation, specialisation and classification to the world of politics and government administration. The prestigious polymaths elected to provincial royal academies, whose genius had already been recognised by the king, did not always welcome this populist approach. One of the reasons for the prolonged, and rather successful, resistance of the Bordeaux parlement to Bertin's plans came from its learned magistrates who were also members of the city's famous Royal Academy, founded as early as 1662. Like so many other academies, it had placed agricultural issues on its agenda for many decades, and thus felt somewhat aggrieved when the intendant cautiously tried to implement Bertin's institutional apartheid between 'academies' and 'agricultural societies'. Provincial *intendants* frequently found themselves caught between a 'rock' (provincial parlements and local elites) and a 'hard place' (Bertin's ministry). Bertin was keen to get practical farming issues on the agendas of his societies; like Arthur Young, he wanted potential 'village Turbillys' to attend their meetings. A glance at the membership of the new agricultural societies in Lyon and Bordeaux, however, suggests that far too many places were eventually taken by local dignitaries – the archbishop of Lyon and the *lieutenant de Roi de la ville de Villefranche* in Lyon; an archbishop and provincial governor in Bordeaux.[24]

The creation of agricultural societies, of course, constituted a relatively minor plank of the reform platform launched by Choiseul and his ministers. They would not have provoked the resentment they did had they not been regarded as instruments of Choiseul's more general reorganisation of the relationship between government and the people, a radical venture that elicited some sympathy from Henri Bertin, former 'protector of the royal purse'. Choiseul believed that it was dangerous for ministers to ignore public opinion, whether in Paris, or the provinces. Bertin's concern, shared by Louis XV and the *dévot* faction, focused on the danger that Choiseul's hand of friendship (including the handing out of bribes) to the parlements was undermining the authority of the monarchy, at a time when the king's infatuation with his new official mistress, the infamous madame du Barry, was draining away what little popular support Louis XV enjoyed. It was the parlements that, all too often, won public acclaim during the constitutional struggles of the late 1760s, leading to Maupeou's royal coup against the parlements in 1771; cautious as ever, Bertin, initially, felt that he had to support this attack on the parlements, given his support for the concept of absolute monarchy. Gradually, however, he would accept the necessity of winning over the hearts and minds of public opinion. One important aspect of the 'Grand Design' would be a move towards transparency, enabling 'subjects' (that word would also have to change!) to explore the history of their past. Moreau's felt that his *dépôt de legislation*, his rapidly expanding compilation of historic charters and documents, should ultimately be made available to scholars and researchers. The 'Grand Design' took time to mature, but we should recall that it would provide an ideology targeted at the reformation of the monarchy, as well as the foundation of the present day *Archives nationales* and the *Bibliothéque du roi*.

The dangers of open government and economic reform, however, became painfully obvious when the regulatory system governing the provision of the nation's staple food, bread, was dismantled. Bread was not just a commodity purchase in mid-eighteenth-century France; it was a matter of life and death. Steven Kaplan, one of the most perceptive analysts of the relationship between the rising cost of basic food supplies and rising curves of social rebellion in eighteenth-century France, has argued that, during the course of the eighteenth century, one can identify 'a double process of popular disenchantment, whose effects were both cumulative and interdependent: a long disaffection of the people with the monarchy, and, conversely, on the part of the king and the government, the growing conviction that the only sentiment people were capable of was ingratitude'.[25] The gradual replacement of a Colbertian regulated economic system with that of a market economic system aggravated the widespread social unrest that peaked during the late 1760s, the mid-1770s, and again during the late 1780s. Bertin, L'Averdy, and Necker, unlike Bertin's disciple, Jacques Turgot, were all aware of the dangers inherent in the process of dismantling a system, which, in the words of the crowd that marched to Versailles in the spring of 1789, could describe the king as 'the baker' and the Queen as the 'baker's wife'. This is why, from 1764 to 1789, and beyond, successive administrations felt they had to intervene in the operation of market economics; this is why the most the most dangerous threat to the monarchy during this period was the accusation that the king himself was involved in a plot to starve his own people – the infamous *complot de famine*. This thorn in the royal crown became yet another contentious issue in the stormy relationships between the monarchy and the parlements, which would end with the execution of the last of the absolute kings of France, Louis XVI, accused, in 1792, of complicity in hoarding grain.

The fear of a famine plot not only formed part of the collective mentality of *ancien régime* society, but also, 'clearly revealed the anxiety of a proto-industrial society that was still subject to the tyranny of wheat prices ... Fear of a food plot mobilised the masses and increased their awareness of politics'.[26] In these circumstances, it took a very courageous, perhaps foolhardy, politician (and the duc de Choiseul was a combination of both) to deregulate the price of bread: the 'politics of the baguette' may still be seen to operate in France today. All the more surprising, then, that Choiseul's ministers chose the critical post-war crisis of the early 1760s to launch their most wide-ranging free-market programme, affecting both industry and agriculture – on 7 September 1762, the end of guild controls over the manufacture of textile products in the countryside; on 25 May 1763, the free circulation of grain, vegetables and flour within French borders; and on 2 January 1764, further legislation allowing freedom to export grain in certain regions, under certain conditions. Bertin, always conscious of a possible popular backlash, thought that his agricultural societies could be used to support the government. On 13 April 1762, he had asked the society created in Lyon to express its views on the merits of free trade. The well-heeled secretary reassured Bertin that his members were convinced that 'the lack of freedom to sell grain is one of the causes that is most detrimental to agriculture', music to Choiseul's ears.[27] However, the changes introduced by Choiseul's administration overturned centuries of state regulation that had been introduced to protect the quality of goods, and the availability of bread to the poor at a price they could afford; they radically altered the relationship between producers, consumers and the police; they also created one of the most serious social crises in the history of eighteenth-century France. For over a century, governments would be forced to introduce, abandon, then re-introduce free-market policies, their decisions dictated by the quality of grain harvests, the scale of popular rebellion, and the impact of political events.

One of the most penetrating analyses of the socio-political dislocation prompted by the introduction of free-market policies in the 1760s and 1770s came from one of Henri Bertin's friends, the abbé Baudeau, who wrote: 'I have long observed that between these two extremes [the rich at court and the lower orders], there exists a great measure of agreement. Enlightenment and virtue can only be found among the bourgeoisie (*l'état mitoyen*). Good government and sound instruction ... tend, increasingly, to diminish the influence of these two extremes and increase that of the bourgeoisie.'[28] Baudeau, like so many other students of the Enlightenment, had discovered that the bourgeoisie could provide the missing link between the aristocracy and the 'irrational' crowd. Trapped again between his high position at court and his profound belief in the doctrine that the king was the 'father of his people', but conscious of the fact that the historic link between the crown and the crowd was visibly being wrenched apart, Bertin chose to seek a compromise solution. This did not prove to be an easy option. On several occasions, Henri Bertin had been forced to defend his sovereign against accusations that the king was involved in a plot to starve his own people – the infamous *complot de famine*. It is ironic, but understandable, that the more the crown involved itself in the process of organising reserve grain supplies to feed the nation in a crisis (the *greniers d'abondance*), the more it was accused of involvement in plots to starve the nation.

The basic problem was that an unreformed, paternalist monarchical system found it increasingly difficult to meet the requirements of a nascent consumerist and capitalist society. As early as the mid-1720s, the influential diarist, Barbier, had written that the origins of the subsistence crisis that had afflicted the nation 'could be traced back to the court'. During the late 1730s, Philibert Orry (*contrôleur général* from 1730–45) had been accused, along with his brother, of making vast fortunes out of the people's misery. The fuel that consistently fed the flames of rumour and revolt was the alleged association between the king's ministers and wealthy merchants and speculators engaged in the purchase of grain for the royal warehouses. The leading physiocrat and free-marketeer, Dupont de Nemours, calculated that Orry had paid out no less than 80,000,000 *livres* to merchants who had organised the purchase of grain imported from the Levant, Pennsylvania and Archangel, one of the biggest royal business operations during the *ancien régime*. De Nemours considered this expense to have been a complete waste of time and money; his solution, as we know, was to introduce the freedom of the grain trade.[29] His belief that the introduction of free markets would solve the problem of producing grain at an affordable price would prove to be ill founded. The interaction of economic, political, moral and social problems during the 1760s enabled the *complot de famine* to secure a greater purchase than ever upon communities and individuals, from princes and parlementarians to the popular masses. During the autumn of 1768 (soon after Louis XV had succumbed to the charms of madame du Barry) when bread prices doubled, some of the parlements, formerly anxious to join the government in a show of national unity, began to sharpen their knives and target ministers such as Henri Bertin, who was not only minister for agriculture but also responsible for the general administration of certain provinces, including Normandy. In Rouen, provincial capital of the province, placards reflecting the increasing politicisation of French public opinion laid the responsibility for the national crisis at the feet of the king: 'Under Henry IV we suffered high bread prices as a result of war', they declared, 'but we had a [real] king in those days. Under Louis XIV we also experienced high bread prices, caused either by wars or poor weather conditions ... At present, however, we cannot attribute high bread costs to wars or a real shortage of wheat. The truth is that we no longer have a king, because the king has become a grain merchant.'[30]

Such inflammatory placards were not uncommon, but the action of a handful of parlements that surfed these waves of popular discontent to indict the king and his courtiers was far more worrying. The parlement of Rouen, for example, reported 'that there was widespread suffering as a result of the high cost of bread; that people blamed *les accapareurs* (grain hoarders) for recent price rises; and, that the crown had gained most from these rises'. What is more they had proof of royal culpability – a copy of the secret 'Malisset convention', agreed with the government on 12 July 1767. It involved four *gros capitalistes* who agreed to share, over a period of twelve years, the profits acquired from the purchase of grain: 'all the [speculative] operations of the company, concerning the organisation and supply of grain to the royal warehouses, were to be made in the name of the king'. In the words of Georges Bussière, 'Voilà le Pacte de Famine!'. On 15

October 1768, the parlement sent the king an open letter, which, although it did not accuse Louis XV of direct complicity with 'monopolists', demanded to know who exactly was involved 'in the kind of trade that was causing such distress to his faithful subjects in Normandy?' It would be hard to imagine a parlement questioning Louis XIV in this manner. Bertin, in his most emollient fashion, sought to soothe the ruffled feathers of the Rouen magistrates: 'I gave the king your letter of the fifteenth of this month. His Majesty struck me as being deeply moved by the misfortunes experienced by the province of Normandy. He instructed me to make sure you knew that he had used a very considerable sum of money from the royal purse to provide supplies for the city of Rouen and the other towns of the province, and that the precautions that he has taken should relieve you of any anxiety on the matter.' Then came a gentle tap on the wrists for the magistrates, 'He was quite surprised that information about your *dépôt* should be so widely known, and he ordered me to inform you of his displeasure.'[31]

Little did Bertin realise that, thirty years later, a remarkable epilogue to this affair would resurrect the ghost of his brother, the unfortunate marquis de Fratteaux who was to die in the Bastille. In November 1768, an employee of the *agent général du clergé*, Leprévost de Beaumont, was arrested for supplying Rouen magistrates with information concerning the Malisset contract, promising to make further enquiries about 'a diabolical pact concerning a monstrous conspiracy', hatched by the king's ministers, to starve the people. Leprévost was eventually locked up in several prisons, including the Bastille, on the not uncommon charge of 'having lost his reason'. During his year in the Bastille, Leprévost claimed that he had befriended the governor, the comte de Jumilhac, Henri Bertin's brother-in-law. Twenty-six years later, at the height of the Jacobin Terror, an elderly prisoner appeared before the Revolutionary Tribunal in Paris. He was Clément L'Averdy, *contrôleur général* at the time of Leprévost's arrest. Accused of being involved in the infamous plot to starve the people in 1768, L'Averdy was offering a reasoned account of his innocence when a man stood up in court and demanded to be heard. It was Leprévost de Beaumont: his long-awaited opportunity for revenge had arrived. His testimony that L'Averdy had been personally involved in the 'monstrous plot' of 1768 sealed the latter's fate. L'Averdy was executed the same day. The Revolution of 1789 provided the stage for innumerable acts of retribution, whether they were founded upon genuine cases of illegal conduct or a matter of settling old scores: accusations of being involved in plots to starve the people were commonplace because so many people had died from starvation.

But had not Henri Bertin acted as the king's defence counsel in 1768? If Louis XV had made money, even indirectly, out of speculating in the import of grain, then was not Bertin, manager of the king's personal and secret accounts, implicated? In his memoirs, Bertin's close friend, Jacob-Nicolas Moreau, agreed that Bertin had indeed been responsible for the king's private purse at this time, but that there was no question of Bertin making money from grain speculation. George Bussière, who made a considerable effort to track down all the documentation relating to Bertin and the *complot de famine de 1768*, concludes that, despite the best efforts of the magistrates of the Rouen parlement, no firm evidence could be found to involve Henri Bertin.[32] Innocent of speculating in grain as he almost certainly was, Bertin's murky role as keeper of the king's private purse, whether it was used to fund the extravaganza of the king's sex life, as Moreau openly admitted, or to launder money which should have gone into the national coffers, would place him in the 'suspect' category when a revolutionary crowd attacked his château in the spring of 1789, as we shall see in our final chapter.

* * *

If agriculture constituted the most important brief in Bertin's wide-ranging portfolio as secretary of state, mining came a close second; indeed, it has been argued that the 'administration of mines must be considered as the most successful of his

157

responsibilities'. The Bertin family had always taken a keen interest in industry and commerce. An entry in the parish register of Saint-Georges for 25 April 1692 records the marriage of a Jean Perret, 'employed currently in the manufacturing works of M. Bertin at Saint-Laurent-du-Manoir'. These works had belonged to Henri Bertin's grandfather, Jean Bertin I, who owned two forges situated quite close to the birthplace of the Bertin family. Five years later, Jean Bertin had joined one of the biggest forge-masters in the region, the baron de Segonzac, in a venture to obtain government contracts for the supply of 100 cannons. Jean Bertin II, Henri Bertin's father, had expanded the family's profile as forge-masters by seizing control of one of the biggest enterprises in the region, the *forge d'Ans*. Henri Bertin, with the assistance of his siblings, would continue to take an interest in the considerable agricultural and industrial holdings of his family.[33] This interest would inform his actions as a dedicated servant of the centralising Bourbon state, represented in the person of a legitimate, if louche, king. Economic change had to be pursued through the institutions of the state, with due regard, of course, for traditional privileges and the authority of powerful provincial interests. The struggle between Paris and the provinces over control of the country's resources has been a constant factor in the political economy of France. Bertin and Moreau would take all these matters to heart when they created their ideological programme for the 'Grand Design'. Nonetheless, the outcome would be an ideology that also reflected the values of the emerging bourgeois class, as opposed to the more traditional, regulated economic system associated with a traditional, aristocratic 'caste'.

The motto that inspired the bourgeois economic policies of the 1760s was '*Il faut calculer en grand*' ('We must think big'), and to do this the government decided that it had to take a more pro-active stance: the idea that 'small is beautiful' belonged to the feudal past. An agronomist, the marquis de Turbilly, and an entrepreneurial mine-owner, François-Pierre Tubeuf, who pressed the all too willing Bertin 'to think big', agreed that progress could only be made through the introduction of larger units of production, the process being assisted by the government. Across the Channel, the British, victors of the Seven Years' War, had embarked upon an 'agricultural revolution': small farms were being replaced by larger estates; cottage industry was being replaced by factories alongside new forms of proto-industrial units of production; in many places, the small drift mines dug into the side of a hill were being replaced by deep mining. Similar developments could be observed in France, but the process of change was far slower. In France, the parlements frequently led the charge against centralising 'government despotism', whilst the massive social dislocation occasioned by the introduction of free-market policies continued to erode the foundations of Bourbon absolutism. Radical change would surely have to include the transformation of traditional forms of absolutist government and the destruction of seigneurial systems of political and socio-economic control. In a recent article, Stephen Miller concludes that, 'The laws upheld by the royal administration and military established burdens on commoners, primarily the peasantry, and reserved titles, exemptions, seigneurial rights, and venal offices for a minority of wealthy subjects, primarily the nobility.'[34] Bertin, although privately very sympathetic to the views of Turbilly and Tubeuf, was convinced that the advance towards a more liberal economic society would have to proceed with due caution; he was wary of head-on challenges to the socio-economic status of the nobility. He realised, however, that for Bourbon absolutism to survive, the bourgeoisie and sections of the robe nobility, alongside a handful of traditional aristocrats, would have to supplant the increasingly embattled sword nobility by offering its unqualified support to the crown. Without the mediation of the bourgeoisie, supported by the more progressive sections of the robe nobility, the monarchy would be too weak to manage, successfully, the emerging capitalist system in France. It is probable that one of Bertin's favourite publications was the abbé Coyer's *La noblesse commerçante* (1756), a work that favoured the creation of a 'business nobility'.

One of the main explanations for Bertin's eventual failure must be found in the contradiction that existed between his defence of Bourbon absolutism at court, and his cautious attack on privileged seigneurial systems of landholding and production in the countryside, described as 'feudal bricolage' by Stephen Miller, an understandable response to the outcry that followed his ill-fated attempt to introduce a new land survey (*cadastre*) in the early 1760s. Much the same could be said of Turgot's policies, and those espoused by the physiocrats in general. The essential difference, however, was that, in Bertin's eyes, Turgot wanted to move too fast, too soon. To understand fully the contradictory course that Bertin often pursued, we need to remember that Bertin's family had roots, on his mother's side, with the nobility of the sword, a fact that Bertin's elder brother, who was to die in the Bastille, had taken all too seriously. The entire family had fed off the decaying corpse of the old feudal system, as so many robe families had done, and were doing. Bertin's father had bought the *forge d'Ans*, one of the most valuable in the Périgord, as part of a feudal estate that included the medieval *château d'Ans*, a prize that Henri Bertin would cling on to until the 1780s.[35] Bertin realised that to survive at Versailles he would be obliged to adopt a somewhat dual approach to the politics of reform – on the one hand, a supporter of some of the old traditions of the French nobility (on a personal front, he tried hard to trace every old noble branch of his family tree) but, on the other, an opponent of the antiquated political and economic *systems* that sustained the sword nobility. As one might expect, he was not always successful. At court, he was obliged to endure the constant disdain of Louis XV's de facto 'first minister', the duc de Choiseul, who had fought to downgrade Bertin's secretaryship of state to the status of a *'petit ministère'*.[36]

As we have seen above, Bertin was fortunate in one regard – both during his period as *contrôleur général*, and during his early years in the *'petit ministère'*, he enjoyed the support of Daniel Trudaine, a 'technocrat' who had played such a formative role in the creation, in 1747, of the famous *Ecole des Ponts et Chaussées*. Philibert Orry's chief lieutenant in the *contrôle général* during the

1740s, Trudaine would continue his work as Bertin's right-hand man during the 1750s and 1760s. Trudaine had been the driving force behind the legislation, introduced on 14 January 1744, which would shape the future of coal mining in France until the twentieth century. It decreed that: (i) every mine-owner, including 'seigneurs throughout the jurisdiction of their fiefs and tribunals', had to obtain permission from the *contrôle général* to operate a mine; (ii) mine-owners had to inform the government of their production figures and the size of their workforce; and (iii) that landowners would continue to be the legal owners of the land under which coal was discovered, but those who did not win concessions to mine the coal would have to be satisfied with an indemnity from the chosen concessionaire. Other articles dealt with security in the mines and the rights of workers. Few royal policies would provoke more resistance in the provinces during Bertin's period in power than the legislation of 1744. Like the land survey that Bertin failed to push through during his period as *contrôleur général*, the 1744 mining provisions threatened the principle of individual property rights that the Revolution of 1789 would declare to be 'inviolable'. The assertion of regalian rights upon which the legislation was founded would clash, especially in provinces such as Languedoc, with individualist interpretations of property rights derived from Roman law.[37] Opponents of the state's centralising policies would cite Roman law when making accusations of 'government despotism'. Among the mining communities of Cransac in the Rouergue, Rive-de-Gier in the Lyonnais and Alès in the Cévennes the question would be asked 'Is the coal merchant (*charbonnier*) no longer master of his own mine?'[38] The answer, in the opinion of the government, was no, he was not. This answer signalled an historic change in property rights as well as in methods of production.

A brief assessment of Bertin's close involvement in the development of three important coal-fields in France, Rive-de-Gier, just south of Lyon, the Alès basin further south in the region of the Cévennes, and Cransac in the Rouergue, will illustrate Bertin's *étatiste* approach to the reform of the mining industry. It will identify his enemies, a contradictory collection of aristocrats, parlements and judicial and seigneurial officials, semi-attached to a decaying feudal system, as well as proto-industrial workers, defenders of a provincial, seigneurial, localised socio-economic system. The struggle that ensued reveals so many of the problems that beset the Bourbon monarchy during its final decades of power, problems that help to explain Bertin's enforced exit from government in 1780.

To clarify the variety and complexity of these problems, we have chosen to address four that recur in any account of mining in mid–late eighteenth-century France, whether it was mining for coal or any other underground deposits such as lead:

(i)   *The length of concessions granted by the government.*
      As in the agricultural sector, short leases did not favour the long-term development of *'l'industrie en grand'*, and this was especially the case with coal mining given the time, investment costs and difficulty involved in digging deep pits and installing the appropriate machinery to deal with the constant threat confronting any miner – underground flooding. Bertin understood the need forlong-term concessions, some of them covering a period of fiftyyears.

(ii) *Government and concessionnaires.*
      There is compelling evidence of an unhealthy relationship between concessionaires and officials in Bertin's office, some of whom had a financial interest in the success of a given contract. Two of his top advisers, La Barberie and Parent, were given a stake in concessions by applicants who wisely thought it was advantageous to have government officials involved in the success of their mining ventures. Parent's financial peculations, over a long period, would help to discredit Bertin, as we shall see in our following chapter. There was also the fact that a lot of money could be made by courtiers and powerful aristocratic landowners who had been advised that 'the age of coal' had arrived. The duc de Bourbon, the prince de Conti, the comte d'Artois, and the maréchal de Castries were just a chosen few of *les Grands* at Versailles who became involved in the new era of French coal-mining.[39]

(iii) *Opposition to government centralisation on the part of provincial parlements, seigneurial and bailliage courts, and local legal practitioners.*

So far as the parlements were concerned, especially the parlement of Paris, Bertin had been obliged to face continual opposition arising from his fierce struggles over taxation during his period as *contrôleur général,* and many parlements continued to oppose Bertin's policies on free trade and mining concessions during the 1760s and 1770s. Local and seigneurial courts of justice were used by local individuals and communities to prevent, or delay, the implementation of government decrees. For the officials of these courts, what is now described by the European Union as 'the law of subsidiarity' should be implemented – local issues should be dealt with, wherever possible, by local institutions.

(iv) *Popular rebellion.*

For concessionaires who had no roots in the community, their greatest fear was a revolt of local workers determined to destroy their machinery, and, on occasions, deliberately flood their mines. This constituted the most intractable problem of all, linked as it often was to the wider issue of popular rebellion directed against the government's free-trade policies, especially the legislation introducing free-trade in grain. As early as 1757, Daniel Trudaine had conceded that, given the scale of local opposition to 'foreign' concessionaires, perhaps it would have been wiser, after all, to have left landowners in charge of the mines on their own property![40] The social and economic consequences of France's defeat in the Seven Years' War changed his mind.

As one can imagine from the above list of formidable problems confronting the early pioneers of modern coal mining after 1744, 'triumph and disaster' were two impostors that were widely recognised in mining circles. The geographic size and duration of government concessions obviously raised major concerns for local landowners, mine workers, and the small businesses that relied upon the coal industry: they transformed external entrepreneurs (*les étrangers*), who had secured financial backing, into '*monopolistes*'. Henri Bertin had been involved, intermittently, in the lengthy struggles between local mine owners and government concessionaires that had characterised the development of mining in the Rive-de-Gier from his time as intendant of the Lyonnais in the late 1750s to his resignation as secretary of state in 1780. One of the first tasks handed down to him as intendant had been a *mémoire*, signed by the local inhabitants of the Rive-de- Gier, rejecting the increasingly widespread accusation that they were incapable of playing their part in the emergence of a modern coal industry. They argued that 'Our ancestors, from time immemorial, have extracted coal efficiently and successfully. Providence has given them the natural understanding and innate gifts ... that enables them to overcome every obstacle confronting them. Someone from outside would not know how to overcome these obstacles.'[41] Wealthy concessionaires, with sizeable capital sums at risk, totally rejected this homespun approach. What they needed was government permission to close the innumerable small drift-mines, dug for a few hundred yards into the hillside until they flooded, in order to concentrate production on the rich seams of coal deep beneath the surface. The company, ('cabal' to the locals) formed by a 'sieur Douin', which sought a long-term concession to exploit the Cransac mines in the Rouergue, knew they were on the right track to win Bertin's support when they highlighted the 'advantage accruing to the state, and to commerce, of a well-ordered exploitation of these mines, given that the local inhabitants had been used to dig around without observing any of the precautions prescribed by the regulations governing mining'. The company was granted a thirty-year government contract. Bertin had also granted a thirty-year contract to the Lacombe company in the Rive-de-Gier during his period as *contrôleur général*. On this occasion, he had introduced a direct measure of government control by insisting that the company should be guided by one of Bertin's close friends during his period as intendant of the Lyonnais, the architect and engineer, Nicolas de Ville.[42]

The most intriguing and revealing relationship between a concessionaire and a government official was that between Pierre-François Tubeuf and Henri Bertin's secretary, Jerôme-

Thomas de La Barberie. It lasted from the time that La Barberie persuaded a local landowner, Douin de Cransac, to employ Tubeuf as director of his mines at Cransac in 1764, to Tubeuf's subsequent ownership of the Alès mines between 1770 and the Revolution. By 1773, La Barberie had become personally involved, as an *'associé secret'*, in the financing of Tubeuf's plans to modernise the Alès mines. A deal was struck which ensured that La Barberie would receive one quarter of the profits on all the coal produced. As Paul Bamford reveals in his study (aptly entitled *Privilege and Profit*) of another pioneering eighteenth-century entrepreneur, Pierre Badaud de la Chaussade, the price of government support for entrepreneurs under the last of the absolute Bourbon kings was high.[43] Not only was La Barberie a shareholder in Tubeuf's mining ventures, but he was also one of the principal guarantors for Tubeuf's mounting debts. In 1776, when considerable local pressure was being exerted upon Tubeuf to restrict his large concession, his first response was to write to write to La Barberie requesting 'une lettre de recommandation'. It duly arrived, and Tubeuf used it in an attempt to end the support given by the Estates of Languedoc to local seigneurs and other property-owners who had always been hostile to Bertin's conces-sion. When, in August 1777, Tubeuf created a society to fund his new mining venture in Normandy, two names on the list of share-holders stand out – *'Louis Morin, commis de M. Bertin'*, and *'M. Parent, premier commis de M. Bertin'*.[44]

The chosen few who benefited from government concessions needed all the official contacts they could secure. Reforming, centralising administrations from the 1740s to the 1770s had to contend with deeply entrenched provincial and local centres of resistance, which included provincial parlements and estates, as well as royal and seigneurial courts of justice. De Tocqueville's thesis on Bourbon centralisation tends to obscure the popularity and power of these regional and local institutions. On several occasions, that historic arbiter between central and local govern-ment, the *intendant*, was forced to explain to Bertin that it was dangerous for concessionaires to ride roughshod over local sensibilities. In the final analysis, local people with cash to spare could always seek justice from their provincial parlement. The sporadic outbursts of violent popular reaction to the introduction of the mining regulations of 1744, together with the granting of long-term concessions, reveal the scale of resistance to government reforms. From the beginning, landowners, bourgeois and noble, had appealed to their local royal and seigneurial courts of justice to curtail the activities of government concessionaires. The following case is untypical in terms of its duration and bitterness, but was by no means exceptional. On 10 March 1760, the seigneurial juge of Senevas in the Rive-de-Gier coalfield rejected a claim by one of the concessionaires belonging to the Lacombe company that the widow of a seigneur, who continued to exploit one of the mines in the Rive-de-Gier basin, was contravening the law of 1744. The case was taken to the *Conseil d'état*, which, naturally, ruled in favour of the company, adding that the case should not be transferred to any other court of justice. In fact, the widow had already taken the case to the parlement of Paris, which not only ruled in her favour but also decreed that the case should not be brought before any other court. The government decided to act swiftly, stating that, henceforth, the *intendant's* office should act as the court of first resort in all contested cases; it also created, under the jurisdication of the *intendant*, a 'commission criminelle' to deal with the rising tide of violence in the coalfield. This judicial chaos was compounded by the fact that other landowners had taken their cases to the local royal judge of the Rive-de-Gier and, at the beginning of 1763, to the *sénéchal de Lyon*. The Lacombe company case dragged on for years before, on 12 May 1767, the government forced the parlement of Paris to revoke its earlier decision on the Lacombe concession and rule in its favour. Even then, as we shall see below, the war over mining rights in the Rive-de-Gier continued well into the 1770s.[45] The troubled history of the Lacombe company reveals the damage that could be inflicted upon central government by the resistance of provincial and local institutions of justice.

Finally, we come to the most persistent and vexatious of all the problems confronting government concessionaires – the scale of popular, often violent, resistance to mining *en grand*. Sporadic clashes with authority had been recorded ever since the announcement of the 1744 legislation on mining, but the scale of the problem widened perceptibly during the 1760s as the government began to support companies that could invest the kind of money that the modernisation of French mining demanded. As the head of the company formed to exploit the potentially rich mines of the Rive-de-Gier coal-field explained to the *Conseil d'état*, it had 'the talents, the experience, and the money to succeed', but it now intended to undertake the necessary work 'to streamline production so that the extraction of coal would be more abundant, and more useful to the community, than it had been hitherto'. To ensure its success it simply wanted long-term exclusive privileges to prevent the flooding of pits that had already been opened by individuals, and permission to prevent the opening of new pits, which would injure no-one 'since the king alone owned the land and could dispose of the mines as he pleased'.[46]

And therein lay the rub. Magistrates in provincial parlements and barrack-room lawyers in scores of villages (*les procureurs des pauvres*) queued up to reject this cavalier, regalian interpretation of property rights. Their influence ensured that hundreds of landowners, both noble and bourgeois, encouraged their tenants and proto-industrial mine workers to organise violent protests against government concessionaires. In the Rive-de-Gier, not only did 'turbulent and greedy' landowners preach violence to workers, but they also 'spread it about that the [Paris] Parlement is all powerful, the *Conseil* [*d'état*] is weak, and *Messieurs les Intendants* have lost all credibility', a damning reflection and indictment of Louis XV's feeble attempts to transmute medieval regalian rights into modern *étatiste* legislation. Even the mounted police was refusing to obey orders. In the Alès coal-basin, where there may have been as many as eighty small mines that ignored the legislation passed in 1744, the 'foreign' concessionaire, Pierre-François Tubeuf had to confront 'the ferocious resistance of the hundreds of seigneurs and small property-owners, often involved in the textile or distilling industries, supported by small business-men operating through the local institutions of the Estates of Languedoc (the *assiettes des dioceses)'*.[47] Tubeuf, a doughty fighter for his rights, would later lose the sight of one eye as a result of one violent confrontation with his enemies.

This degree of popular resistance to mining concessionaires cannot be fully understood without realising the degree of contempt with which royal officials in many local communities were treated, a widespread phenomenon that contributed to the launch of Maupeou's coup in 1771, as well as the socio-economic problems experienced by rural and small town communities confronted, on the one hand, with the expansion of industry in the countryside (encouraged by the decree of 7 September 1762 which helped to transform the traditional patterns of domestic industry in France), and, on the other, the impact of the liberal economic policies introduced by Choiseul's administration during the 1760s. The political consequences of the massive proto-industrialisation of the French countryside, especially its impact upon popular resistance during the Maupeou 'revolution' (as well as during the Revolution of 1789), require further investigation. Roger Dugrand described the type of capitalism that operated in the mining communities of lower Languedoc during this period as one 'which rests more upon the old world of woollen stockings than the new one of laissez-faire confrontation'.[48] Henri-Léonard Bertin was, at times, a rather reluctant champion of the new laissez-faire political economy, but it was his involvement in this evolving form of free market capitalism that would explain, in large measure, his fall from grace in 1780, by which time the French economy had waved goodbye to the *'âge d'or'* of the eighteenth-century French economy.

Bertin and Moreau were not as misguided as they might appear when they fought, to the bitter end, to defend the need for an 'absolute' monarch. Many of the government's supposed enemies, the *philosophes* and *physiocrats*, including Jacques Turgot, were also convinced that, confronted with a society experiencing rapid and unwelcome change, the strongest hand possible would have to be placed on the tiller of the state. This was also why, for almost thirty years, Bertin would pay tribute in his correspondence with the French Jesuit colony in Peking to the great, absolute, emperor of China, Kien-long. Peking was a long way, in geographic terms, from Paris, but Bertin and Moreau's 'Grand Design' would prove to be a product of a global, not a local, Enlightenment.

Notes

1 Bussière, *'Etude sur Henri Bertin'*, BSHAP, vol.35 (1908), pp.441–2.
2 Baker, *Inventing the French Revolution*, p. 31.
3 Duc de Richelieu, *Mémoires du maréchal duc de Richelieu* (Paris, 1792), ix and p.361.
4 Baker, *Inventing the French Revolution*, p.85.
5 G. Lewis, 'Henri Bertin and the Fate of the Bourbon Monarchy: the Chinese Connection' (Aldershot, 2004), pp.69–70.
6 Guy Chaussinand-Nogaret, *Choiseul, Naissance de la Gauche* (Paris, 1998), p175.
7 Lewis, 'Henri Bertin and the Fate of the Bourbon Monarchy', pp.92–6 and pp.180–1; Lewis, *France 1715–1804*, pp.178–87; J. H. Moriceau, *Les fermiers de l'Ile de France XVe-XVIIIe siècle* (Paris, 1994), pp.781–3.
8 Daniel Roche, *La France des Lumières* (Paris, 1993), pp.438–41.
9 Harold Parker, *The Bureau de Commerce in 1781 and its Politics with Respect to French Industry* (Durham, 1979), pp.20–8.
10 Richard Bonney, 'Early Modern Theories of State Finance', in Bonney (ed.) *Economic Systems and State Finance* (Oxford, 1995), p.203.
11 A. Bourde, *Agronomies et agronomes en France au XVIIIe* (Paris, 1967), ii. pp.1087–9.
12 David Parker, *Class and State in Ancien Régime France: The Road to Modernity* (London, 1996), p.278. See also Peter Jones, *Reform and Revolution in France: The Politics of Transition, 1774–1791* (Cambridge, 1995), pp.50–66; Lewis, *France, 1715–1804*, chap. three.
13 Roche, *La France des Lumières*, pp.447–54.
14 Bourde, *Agronomies et agronomes*, i, pp.47–50.
15 Jean-Pierre Poirier, *Turgot* (Paris, 1999), pp.102–14; Marx, 'Theories of the Plus Value', in François Furet, *Marx and the French Revolution* (Chicago, 1988), p.218.
16 Bussière, *'Etude sur Henri Bertin'*, BSHAP, vol.36 (1909), p.216.

17 Bourde, *Agronomies et agronomes*, ii, p.1083 and p.1102.
18 Davidson, *Voltaire in Exile*, p.61.
19 Arthur Young, *Travels in France During the Years 1787, 1788, and 1789* (Gloucester, Mass., 1976), p.108.
20 Antoine, *Louis XV*, pp.196–201.
21 Bussière, 'Etude sur Henri Bertin', BSHAP, vol.36 (1900) p.213; Swann, *Politics and the Parlement of Paris*, p.249. Swann argues that the magistrates of the parlement 'were genuinely troubled by what they perceived as arbitrary and inconsistent methods of government'.
22 Bussière, '*Etude sur Henri Bertin*', vol.36 (1909), p.213 and p.225.
23 Jones, *Reform and Revolution*, p.76.
24 Bussière, '*Etude sur Henri Bertin*', BSHAP, vol.36 (1909), p.213 and p.225.
25 Steven Kaplan, *Le complot de famine: histoire d'une rumeur au XVIIIe siècle* (Paris, 1982), pp.55–6.
26 Kaplan, *Le complot de famine*, p.55.
27 Bussière, '*Etude sur Henri Bertin*', BSHAP, vol.36 (1909), p.215.
28 Pierre Foncin, *Essai sur le ministère de Turgot* (Geneva, 1976), p.107.
29 Kaplan, *Le complot de famine*, p.33.
30 Kaplan, *Le complot de famine*, p.40.
31 Bussière, '*Etude sur Henri Bertin*', BSHAP, vol.36 (1909), pp. 215–18.
32 Bussière, '*Etude sur Henri Bertin*', BSHAP, vol.36 (1909), pp.216–24; Kaplan, *Le complot de famine*, pp.39–43.
33 Bussière, '*Etude sur Henri Bertin*', BSHAP, vol.32 (1905), pp.394–406.
34 Stephen Miller, 'The Absolutist State of Eighteenth-Century France: Modern Bureaucracy or Feudal Bricolage', *Socialist History*, vol.33 (*Origins of the French Revolution*), p.40.
35 Bussière, '*Etude sur Henri Bertin*', BSHAP, vol.33 (1909), pp.220–3.
36 Choiseul, in a letter to Louis XV, had included Bertin in a group of ministers he described as 'a miserable mob' (*ces espèces misérables*) whose right to question his actions 'elicited disgust among us all'. Chaussinand-Nogaret, *Choiseul*, p.171.
37 Lewis, *The Advent of Modern Capitalism in France*, pp.22–3.
38 Bussière, '*Etude sur Henri Bertin*', vol.34 (1907), p.273.
39 A. N., E 2660, decisions by the *conseil d'état* on the granting of concessions, 1763–5.
40 Gwynne Lewis, *The Advent of Modern Capitalism in France, 1770–1840: The Contribution of Pierre-François* (Oxford, 1993), p.24.
41 Bussière, '*Etude sur Henri Bertin*', BSHAP, vol.34 (1907), p.273.
42 A.N., E 2660, *arrêt du conseil d'état*, 18 June 1765; contract agreed by the government on 10 Apr. 1759 in favour of the 'société Lacombe, Bertelot, Grange et Chambeyron'.

43 Paul Bamford, *Privilege and Profit: A Business Family in Eighteenth-Century France* (Philadelphia, 1988), pp.177–80.
44 Lewis, *The Advent of Modern Capitalism*, pp.51–2, n.131.
45 Bussière, '*Etude sur Henri Bertin*', *BSHAP*, vol.34 (1907), pp.279–91.
46 Bussière, '*Etude sur Henri Bertin*', *BSHAP*, vol.34 (1907), p.282.
47 Lewis, *The Advent of Modern Capitalism*, p.24.
48 Roger Dugrand, *Villes et compagnes en Bas-Languedoc* (Paris, 1963), p.40.

Chapter Five

'Back to the Future': From Maupeou to Maurepas

During the 1770s, Henri Bertin's *petit ministère* began to fall apart at the seams. We raised two of the crucial issues that accelerated the collapse of Bourbon absolutism in a previous chapter – the historic, constitutional conflict between the crown and the parlements, and the widespread, popular resistance to the introduction of Choiseul's liberal policies, a consequence of the socio-economic and intellectual revolution that was creating a more critical and informed public. Bertin's position as a personal favourite of Louis XV and madame de Pompadour had placed him in the front line of ministers charged with the responsibility of defending the monarchy, especially during the Seven Years' War. It is also not surprising, therefore, that with Pompadour's death in 1764, followed by the demise of Louis XV a decade later, Bertin's situation at court should have become increasingly problematic. The accession of the young, timid Louis XVI in 1774, accompanied by the intelligent, but rather irresponsible, and Austrian, Marie Antoinette as his queen, did little to strengthen Bertin's precarious position. Nonetheless, he would manage to survive at court after his enforced resignation as secretary of state in 1780, acting as one of Louis XVI's ministers of state, until the onset of the Revolution of 1789. Any explanation for the longevity of his political career must include Bertin's readiness to take on a daunting array of official responsibilities, his personal relationship with Louis XV, together with his impressive contribution to Enlightenment reform, and the ideological development of the 'Grand Design'. These four achievements mark the staging-posts of his long career as a servant of two Bourbon kings.

Bertin's efforts were often achieved against a background of continual abuse from his many enemies. On 31 August 1772, the abbé Georgel (attached to the princely house of Rohan) described Bertin as 'the minister for stud farms, lotteries, and the private pleasures of the king', his ministry nothing more than 'a fifth poorly constructed department of state, created to compensate [him] when he lost his post of *contrôleur général*'.[1] This statement clearly contained more than a grain of truth, especially the reference to his 'poorly constructed department'. The only coherence one can discover is that most of these responsibilities came from the portfolio of another royal favourite and protector of the king's private life, the comte de Saint-Florentin, which did little to add credibility to the *petit ministère*. Saint-Florentin, one of the few ministers Bertin could rely upon at court, had been running the King's Household for decades, and, given his advancing years, he needed to jettison some of the work that ended up on his desk. Apart from the continued management of Louis XV's private life, and his involvement in agricultural and mining reform, Bertin's brief would include a ragbag of administrative and managerial responsibilities – public lotteries, postal services, stage-coaches, freight wagons, whether by road, river or canal (though not royal carriages), the management of stud farms (though not those in the provinces of the Auvergne, Normandy, and the Limousin), and some authority over various civil affairs in several intendancies and *généralités*.[2] In addition, a mere scan through the many volumes of Bertin's official correspondence reveals the extraordinary variety of minor issues that landed up on his desk. There was the request from the chevalier Courtin that he should be allowed to keep two of the six black slaves 'belonging to him', and that the remaining four should be repatriated on the next ship sailing under the flag of the

Compagnie de Indes. There were hundreds of requests for the issue of royal arrest warrants (*lettres de cachet*), most of them from men who wished to place their sons, wives or daughters in prison or convents. However, it seems that a minister's lot was not always an unhappy one. Between 5 November 1771 and 1 February of the following year, Bertin received a number of gifts, or bribes – 50 bottles of 'vin du Cap Constance', a turkey stuffed with truffles, a basket of game from a M. de Bouilhac – and, on 7 February 1772, a request from a 'mademoiselle de Charlière' for 'une gravure du portrait du ministère'.[3]

All this did not complete the official list of Bertin's responsibilities as *'le petit ministre'*, but if reading it so far has elicited feelings of disbelief and confusion, then we are closer to an understanding of the manner in which the administrative jigsaw of *ancien régime* government was pieced together during the reign of Louis XV. It would be very misleading, however, to conclude that Henri Bertin, by accepting responsibility for this accumulation of affairs that were surplus to requirement, had lost real influence over government policy. He was one of only a handful of secretaries of state serving under Louis XV; he was a member of the royal *conseil d'en Haut*, or *conseil d'état* as it became under Louis XV. We have already established the importance of Bertin's pioneering involvement in the reform of agriculture and mining: to itemise and evaluate all the remaining responsibilities that were included in his portfolio as secretary of state would be tedious and unproductive. We shall, therefore, focus on just three, which, when combined with his work in the spheres of agriculture and mining, may be thought to justify the description of Bertin as one of Louis XV's principal reforming ministers – the expansion of the French silk industry, the establishment of a national veterinary service, and, a cultural initiative that had been close to madame de Pompadour's heart, the creation of the royal porcelain factory at Sèvres.

* * *

Bertin's prolonged interest in the success of the silk industry reflects its emergence as one of the leading French luxury products to assume global significance by the second half of the eighteenth century. It also identifies a thread that runs throughout Bertin's career – the interdependence of his private and public lives, a characteristic of many *ancien régime* public figures during the experimental 'Age of Enlightenment'. Voltaire, as we know, liked to practise a little of what he preached on his estate of Ferney; the marquis de Turbilly did much the same on his far more extensive property.

Bertin's involvement in the silk industry had begun with his brief experience as an *intendant* of the Lyonnais, a region renowned for the production and manufacture of silk. It was personalised by his close relationship with John Badger, one of the many British pioneering inventors and manufacturers to cross the channel during the second half of the eighteenth century. An Irishman, John Holker, had been appointed as an inspector of foreign manufactured goods during Daniel Trudaine's period in control of French trade and industry.[4] John Badger was an inventor and entrepreneur who chose to spend his entire adult life in France. He had initiated Bertin, supported, as ever, by Trudaine *père*, into the mysteries of producing the increasingly fashionable silk material, for the increasingly fashion-conscious bourgeoisie of Europe. The government had expressed its support with a gift of 5,000 *livres*, a monthly pension of 100 *livres* and the provision of accommodation for Badger and his family. Unfortunately, Badger proved to be a very difficult man to deal with, obsessed with the task of keeping his production methods secret. In his defence, he argued that he was not receiving the support he had been promised, either from local silk merchants and manufacturers, or the government in Paris. Bertin was once again confronted with the dilemma he had faced following the launch of his new *sociétés d'agriculture* in France – individuals and local authorities had their own agendas, often revealing a negative reaction to modernisation that was based upon opposition to government interference and the introduction of free-market schemes. The silk manufacturers in Lyon wanted Badger to share his secrets with the rest of the textile community, but Badger fought hard to protect his patent, and his family. Bertin, as always, sought compromise,[5] convinced that the state should play a decisive role in the expansion of trade and industry: at heart, he would remain a flexible, *'homme de l'ancien régime'*, *absolutiste* and *étatiste*; as a reforming minister, however, he tried to work within the boundaries established by physiocratic, free-market principles. It was not an easy balancing act to perform.

Although the burdens of high office prevented him from devoting too much of his time to the day-to-day running of his own estates (he left this to his brother, Louis-Augustin, abbé of Brantôme, and their two sisters), Bertin was keen to practise what he preached when the opportunity arose. The government and certain provincial estates had offered rewards in the 1750s to those who had contributed to the expansion of the silk industry by planting mulberry trees: the intendant of Bordeaux, for example, Aubert de Tourny, had encouraged his constituents to take up these offers. Bertin had followed suit in the mid-1750s by planting mulberry trees on his own land, eventually setting up a spinning and weaving business in some of the rooms of his massive, crumbling, feudal château of Bourdeille in the neighbouring Périgord. His interest in his silk workshops would continue after his term of office as *contrôleur général* had ended, and by the 1770s, they were turning out fine silk cloth, on a small scale, as well as more popular cotton and woollen products. On the national platform, Bertin also encouraged the publication and distribution of Henri Goyon de la Plombanie's *La France agricole et marchande*, a work that sold well in the 1760s; it popularised many of the reforms that Bertin was advocating, and initiating.[6]

The second achievement that increased Bertin's status as a reforming minister was his contribution to the creation of a modern veterinary system in France; it must count as one of his most beneficial and enduring achievements, given the ravages that afflicted the farming sector. We have discussed his support for the cautious introduction of free trade policies, and the improvement of agriculture and industry; Emma Spary's intriguing work on 'political, natural, and bodily economies' opens up a new avenue of enquiry into the link between political, economic and moral imperatives that underpinned Bertin's political philosophy. It also helps to explain his unqualified support for a new approach to the study of veterinary medicine. For example, Spary's work establishes the connections between political economy, natural history and animal welfare: 'Improvement became immensely popular in the latter half of the eighteenth century' she writes, 'as Europe's monarchs and ministers came to see natural history and the introduction of new species of plants and animals as a certain way to increase national revenue and private wealth. Enlightened proprietors began to improve their own lands; implementing the new agricultural and industrial practices was seen as a route to moral self-improvement, which simultaneously served the nation.' These remarks are both illuminating and of considerable significance to the evolution of Bertin and Moreau's 'Grand Design', which would place morality at the centre of its political ideology: as we shall see, it also helps to explain his increasing fascination with Confucian philosophy.[7] It is all too easy, and very misleading, to associate the Enlightenment with a western, materialistic, philosophy of the world. Bertin, despite the fact that he never really lost the Catholic faith in which he had been raised, would quarry Enlightenment publications, the Bible, and the works of Confucius in his search for a personal answer to the problems confronting Bourbon absolutism. This eclectic approach was consistent with the beliefs of many Enlightenment scholars.[8]

Bertin's political methodology was to implement his reform programmes with the support of several trusted mentors and advisers, especially Daniel Charles Trudaine. Bertin chose Claude Bourgelat, director of the *Académie du Roi* in Lyon, to pioneer the academic development of veterinary studies, which led to the creation, or expansion, of veterinary schools in Lyon and Alfort (Paris). Bourgelat, like Bertin, was the son of a robe noble, an habitué of the academies and salons in Lyon. His early written work, published in 1750, *Eléments d'hippiatrique ou nouveaux principes sur la connoissance et la médecin des chevaux*, had confirmed his position as a leading authority in his field. Bertin and Bourgelat were both sustained by the strong conviction that radical improvement in animal husbandry, especially the control of the epidemics that periodically devastated entire regions of France, would make a significant contribution to the reform of French agriculture. Until the death of Bourgelat in 1779, the *Ecole royale vétérinaire* de Lyon, not the Alfort school, would promote the study of veterinary medicine. Success was not achieved overnight: it was not until Bertin was appointed *contrôleur général* in 1759 that early plans for a veterinary school were actually implemented. He managed to convince Louis XV that Bourgelat was the right man to create an institution to study animal medicine in France, with the result that he was duly appointed as the director of the first veterinary college at Lyon, as well as *commissaire général* of all the nation's stud farms. The first student entered the 'Ecole pour les maladies des bestiaux' on 25 February 1764. Over the next few years, the college would establish a European reputation. Most of the students were recruited, as one would expect, from the Lyonnais, but a few came from outlying French provinces and even neighbouring countries, including Frederick the Great's Prussia.[9]

The epidemic of 1774–6, which proved to be one of the worst to afflict France during the eighteenth century, provided an opportunity for Bertin and Bourgelat to test the progress of their work. Students were despatched to some of the worst affected areas; all to no avail, unfortunately, which is not surprising given the difficulties encountered today by veterinary experts when confronted by animal epidemics. What does strike the student of epidemiology is the fact that many of the measures introduced to contain the outbreaks in the 1770s are still being employed today – the disinfection of stables, restrictions on the transport of animals to and from infected areas, the slaughter of diseased animals and a solution that continues to alienate farmers, the culling of entire herds. Although scattered reports of sick and dying cattle were reaching the government from January 1771, confirmation that it was facing a serious epidemic, affecting several regions of the south-west around Bayonne and Bordeaux, did not reach Paris until the early spring of 1774. Reports of cattle exhibiting the signs of disease persisted throughout the year, reaching the province of Roussillon and the countryside around Poitiers and La Rochelle by the spring of 1775. By the autumn of the same year, the epidemic had moved west to many areas of the Midi and north as far as the towns of Boulogne and Calais, before threatening the livelihoods of farmers in Flanders early in 1776. It was not contained until the early spring of the same year.[10]

The history of the epidemic is one of failed endeavours, symptomatic of a time when modern science and medicine was still in its infancy: in many villages, it was the blacksmith who doubled up as the local vet. Nonetheless, the pressure exerted by the state on hostile communities, pressure that was again frequently challenged by provincial parlements, explains much of the success that was eventually achieved. Bourgelat, Bertin and Jacques Turgot (appointed *contrôleur général* in August 1774), were all prepared to use centralised state power to tackle the epidemic. But the incursion of the modern state continued to provoke howls of protest from local and provincial institutions. Reform during the 1760s and 1770s was 'top down', provoking accusations of 'government despotism' that fuelled the political struggle between the parlements and the crown. The 'despotic' Maupeou coup of 1771, a landmark in the evolution of Bertin's political ideology, has to be studied within the context of an expanding bureaucratic state, and the introduction of liberal economic policies, policies that would provoke social rebellion in many areas of the country. Government commissions were created to chart the course of the epidemic and offer advice to local authorities.[11] One of the more fascinating aspects of medical involvement in the epidemic of 1774–6 concerns the major contribution of Félix Vicq d'Azir, an influential figure in the Royal Society of Medicine. Here again, D'Azyr's opinions have considerable contemporary resonance, especially in the field of animal experimentation and vivisection. He argued that 'the degree of sensibility an animal possessed was related to its brain structure and to the degree of complexity of the nervous system'. He also conducted experiments with inoculation, collecting a virus on absorbent cloth from a diseased animal, then slitting the skin of a healthy animal and rubbing the cloth over the open wound. The results are not recorded.[12]

On 1 October 1770, the *philosophe* Melchior Grimm wrote that, in just a few years, the veterinary schools of Lyon and Alfort had become famous throughout Europe, although he was still of the opinion that, in general, 'the treatment of animals has hardly advanced further than that given to human beings'.[13] Nonetheless, by the end of the 1770s, Bertin and Bourgelat had at least laid the foundations for modern veterinary studies in France. The overall cost of dealing with the epidemic of 1774–6, however, was worrying, particularly as it was published at a most inopportune time – during the early stages of France's involvement in the War of American Independence. For one historian, the epidemic represented 'a cruel misfortune for French agriculture, already suffering from the heavy weight of government taxes; it meant a ruinous increase in the burden placed upon the state, whose financial position was so precarious'.[14] As for the political cost, it represented yet another burden on the shoulders of Bertin's former disciple, Jacques Turgot, who would be forced out of office in May 1776, a date that also marks the end of the epidemic. More attention should be paid to climatic conditions, the cost of serious animal epidemics and rising state debt when assessing the causes of the 'Maupeou revolution' and the collapse of Turgot's radical programme of reform.

The third achievement we have chosen to highlight is Bertin's participation in the establishment of the royal porcelain factory at Sèvres, reminding us that Bertin was living through 'a privileged period in the history of French art'.[15] It was a period that was synonymous with the reign of madame de Pompadour, fashion-icon of her times. Sèvres was one of her greatest legacies to French culture, as a visit to the museum at Sèvres today will confirm, but a facet of the splendour that has always been attached to the output of the Sèvres factory should be attributed to Henri Bertin, who, in this instance as in so many others, helped to turn one of Pompadour's projects into a working reality. The history of Sèvres is indistinguishable from the eighteenth-century fashion craze that exalted the arts and crafts of Chinese culture, *la chinoiserie*. China had been manufacturing porcelain since the eighth century, but it was not until Portuguese and Dutch ships began to unload their precious cargoes of Chinese prints, porcelain and furniture in European ports that the blue and white crockery of China became a familiar sight on European tables and dressers. Small factories in Rouen and Chantilly had been producing porcelain since the beginning of the eighteenth century, but the soft white clay known as kaolin (Chinese for a hill in the Jiangxi province of China where it was to be found in some abundance), which formed the basis of fine porcelain, would not be discovered in France until the 1760s. Twenty years earlier, the *contrôleur général*, Philibert Orry, friend of the Bertin family, had encouraged the establishment of a royal porcelain factory in the château de Vincennes, which proved to be the inspiration for Pompadour's far more famous, royal factory at Sèvres. The appointment, in 1749, of Pompadour's favourite painter, François Boucher, who added his popular images of children and rural family idylls to the design catalogues of the factory, marked a significant advance in the early success of Vincennes-Sèvres porcelain.

When Pompadour first approached Henri Bertin with her Sèvres project, she was addressing a minister who was more than favourable to the notion of increasing trade, and cultural relations, with the Far East. Control over the French *Compagnie des Indes* was one of the many responsibilities that Bertin had packed into his portfolio as secretary of state, and, at this stage in its history, the company was making record profits, much of it from the import of Chinese porcelain. In 1766, just one convoy of the company's ships docking at the port of Nantes unloaded, apart from fabrics and spices, 308 cases of blue and white porcelain, 295 cases of coloured porcelain, and 1,272 tea services.[16] As we shall

see in the following chapter, Bertin, like so many of his contemporaries, was attracted to all things Chinese. He would prove to
be far more than a mere diplomatic bag-carrier for Pompadour's
projects, playing a significant role in the discovery of kaolin (*pâte
tendre*) in the Limousin, and enhancing Sèvres' reputation as a
world-famous centre for the production of fine porcelain,
enabling it to compete with the famous Meissen factory in
Saxony. The fact that Sèvres established a global reputation for its
porcelain throughout the 1760s and 1770s was due, in no small
measure, to Bertin's stature as a European figure. His duties as
contrôleur général between 1759 and 1763 had brought him into
contact with kings, queens and emperors, not only in Europe, but
also throughout the trading world. In September 1764, he
arranged for a shipment of porcelain *'groupes de Boucher'*, to be
delivered to the Chinese Emperor, Kien-long, an eighteenth-
century version of 'taking coals to Newcastle'.[17] As we saw in our
previous chapter, Bertin had a particular interest in the new 'black
gold', coal, and he used it to promote the technological changes
that were taking place in the manufacture of fine porcelain. On 4
September 1768, one of his staff explained to the government that
Bertin had entrusted him with the task of promoting the use of
hard wood, particularly *le charbon de terre* (coal), in the manufacture of porcelain at Sèvres.[18] In 1766, Bertin was able to issue a
decree that gave Sèvres the exclusive *privilège* to manufacture fine
porcelain, although it appears to have been 'more honoured in the
breach than the observance'.

The discovery of kaolin in France, together with more scientific
methods of producing fine china, created something of a boom in
the production of porcelain products. The famous scientist, René-
Antoine de Réaumur, wrote in one of his *mémoires à l'Académie des
Sciences*, that 'a prodigious amount of porcelain in Europe' had
been imported to Europe, adding that 'everyone has something,
from the Grand Seigneur to the most insignificant individual'.
This was, after all, the dawn of the age of modern consumption;
'The world of ephemeral consumptions and rapid ageing of
needs had begun. Among the rich it was symbolised by the

triumph of porcelain'. Daniel Roche discovered in his study of household inventories in several Parisian parishes references to 'cups in porcelain or faience (earthenware), and complete services *à la chinoise* in the houses of the rich'.[19] The Sèvres' archives contain many interesting letters to Bertin, dating from the late 1760s, written by individuals seeking the royal *privilège* for manufacturing porcelain. On 13 August 1769, the owner of the '*manufacture de Vaux*' explained to Bertin that he would 'see from the price of our products that we will never be in competition with Sèvres ... we only wish to sell to ordinary households [*les petits ménages*] and the lower middle-class [*pauvres bourgeois*]'. A porcelain dinner service was sent along with the letter. The correspondent from Vaux might have decided not to send the dinner service if he could have read Bertin's reply to another suppliant, refusing the offer of a dinner service because, 'I know enough about the materials used in its manufacture and I have absolutely no doubt about its beauty'.[20] Bertin only agreed to take full control of Sèvres in 1767. His decision, as we shall see below, could be described as unwise, given the burden of his many other responsibilities as secretary of state.

* * *

Praising Bertin's achievements may appear inconsistent with his dismissal in 1780, but, by this time, the political scene had been transformed by a series of events that would bring the monarchy into further disrepute, posing a challenge to the traditional beliefs that underpinned the 'Grand Design'. They began with the dismissal of Choiseul in December 1770 and the subsequent Maupeou 'coup' against the minority of 'constitutionalists' in the French parlements in 1771. They continued with the death of Louis XV in May 1774, followed, a few weeks later, by the dismissal of Maupeou. These early years of the 1770s, which included the accession of Louis XVI, constitute a period that would determine, along with the later decision to intervene in the American War of Independence, the direction of French politics until the early 1790s. Bertin and Moreau, conscious that the 'Maupeou Years' constituted something of a watershed in the history of the period, decided, in 1775, to publish what one might describe as 'the first manifesto of the "Grand Design"'.

Ironically, it was the duc de Choiseul who had appointed an ex-president of the Paris parlement, René Nicolas de Maupeou, as chancellor of France in 1768, a sign of his 'open door' approach to the parlement of Paris. Unfortunately, Maupeou proved to be more interested in his own political advancement than Choiseul's survival, helping to coordinate the coup that marked a critical stage in the conflict between the crown and the parlements.[21] Louis XV had made things more difficult for Choiseul by deciding to end his reign as he had begun, with a spot of sexual debauchery. Towards the end of 1768, the king had been 'presented', by the usual suspects at Versailles, with a young, extremely attractive and sexually mature lady, guaranteed to rekindle the dying embers of his sexual desires. She was Jeanne Bécu, better known to history as 'madame du Barry', a lady of loose virtue conveniently married to her procurer, the flamboyant comte Jean du Barry. Louis' wife, Marie Leszczynska, had died just a few months earlier (24 June 1768). To the disgust of Choiseul's 'patriot' followers, and many more, both inside and outside the corridors of power at Versailles, madame du Barry, heavily burdened with the diamonds that Louis XV had bought for her, had been presented to the court as his official mistress on 22 April 1769.[22]

Hovering over all these events was the *dévot* cabal that hated the very ground upon which Choiseul walked – the politician who had supported the successful assault on the Jesuit Order, a favourite of the king who was more than happy to negotiate with *philosophes* and *parlementaires*. A few of the *dévots*, bent on revenge at any price, were even prepared to accept du Barry as an accomplice. Seizing what he regarded as an opportunity for advancement through the king's mistress (a well-worn route at Versailles), Maupeou, temporarily converting himself into a *dévot*, began to address du Barry as 'ma cousine', claiming to have discovered a

184

distant relative of his who was, allegedly, related to the king's new mistress. The duc d'Aiguillon, nephew of the powerful maréchal de Richelieu, also joined the *dévot* bandwagon, along with the abbé Terray, who had been the given the post of *contrôleur général* by Maupeou. Despite their links with court cabals, however, Maupeou, d'Aiguillon, and Richelieu would continue to pursue their own private agendas: in this respect, the court of Louis XV became more Byzantine than Bourbon during the final years of the king's life. Through the alluring, but politically innocent, du Barry, cabals and individuals did their best to convince Louis XV that Choiseul was using the parlements to create a constitutional monarchy on the English model. Louis was not easily convinced: Choiseul had been a close confidant, a partner on many of his hunting expeditions. On the negative side, however, there was the threat of war between Britain and Spain over possession of the Falkland Islands, which Choiseul, contrary to the king's deepest wishes, appeared to support: it was an opportunity for Choiseul to prove that the 'family pact' he had constructed between Spain and France had real substance. This arrogant approach, when coupled with Choiseul's plotting with the parlements, led to his dismissal from Versailles on 24 December 1770, along with his equally feisty and freewheeling sister, the duchesse de Gramont. The Choiseul clan immediately set up an opposition court at their palatial residence of Chanteloup: Choiseul was the last man to let bygones be bygones, and the political influence of his *'parti patriote'* would be felt until the Revolution of 1789. France was now saddled with a government team composed, in the opinion of his supporters, of 'Choiseul's odious successors [Maupeou–Terray–d'Aiguillon–Saint-Florentin], allegedly the most reactionary, most imbecile servants of Louis XV'.[23]

Where did Henri Bertin stand, confronted by this rather sudden lurch towards the reaffirmation of Bourbon absolutism? The answer is obvious – at his royal master's side, where he had always stood. Bertin was not a loyal supporter of Choiseul, even if they had both contributed to the introduction of many liberal economic policies. In any case, Choiseul had always treated him, and his patron, the comte de Saint-Florentin, with some disdain. This had not prevented the king from elevating Saint-Florentin on 22 June 1770 to the status of 'duc de la Vrillière' for his unfailing, one might say obsequious, loyalty to the crown.[24] Perhaps Bertin, only marginally less loyal than Saint-Florentin, could expect similar treatment? If this did not appeal to him, and there is no reason to suggest that it did not, there was Bertin's distrust of the parlements in their adopted role of 'guardians of the nation'. He eventually decided, despite his personal dislike of Maupeou, that he had no option but to support him, if half-heartedly, during this great crisis in the epic struggle between the crown and the French parlements.

During the night of 19–20 January 1771, royal musketeers, furnished with arrest warrants, were despatched to the homes of over 150 magistrates of the Paris parlement. They demanded that each magistrate should sign a statement of their willingness to accept the king's orders – absolutism in action. Maupeou had been driven to this dramatic act, one that transformed 'Bourbon absolutism' into 'Bourbon despotism' almost overnight, by persistent opposition from the parlements, encouraged by the growing ranks of his critics in the wider public sphere. Disagreements over the implementation of government policy in the recalcitrant province of Brittany had poisoned relationships since 1766. They had culminated in the trial of the duc d'Aiguillon (the government's military commander in the province) by the Paris parlement, and the imprisonment by the government of d'Aiguillon's principal antagonist, and personal enemy, the *procureur* of the Rennes parlement, Louis René de Caradeuc de La Chalotais. La Chalotais had become embroiled in the private sex life of the king when some of Louis' letters to his beloved mistress, mademoiselle de Romans, had mysteriously come into his possession. The 'Brittany Affair', when stripped of personal antagonisms and accusations of royal blackmail against La Chalotais, confirmed the existence of two opposed schools of political thought, the first moving forward to a more constitutional form of monarchical government, which a few radicals sought to base on the English model, the second defending a reformed French monarchy, which supporters like Bertin and Moreau believed would silence the continual criticisms of the parlements, along with the more radical *philosophes*, as well as hostile sections of the general public. Voltaire, always inclined to be his own man in these matters, and hopeful that Maupeou would introduce a less corrupt and more humane form of justice in France, actually wrote a eulogy of Maupeou – not all *philosophes* were anti-absolutist.

Flexing its muscles on behalf of the first school, the Paris parlement had invoked the *union des classes* by decreeing that d'Aiguillon's trial should be transferred to the 'mother parlement', the parlement of Paris, which is what d'Aiguillon wanted. Surprisingly, Louis XV, exercising his rather wasted muscles, massaged on this occasion by chancellor René Maupeou, struck a series of blows for the second school during the second half of 1770. On 3 September, he refused to allow the Paris parlement to continue its trial of d'Aiguillon; on 7 December, he held a *lit de justice* following the refusal of the parlement to register Maupeou's draconian plans to emasculate its powers; and, as we noted above, he decided to end Choiseul's lengthy spell in power on the twenty-fourth of the same month. By the spring of 1771, Maupeou had also exiled the majority of magistrates in the parlement of Paris, creating in its place what amounted to a new 'royal parlement', and seized the opportunity to reform many of the abuses associated with the old system. The extensive judicial powers of the Paris parlement, which covered almost half of the country, were drastically curtailed, and new courts of appeal were set up in Arras, Blois, Châlons-sur-Marne, Clermond-Ferrand, Lyon and Poitiers. The new magistrates, some of whom had to be drafted in to the reformed parlements from other quasi-judicial courts, would no longer enjoy hereditary status; they were to be paid by the state and appointed by the king. Finally, the right to issue *remonstrances* against government policies considered to be 'unconstitutional', one of the most powerful weapons in the political armoury of the old parlement of Paris, was to be significantly restricted. In the provinces, the authority of most of the twelve parlements was also curtailed; the parlements of Rouen, Metz and Douai were abolished. For those who cherished the historic tradition of a French monarchy, absolute but not despotic, checked and balanced by the legal authority of the Parisian and provincial parlements, this was a step too far in the direction of 'eastern despotism', posing a problem for both Bertin and Moreau.[25]

* * *

Bertin's behaviour during the period of Maupeou's chancellorship, which lasted from 1771 to a few weeks after Louis XV's death in May 1774, was both instructive and revealing. Was he simply fighting for his survival at court, or did his actions provide further evidence of his long-standing commitment to a regenerated ideology of Bourbon absolutism? His attitude towards the king's new mistress, madame du Barry provides us with an important indication of Bertin's unswerving attachment to the latter. Given du Barry's humble, even disreputable, background, and, of far greater importance perhaps, her relative lack of intelligence, one might have expected that Bertin's relationship with her would have been far less intimate than the personal rapport he had forged with madame du Pompadour. It seems, however, that Bertin made every effort to please the king by exhibiting a friendly disposition towards du Barry. Moreau tells us that Bertin was 'on good terms' with the king's highly controversial mistress, 'at whose apartments "anti-parlement committees meet"'. Moreau had also thrown his hat into the Maupeou ring, having become the indispensable confidant of the chancellor.[26]

It soon became obvious, however, that Bertin, anxious to retain some political space for the personal reformist projects contained in the 'Grand Design', was reverting to type by advocating a conciliatory approach to those who found the chancellor's uncompromising stance both illegal and unacceptable. By the spring of 1772, Bertin's backbone was already beginning to exhibit something of its old pliability. We know that he attended private meetings organised by a magistrate, Lefèvre d'Amécourt, who had been exiled to Argenteuil for rejecting Louis XV's ultimatum of the 19–20 January. It seems that d'Amécourt often invited Bertin to dinner at Argenteuil, which was not far from Bertin's new residence at Chatou. Just as surprising was d'Amécourt's decision to add the names of the prince de Soubise, the maréchal de Richelieu, and the duc d'Aiguillon to his guest list. All three now joined Bertin and d'Amécourt in their efforts to find an acceptable solution to the wearisome confrontation between the parlements and the crown: they were probably banking upon Louis XV's legendary inconsistency when taking flak from all sides. On this occasion, however, Louis refused to back down.[27] His resolve to provide unreserved support for Maupeou and the anti-parlement lobby at court was made abundantly clear in a meeting of the *conseil d'état* held in January 1773. Resistance had been widespread in the province of Normandy, one of the provinces that came under Bertin's jurisdiction. At a meeting on 4 November, Bertin raised the temperature of the discussion by referring to a protest against Maupeou's reforms by 271 Norman nobles. His contribution was followed by interventions from the duc d'Aiguillon and the *contrôleur général*, the abbé Terray, both supporting Bertin's conciliatory line. Maupeou's own account of the meeting states that Louis XV first turned on Bertin, telling him 'I can see exactly what you have in mind, but the [old] Paris parlement will never be reconstituted so long as I am alive'. The meeting broke up after an angry attack by Louis on the abbé Terray. According to Maupeou's *Journal*, members of the *conseil* could hardly believe that Louis XV was capable of such fierce determination, 'which, in the eyes of his courtiers, wonderfully augmented the enigma of this indecipherable Prince's character', a most revealing comment on this most deliberately enigmatic of French kings.[28]

Throughout the year of 1773, arguments over foreign policy

and domestic issues, together with the continuing animus against madame du Barry, combined to undermine what unity still existed of Louis XV's government. At the end of September, the comte de Broglie, head of Louis XV's infamous *secret du roi*, was exiled after the duc d'Aiguillon had unmasked three of his subordinates. D'Aiguillon claimed that a plot had been hatched to dismiss him 'and to subvert the whole of French foreign policy'. In order to cover his own complicity, Louis XV threw the three men into the Bastille. An attempt by the comte de Vergennes, a long-term member of the *secret du roi*, to graft Louis XV's secret foreign policy onto the official foreign policy of his successor would be rejected, on the grounds that this would be the last thing Louis XVI would want for the *secret* and its agents 'because it painted [Louis XV] in a poor light'.[29] Once again, the interests of Bourbon monarchs were taking precedence over those of the nation. On the domestic political front, the government was pursuing a very repressive policy against demands for greater freedom of the press, and of the political system in general, while the Choiseulistes were doing everything they could to weaken Louis XV's government even further. The most revealing evidence that the political scene in France had changed forever, however, can be found in Maupeou's own stance. Once a firm supporter of the Jesuits, by 1772 his conduct revealed 'a remarkable absence of strong religious themes ... there was little dwelling on divine right'. In more general terms, the expectation of deferential obedience to the crown 'was grounded in historically derived, social utilitarian arguments which reflected the enlightened temper of the times, and not on the basis of theological doctrine. This secular discourse that had been developing since the Seven Years' War proved to be one of the enduring legacies of Choiseul's ministry.'[30] This was the quiet secular, democratic revolution that deeply disturbed Bertin and Moreau: their reflections on, and realisation of, its significance would eventually lead to the publication, in 1775, of their 300–page manifesto of the 'Grand Design', the *Mémoire sur la constitution de la ville et cité de Périgueux* (Bertin's home town).

Louis XV, who had done so much to support the venture, did not live to read it. He died on 10 May 1744, after a relatively short and painful attack of the dreaded smallpox virus (he had been 'bled' on three occasions at least). He died having received the rites of the Roman Catholic Church, an intelligent and religious man whose personal failings had compromised his position as 'a most Christian King': madame du Barry had been hastily removed from Versailles before Louis died. It was appropriate that Henri Bertin and the duc de la Vrillière (Saint-Florentin) should have been given the honour of reading out Louis XV's will; their careers had depended upon his patronage. Michel Antoine concludes that de Vrillière, 'having survived so many changes in the course of his career since his appointment as a secretary of state in 1720s, considered himself to be irremovable'.[31]

Bertin, on the other hand, was very pessimistic about his chances of being retained as secretary of state by Louis XVI, which may explain his rather surprising courtship of madame du Barry. Whether it does or not, he felt that he would have to act very circumspectly indeed if his political career were not to end with the king's funeral, which he thought would also be bad news for his friend, Jacob-Nicolas Moreau. In fact, Moreau would be offered the post of librarian to Marie Antoinette, which suggests that he might well have survived without Bertin's patronage. Moreau had his own slant on these events, suggesting that there was an element of political calculation in Bertin's apparent lack of concern for his position at court: 'he was the only minister who had not asked Louis XVI for a post; he felt that his department would not be of any real interest to Louis XVI and that he ought to attract his attention by being modest and not over-eager'. The young monarch, in fact, did notice his reticence and asked what reasons lay behind it, to which Bertin answered, tactfully: 'Sire, I thought that you had far more pressing problems to deal with than those that concerned my future.' It was the right reply: Louis XVI, a moral and religious man, proved to be more interested in Bertin than most courtiers thought appropriate. To Moreau's

191

relief, Bertin was retained in office.[32] As for his new master, Louis XVI was only nineteen years of age and had never really relished the idea of being a king. Tradition has it that he was even more timid and more indecisive than his predecessor, although well-informed historians have challenged this description of his character.[33] The choice of ministers, however, including, possibly, a 'first minister' to guide the inexperienced Louis XVI, had to be left to older heads at court. Enter Louis' aunt, madame Adélaide, who presented Louis XVI with a list of possible candidates. She placed the comte de Maurepas, a favourite of her recently deceased mother, Maria Lesczynska, at the top of her list. To the surprise of many people at court, the seventy-three year old Maurepas, thrown out of office by Louis and Pompadour in 1749, was actually chosen as the man to lead the monarchy out of the critical position in which it found itself in 1774.[34] Again, this was hardly a sign that Bourbon absolutism was moving forward along with the rapidly changing times.

*   *   *

Maurepas reassured the old guard at Versailles because he represented a return to traditional values: 'back to the future' in other words. His re-appearance also highlights the incestuous nature of Versailles politics. The courtier who informed Maurepas on 12 May 1774 of his return to power after twenty-five years in the political wilderness was the duc de la Vrillière (Saint-Florentin), Louis XV's longest-serving minister. De Vrillière was Maurepas' brother-in-law, and there can be little doubt that he was involved in the appointment of Maurepas. Bertin was one of the first members of the government that Maurepas contacted as soon as he was settled in his post – Maurepas, de Vrillière, Bertin, three robe nobles, representing two different generations of the robe nobility, but all equally intent upon defending the absolute authority of the monarchy against repeated challenges from princes, peers and the encroachments of the parlements. To strengthen their hand, they could call upon the duc d'Aiguillon, minister for war and foreign affairs, although they knew that they would have to watch him like a hawk. Here again, family relationships formed the background to court intrigues: d'Aiguillon was Maurepas' nephew who was also related to the powerful court noble, the maréchal de Richelieu. Hué de Miromesnil, who was given the ministry of justice (*garde des Sceaux*), was another one of Maurepas' nephews. No wonder Maurepas could adopt this rather lofty tone towards Louis XVI at their first meeting: 'As for your present ministers, I have not much to say: some are my close relatives, the others are known only to me by public repute.'[35] Bertin had no close links with either the old court aristocracy, or indeed the old robe families, which, in part, is why his hold on power was becoming increasingly untenable. There was also the indisputable fact that Bertin did not enjoy the same intimate relationship with Louis XVI that he had enjoyed with Louis XV.

Nonetheless, for Bertin and Moreau, Maurepas' appointment left some room for optimism. Maurepas was, after all, despite his previous reputation as a cynic and court gadfly, a firm supporter of the traditional monarchy, with the robe nobility administering the great offices of state, and the thirteen parlements of the realm acting as supreme courts of justice and guardians of the *unwritten* Bourbon constitution. The essential point for us is that these fundamental principles were by no means incompatible with the way in which the 'Grand Design' was evolving. Indeed, Maupeou's political programme from 1771–4 had included many of Bertin and Moreau's ideas on the regeneration of the monarchy, especially the attempt to strengthen its absolutist stance. In 1772, Moreau was actually accused by the *Choiseulistes* of acting as Maupeou's scriptwriter.[36] As for Maurepas' ambitions, early indications were that he was content, temporarily perhaps, to act as Louis' mentor; he was not given any ministerial office in the new ministry that was constructed during the summer of 1774, nor did he receive the coveted title of 'first minister': the king, alongside his ministers and royal committees, which the abbé de Bernis had advocated in the late 1750s, would run the government. The ambitious duc d'Aiguillon had decided to resign on 2 June, pushed in that direction, perhaps, by a distinct lack of support from his uncle, Maurepas. Maupeou and Terray were both dismissed on 23 August after Maurepas had issued Louis XVI with what amounted to a personal ultimatum – either they went or he would. The d'Aiguillon–Maupeou–Terray triumvirate had failed, despite its commitment to a strong monarchy and more pliant parlements. It is interesting to note the existence of yet another 'triumvirate', after the two triumvirates of the fifties and sixties, and twenty years before the infamous Jacobin triumvirate of Robespierre, Couthon and Saint-Just. It is just possible that French politicians of this period, many well versed in classical history, were attracted to the republican triumvirates of the Roman Empire – the author responsible for the entry in the *Encyclopédie* on 'Triumvirs' devoted several pages to the subject. The crucial point to note is that for its many enemies, the Maupeou triumvirate had represented 'the Hydra of Despotism', a depiction that seriously damaged the image of the Bourbon monarchy.

An assessment of the ministry that was formed during the summer of 1774 confirms first impressions that Maurepas was perhaps seeking a return to a time when the administration of government was placed firmly in the hands of the *noblesse de robe*, an approach to good government that looked back to the reign of Louis XIV. Ministers trained in the law would occupy five of the six most important departments in Maurepas' new administration. Sartine, 'this great servant of the *ancien régime*', who had served as *lieutenant de police de Paris* from 1759 to 1774, was appointed as minister of the navy. The comte Du Muy, a career soldier and old friend of Louis XVI's father, was placed in charge of the war ministry. He had been heard to say that he was now 'counting on the coming moral revolution', words that must have warmed the heart of the Jansenist-moralist, Jacob-Nicolas Moreau.[37] To the dismay of the old guard at Versailles, the man who had guided the publication of the *Encyclopédie* through early stormy waters, Lamoignon de Malesherbes, was chosen as minister of the King's Household, replacing Bertin's patron and Louis XV's trusted friend, the duc de la Vrillière. The latter, unlike Shakespeare's cardinal Wolsey, had served his king far more diligently than he had ever served his God, and had recently been rewarded with a dukedom for his pains. Miromesnil, who was given the office of *garde des Sceaux*, was an ex-*premier président* of the Rouen parlement; and Vergennes, who was placed in charge of foreign affairs, was a loyal career diplomat who would remain in post until his death in 1787.

Bearing in mind the title of this chapter, we must pause here to emphasise the real significance of Vergennes' appointment. He had been a key member of Louis XV's *secret du roi*, and his membership would continue under Louis XVI, as was the case with the comte Du Muy.[38] This 'back to the future' approach to the foreign policy of Louis XV, together with Vergennes' appointment as 'official' minister of foreign affairs by Louis XVI, did little to repair the dislocation of French foreign policy since the 1740s. To no-one's surprise, Bertin did not receive a dukedom, but he was called to Versailles, where Louis XVI asked him to deputise for the comte de Vergennes until the 21 July, the date Vergennes was due to return from his post of ambassador to Sweden. Even then, Bertin was obliged to wait until the dismissal of Maupeou and Terray on 23 August before he knew for certain that he had retained his *petit ministère*, much to Jacob-Nicolas Moreau's relief. Finally, we must signal the arrival at Versailles of the most radical figure in the new ministry of 1774, and sometime disciple of Henri Bertin, the intendant of the Limousin, Anne-Robert-Jacques Turgot, who was appointed *contrôleur général des finances* on 24 August, after just over a month in charge of the navy. When the appointment of both Malesherbes and Turgot was announced, Julie de Lespinasse, niece of the famous *salonnière* madame du Deffand, was beside herself with joy. She told her absent lover, the comte de Guibert, that he should have been with her – 'you could have shared in the universal explosion of joy'.[39] An exaggerated reaction to Malesherbes and Turgot's promotion no doubt, but

Voltaire was only slightly less effusive, and for good reason. Their appointment made it clear that, in one sphere at least, 'the old order changeth, yielding place to new'. The rapid collapse of Turgot's administration between 24 August 1774 and 12 May 1776, however, highlighted the fact that changing the 'old order' would be an almost impossible task. After 1776, the political tide would slowly move, or stagger, in the direction of revolution and a constitutional, as opposed to an absolute, monarchy, a development that was anathema to both Bertin and Moreau. According to Chaussinand Nogaret, the declining support for Bourbon absolutism, discredited by Maupeou's 'despotic' experiment, represented 'the posthumous victory of Choiseul and the realization of a national desire that he, with the limited means at his disposal, had tried to satisfy'.[40]

On 27 September 1774, following weeks of pressure on, and much procrastination from, Louis XVI, the edict that led to the recall of the pre-Maupeou parlements was signed. Turgot, a sympathiser with the widely accepted concept of 'Enlightened Despotism', had real reservations about the role of the parlements in his personal vision of the 'Grand Design', but chose to accept Louis XVI's promise that they would not interfere with his reforms. However, given Louis' inexperience, it was Maurepas who was calling the shots in 1774, and it had always been a tenet of faith for Maurepas that the Bourbon monarchy and the parlements were 'joined at the hip': he knew, from bitter experience, that the parlements were popular with many peers as well as with sections of the general public.

Had he been talking to Bertin and Moreau whose manifesto of the 'Grand Design' was shortly to be published? As Keith Baker has established, Moreau had been arguing for over a decade that the crown had been seriously weakened because it 'had allowed the magistrates to capture those central symbols of monarchical authority without which any act to reassert the royal will could be construed as recourse to arbitrary and despotic power'. He had advocated a policy of taking the fight to the enemy, since, to 'recapture the political initiative against the parlements, the crown needed, first and foremost, to succeed in the battle for public support'.[41] In 1774, it was Bertin who supported the notion that the rules governing the procedures of the post-Maupeou parlements would have to curb the excesses that he had been forced to confront during his time as *contrôleur général* in the early 1760s. For example, they could retain the right of *remonstrance*, but the potential for delaying royal edicts would have to be curtailed. Maurepas agreed, and the reforms would be implemented by Maupeou's reconstructed parlements. Historians have provided conflicting verdicts on the performance of these parlements. Julian Swann has argued that William Doyle reached the right conclusion: the parlements returned, but they were 'badly chastened ... neither willing nor able to resist the crown'. Not everyone, however, agrees with this assessment. Peter Campbell, for example, argues that the return of the parlements was a mistake, and that they returned 'defiant and vindicated'. In his depiction of the parlements as conservative, legally minded members of a privileged corporation, Campbell cites the work of Bailey Stone who provides another reason for Bertin and Moreau's qualified support of the parlements: the fact that they were 'attached to the division of society into three orders', and that the parlements were strong believers 'in the justness of privilege'.[42]

It may be surprising to learn that Bertin and Moreau had embraced these principles in the 1760s, alongside their support for the traditional alliance between the monarchy and the Catholic Church, which demonstrates that they both realised that, in the aftermath of the Seven Years' War, Bourbon absolutism would have to be given a royal face-lift. They worked to improve the foundations of the system by finding an alternative to the old supports supplied by the more recalcitrant ranks of the aristocracy. By the mid-1770s, long before the birth of Karl Marx, but around the time that Adam Smith was working on his *An inquiry into the Nature and Causes of the Wealth of Nations* (1776), both men recognised the significance of what is now commonly referred to as 'the rise of the bourgeoisie'. This did not necessarily entail the destruction of the three estates of the realm; social and cultural distinctions could still be observed. Bertin and Moreau's principal enemies were not the 'emerging bourgeoisie', but 'feudal' and 'anarchic' nobles. These 'proto-revolutionary' ideas were contained in the document we have referred to above as the 'manifesto of the "Grand Design"'. It was published under Moreau's name in 1775 as the *Mémoire sur la constitution politique de la ville et cité de Périgueux,* and it represents the first draft of what would evolve into the 'Grand Design'.

On *public opinion*, Moreau had argued that the monarchy would have to engage more enthusiastically with the public as early as the 1750s. This did not mean, however, that 'the people' should constitute the sovereign power in the state; sovereignty should remain the prerogative of the king. By the same token, the suggestion that the parlements should 'represent the nation' is dismissed out of hand; the king was the true 'father of his people', the function of the parlements had to be exclusively legal and advisory.

On *class and caste*, the *Mémoire*, written, originally, for the wealthy city fathers of Bertin's home town, Périgueux, argued that towns were the 'cradles of the bourgeoisie', which had secured their freedom by fighting the 'feudal nobility' since medieval times. It was now time for the bourgeoisie to join the robe nobility in a new political and economic power bloc. This new elite would provide a counter-balance to the dominance of the sword nobility, thus providing the socio-economic and political foundation for a modernising, Bourbon monarchy. Some of these ideas had been aired, in 1756, by the abbé Coyer in his very popular work, *La noblesse commerçante.* During the early years of the Revolution, Bertin would bemoan the fact than neither Louis XV, nor his successor, had chosen to adopt a more critical approach towards the political and socio-economic power of the traditional aristocracy. He believed that if only the crown had embraced the cause of a Third Estate *that included the liberal and robe nobility*, the Revolution might never have happened.[43]

On *political and public morality*, Moreau thought that boosting the image of Louis XV as a 'patriot' would not reconcile the monarchy with the people (the Choiseulistes had seized the franchise for 'patriotism' anyway): given the legacy of madame de Pompadour's reign, the calamity of the Seven Years' War, and the scandalous behaviour of Louis XV in his Deer Park, rather more would be required to regain the popularity of Bourbon absolutism: the immorality of the French monarchy, and French society in general, would be a common topic of revolutionary political and social discourse. The *Mémoire sur la constitution* would provide an agenda for many supporters of the reformed royalist right during the heated debates that characterised the early 'moderate' phase of the Revolution. Bertin and Moreau would participate in that epic struggle until Bertin's emigration in 1792.

*   *   *

Jacques Turgot, appointed to the post of *contrôleur général* in August 1774, adopted a far more radical approach to reforming Bourbon absolutism than his early mentor, Henri Bertin. We have already discussed Turgot's guarded reaction to the recall of the old parlements at the beginning of his brief ministerial career: his implementation of two major policies – the reintroduction of the freedom of the grain trade within France's borders, and the intro-duction of a more representative system of government – reveal his uncompromisingly radical agenda. It comes as no surprise that Bertin was very suspicious of Turgot's 'revolutionary' cures for the ailing Bourbon regime, founded, as they were, upon current, 'social scientific' principles. Turgot was one of those enlightened intellectuals who would make the term 'socio-economic' a meaningful concept. Bertin's relationship with his former disciple would become increasing complex, reflecting, in many ways, the unpredictable political situation that charac-terised the early years of the Revolution. The two men had shared many of the ideas that, before 1763, were associated with the physiocrats, led by François Quesnay. They had continued to walk more or less in step until the formation of a breakaway sect, the *économistes*, in late 1763. During the 1760s and early 1770s, Turgot had developed an interest in political economy, which actually brought him into contact with Adam Smith. The abbé Morellet recalls an evening in the company of Smith, Helvétius and Turgot during which they discussed a few of Smith's ideas on 'commercial theory, banking, public credit and several other points relating to the great work he had conceived'.[44]

Turgot, unlike Bertin, was a revolutionary thinker; he supported the creation of a new social and political system, a system that looked forward to Karl Marx, rather than back to François Quesnay, a *scientific* social and political system that would transform the public from spectators to participants in the great enterprise of creating the good society; 'subjects' would become 'citizens' of the state; the monarchy could retain a measure of absolutism, but transmuted for the times into 'enlightened despotism'. A powerful head of state was very much *à la mode* in Europe during the second half of the eighteenth century, which meant that Bertin and Moreau did not lack considerable support for their 'Grand Design', but Turgot was eager to go where Bertin and Moreau feared to tread, and his radicalism clearly unnerved some of his own supporters, which may explain why he was wary of being associated with any particular 'sect'. In January 1770, he launched a bitter attack upon one of the leading figures in the *économiste* group, Dupont de Nemours. The latter had altered the text of one of Turgot's most influential works, *Réflexions sur la richesse*, to make it more suitable for publication in the *économiste* house journal, the *Ephémérides du citoyen*. Turgot, not a man to be trifled with, threatened to denounce de Nemours in print unless he disavowed 'all the alterations to my text that transform me into an *économiste*, something that I have no more interest in being than an *encyclopédiste*'. Turgot regarded himself as an original thinker; Louis XVI thought that he wanted his job – 'M Turgot wants to be me, and I do not want him to be me'.[45]

Turgot's 'social scientific' approach to reform became crystal clear with the launch of his reforms to free the grain trade, one of those defining policy issues that would test the resolve of every *contrôleur général* during the second half of the eighteenth century. In Turgot's case, admiration for political economists like Adam Smith meant that basic notions concerning the benefits of free trade were to be incorporated into a more general philosophy of government that linked economic progress with the problem of solving the fundamental social issue of mass poverty: this is what made him a revolutionary figure. Bertin had been a pioneer in introducing free trade legislation, deregulating, on 26 May 1763, the internal trade in grain, followed in August of that year with a relaxation of the laws governing the export and import of grain. In July 1770, the abbé Terray had reversed much of this legislation, abolishing the laws relating to the export of grain, as well as placing restrictions on internal trade. Terray's volte-face was itself a response to the increasingly violent, popular protests against the implementation of free trade principles. Bertin, unlike Turgot, was an experienced campaigner in these matters, which prompted him to suggest a Machiavellian method of avoiding renewed violence when Turgot re-introduced the freedom of the grain trade in 1774: 'I would advise you,' Bertin wrote, 'to adjust your speed by being prudent. I would go as far as to suggest ... that you hide your thoughts and opinions from the child that you have to govern and restore to health. You cannot help playing the role of a dentist, I agree, but, if you can, try to pretend, not that you have abandoned your treatment, but that you have decided to apply it more slowly'.[46]

But Turgot was a man in a hurry, and, on 20 September 1774, he published the edict that abolished important restrictions on the sale and movement of grain, which, together with the unfortunate coincidence of the failure of the 1774–5 harvest, and the outbreak, the previous winter, of the deadly cattle epidemic discussed above, provoked one of the most serious popular uprisings of the eighteenth century – the *guerre des farines* (Flour War). By the spring of 1775, the price of a four-pound loaf in the grain belt around Paris had risen to 14–16 *sous*, double the normal price. Serious riots occurred from Champagne to Burgundy, as well as in small market towns around the capital. At the end of April, the riots, often led by women, reached the gates of Versailles, where Louis XVI was forced to address angry crowds, a disturbing rehearsal of the 'March to Versailles' that would take place in the autumn of 1789. Confronted with this massive popular revolt, Turgot kept his nerve, as did the king – on this occasion. The execution of two rioters in the place de Grève on 11 May signalled the end of the uprisings, but a crippling blow had been struck against Turgot's reform programme.[47] Nonetheless, the issue of mass poverty would now play a more significant part in determining political practice until Napoleon Bonaparte created the military dictatorship that, temporarily, changed the rules of engagement.

The second major policy issue that reveals Turgot's attitude towards Bourbon absolutism by the mid-1770s, the introduction of a more democratic form of representative government, was probably the most pivotal in the Bourbon monarchy's reluctant move from an absolutist to a constitutional form of government. Before the piecemeal reforms of L'Averdy in the mid-1760s, again reversed by Terray in 1771, 'Oligarchy and also venality were the defining characteristics of urban municipal government.'[48] In 1775, Turgot published his ideas on local government in a *Mémoire sur les municipalités* that had originally been drafted by Dupont de Nemours. It included some of Turgot's most profound reflections on the exercise of democratic power within the confines of the absolute state, and was therefore of great interest to Bertin. Turgot offered a 'vision of a transformed administrative system that would implement the rights of man and bring about the rule of reason', without, necessarily, mortally wounding Bourbon absolutism.[49] According to his proposals, *citoyens propriétaires* (interesting that as early as the 1770s, 'subjects' had been transformed into 'citizens') paying over 600 *livres* a year in taxation would choose the members of parish municipalities; each parish municipality would then choose one delegate to the municipality of the *arrondissement*, election or district; these bodies, in turn, would choose delegates to a provincial municipality. Finally, to the dismay of the clergy and nobles representing the first and second estates of the Estates General, a *grande municipalité*, composed of delegates from the provincial municipalities, would discuss the financial affairs of the nation with the government. This, again, was clearly a truly revolutionary proposal, impinging as it did on the vexed issue of national sovereignty.

Turgot was attempting to square the circle, accepting, with Jean-Jacques Rousseau, that sovereignty ultimately lay with the people, but realising, with Henri Bertin and Moreau, that it was not yet possible, or perhaps desirable, that executive power should lie with anyone but the monarch. In 1861, a government lawyer would spot, with the benefit of hindsight, the real significance of Turgot's proposed reform: 'It was a profoundly revolutionary programme that sought to absorb the two first estates into the third estate. Doubtless, the great number of properties that they possessed would have guaranteed that the clergy and nobility would have exercised a considerable influence on elections, but they would have ceased to be separate orders, deriving their rights from their birth and their clerical position.'[50] This premature attempt to incorporate the first two estates into the third estate (it would only be achieved during the Revolution, on 27 June 1789) explains why Turgot's proposals on municipal government never reached the statute book. Once again, the influence of the clergy, princes, peers, and other privileged groups was still too great for the implementation of truly representative and democratic reforms, as Bertin had warned. Karl Marx could have been paraphrasing Moreau when he wrote that 'absolute monarchy appears in those transitional periods when the old feudal estates are in decline and the medieval estate of burghers is evolving into the modern bourgeois class, without [either] of the contending parties having as yet disposed of the other'.[51] Marx was a voracious reader and may well have read some of Moreau's many publications.

Turgot had produced his *radical* version of a reformed absolutist system, and Bertin and Moreau had to respond accordingly. The archival foundations for their 'Grand Design' had already been laid by the creation of Moreau's *dépôt de législation*. As early as the 1760s, Moreau, supported by Bertin, had created a dedicated team of Benedictine 'scholar-monks', selected to unearth documents relating to the history of the French monarchy (some of which dated back to the time of Charlemagne) in French and English archives. Moreau would refer to this enterprise as his *'Travaux littéraire'*; Bertin would refer to his thirty-year exchange of ideas with French Jesuit priests in China as the *'Correspondence littéraire'*: together they would constitute the 'Grand Design'. We must remind ourselves that both men were both working in the over-heated, intellectual hothouse that encouraged the rapid growth of new ideas and projects. It was during the 1770s that the *Encyclopédie*, that world-famous compendium of human knowledge, moved 'into a phase that represented the diffusion of Enlightenment on a massive scale'.[52] In 1776, Pierre-François Boncerf published his widely read *Les inconvénients des droits féodaux*, which reinforced Bertin and Moreau's attack on 'feudal nobles' that was contained in their *Mémoire sur la constitution politique de la ville et cité de Périgueux*.

The pressure for radical change was rising, and Turgot was only too eager to respond to the challenge: on the religious front, he went as far as to question the purpose of the traditional alliance between 'Throne and Altar'. His suggestion that Louis XVI should not include the traditional promise that he would 'exterminate heresy' during his coronation address in Rouen on 11 June 1775 immediately lost him the support of many clerics. On taxation, Turgot provoked alarm amongst both clerics and nobles by his sympathy for the old physiocratic hobbyhorse – a single tax to fall on all landowners, *irrespective of their social rank*. Early in 1765, he began working on his 'Six Edicts', which included the further deregulation of markets in the capital, the abolition of trade guilds, and the substitution of peasant labour on roads (*corvée*) with a new property tax, *designed to fall upon bourgeois and noble landowners alike*. To pursue Bertin's description of Turgot as a dentist, it seemed to many at Versailles, as well as in the wider community, that Bertin was intent upon extracting too many decaying teeth at one sitting. Evidence of the pain being inflicted upon the privileged orders surfaced at the beginning of 1776, when a *'ligue pour les abus'* attracted a wide spectrum of social and political opposition to Turgot's reforms. It included guild masters, financiers, tax-farmers, members of the clergy and the nobility, as well as the queen, the princes of the blood, and the parlements. The prince de Conti led the revolt of the privileged orders in the Paris parlement. By this time, Maurepas himself had lost confidence in Turgot, declaring that his reform programme contained more *'esprit de système'* than sensible, administrative measures: 'the only thing that entered his head were speculations and philosophic dreams ... a *système de perfection* that did not belong to this world, but only existed in books, a point by point analysis of a noble ideal that could never be put into practice ...'. In other words, Turgot and allies were seeking to replace the biblical, and historically validated, supremacy of the crown and the aristocracy with the theoretical supremacy of the social sciences, the intellectual revolution that preceded the social and political revolution of 1789. For Michael Sonenscher, the failure of Turgot's *'système'* would produce a 'new implementation strategy [that] was based on a number of claims about the reforming power of public credit'. This new strategy, according to Sonenscher, contained the seeds of nineteenth century 'socialism'.[53]

By the mid-1770s, Bertin and Turgot had drifted, or been driven, apart by Turgot's uncompromising radicalism; Bertin had even toyed with the possibility of resignation in 1775, following the death of his brother, Charles-Jean Bertin, bishop of Vannes, the previous year. One of Bertin's more critical acquaintances at court tells us that he had survived, 'only because of his ability to bend with the prevailing wind and the fact that no-one took much notice of him'.[54] The prevailing mood among ministers in Versailles in 1775–6 was, according to Malesherbes, distinctly pessimistic: 'M. de Maurepas ... laughs at everything, M. Turgot doubts nothing: I doubt everything and laugh at nothing. What a bloody awful ministry!'[55]

Whether it was 'bloody awful' or not, by the spring of 1776 Maurepas' administration was beginning to split down the middle over French involvement in the American War of Independence (1775–83). Hardman and Price, following a very detailed examination of the main arguments, based on an impressive array of royal and ministerial correspondence, conclude that Vergennes (in charge of foreign affairs and de facto first minister) and Sartine (navy minister) were 'the hawks', that is in favour of intervening on the side of the American colonists, while Turgot and Montbarey (War Office) were 'the doves', with Louis XVI and Maurepas 'somewhere in between'. From our research, Henri Bertin stood (on one leg perhaps!) in Turgot's corner.[56]

There is little doubt that, for die-hard Anglophobes at court and in the country, the conflict presented France with a wonderful opportunity for revenge against the British for her catastrophic defeat in the Seven Years' War. Led by the romantic celebrity of his day, the marquis de Lafayette, and encouraged by the gunrunning popular playwright, Beaumarchais, opinion began to swing in favour of intervention. In 1776, America's version of the 'common man', Benjamin Franklin, arrived in Paris to sell the story of his fledgling country's noble struggle for independence to the French public. By 1778, when Louis XVI and Vergennes decided, officially, to intervene in the American War, encouraged by the British defeat at the battle of Saratoga in December of the previous year, informed French opinion appears to have accepted Vergennes' belief that, once the American conflict was over, Britain would attack France, therefore, it was best 'to get one's retaliation in first'. But what about the parlous state of the nation's finances? The duc de Choiseul, sniping from the sidelines as usual, thought that taxpayers would continue to foot the bill: his line was that 'a great state cannot survive without credit'. Turgot, Bertin, and, far too late, Louis XVI, agreed that the cost of French participation on the side of *republican* rebels in the American War of Independence precipitated the Revolution of 1789.[57]

The issue of escalating public debt, all too familiar to governments throughout the world since 2009, has recently attracted the attention of historians of France. Michael Sonenscher, who has recently published a major study on the subject, reveals that David Hume had written, as early as 1752, that 'either the nation must destroy public credit, or public credit will destroy the nation'. During the Maupeou coup of 1770–74, Edmund Burke, in apocalyptic mood, sought to establish the relationship between public debt and 'revolutions'. He argued, predicatively, that the cost 'of supporting great standing armies' could lead to the destruction of liberty, or 'a convulsion that will shake the globe to its centre'.[58] Turgot had followed this controversy closely, choosing to side with Hume and Burke on the grounds that 'the disadvantages of public credit remained too strong, *especially under an absolute government* [emphasis added]. The unitary character of sovereignty, even if modified by a subordinate network of provincial assemblies, ruled out something as divisive and as potentially damaging to productive investment as a public debt.'[59] It was a courageous conclusion, given that Britain had depended on 'national debt' to finance her involvement in the Seven Years' War. The problem for the French government, as David Parker has observed, was that France simply did not have the modern financial structures to support the development of the modern state. He cites the case of the Bank of England, which had statutory rights to borrow money on the security of parliamentary revenue, and whose investors were guaranteed interest from additional customs and excise duties: 'Such a modern articulation of private interest and investment with public utility and control could not be replicated within the structures of *ancien regime* France.'[60]

The issue of public debt was closely linked to the cost of waging war. From the time of Louis XIV to that of Louis XVI, 'the motor of fiscal change in France, as for all the leading European countries, was expenditure on war'.[61] But this increased income did nothing to ease the nation's deficit. Between 1740 and 1783, France had participated in three wars, which, together, had lasted for twenty-two years. Pompadour and Bertin had saddled the country with massive debts, created, in part, by the high interest loans they contracted to finance the Seven Years' War. In 1786, Calonne would inform Louis XVI that, primarily as a result of the huge loans raised by Jacques Necker to finance the American War of Independence, the deficit had risen to *c.*115 million *livres,* representing almost a quarter of the government's income for that year.[62] Turgot's experience in 1776 would be repeated when Calonne's radical reform programme was sabotaged by *les privilégiés,* thus opening the floodgates of revolution even wider. Only the Revolution of 1789 would redress the situation by securing the nationalisation of church property and fairer tax distribution.[63]

*   *   *

One of the consequences of Turgot's shock therapy for the monarchy was his dismissal in May 1776. Keith Baker argues convincingly that Turgot's failure was related to the 'tension [that existed] between the traditional foundations of royal absolutism in a particularistic social order, and the universalist implications of the growth of more centralised government'.[64] These words aptly sum up the two major themes of this study. Henri Bertin was both a contributor to, and a victim of, the growth of a more centralised and bureaucratic government. His bespoke *petit ministère,* primarily created in 1763 by Louis XV and Pompadour to keep Bertin 'on side', had become a bureaucratic anachronism. By the late 1770s, the administration of government was no longer a matter of the royal prerogative: 'All sorts of bodies exercised powers of administration, sometimes on behalf of the crown and sometimes independently. The Church, the parlements, the Provincial Estates and secular seigneurs generally, all performed considerable administrative tasks.'[65] We noted in previous chapters that Bertin had to confront serious and persistent elite, institutional and popular resistance to his centralising policies, which included the introduction of regulations governing free trade, the creation of agricultural societies, the modernisation of coal mines, even the introduction of a modern veterinary service. The scale of this resistance, frequently encouraged by influential figures in Versailles and beleaguered intendants in the provinces, explains the limited success that Bertin managed to achieve, and this entrenched resistance showed little sign of weakening during the 1770s.

Undermined by the rising profile of aristocratic ministers at court, associated with the unpopular liberal economic policies of Choiseul and Turgot, regarded by many critics, outside as well as inside Versailles, as a crony of the two 'leeches' who had drained the country of its life-blood, Louis XV and madame de Pompadour, the writing had been on the Versailles wall, so far as Bertin's career was concerned, since the early 1770s: it had become more legible with the death of Louis XV in 1774. The previous year, the *contrôle général* had removed the management of canals and river navigation from Bertin's *petit ministère*; two years later, Turgot deprived the ministry of its control over public carriages and freight services. Further evidence of Bertin's dwindling authority at Versailles can be found in the two spheres of government policy we highlighted in our previous chapter – agriculture and coal mining. For all the early energy he had expended on the creation of agricultural societies, the programme had suffered a serious reversal by the late 1770s.[66] Bertin's dismissal in 1780 represented a delayed victory for the *contrôle général* and its new director, Jacques Necker. The increasingly powerful finance ministry had never really come to terms with the creation of Bertin's '*petit ministère*' in 1763. Nonetheless, André Bourde is surely right to conclude that despite the fact that Bertin was never in a position to pursue a coherent and comprehensive rural policy, many of the major agricultural reforms of the 1760s and early 1770s bear testimony to his reforming zeal.[67]

Pursuing the same departmental imperialism, the *contrôle général* had, grudgingly, allowed Bertin to control the granting of concessions to mine owners in 1764, but here again he was never given the opportunity of developing an overall commercial strategy for the coal industry in France, despite the leading role he played in the eventual creation of the *Ecole des mines* in 1783. If we take the example of Bertin's constant support for Pierre-François Tubeuf, one of the early pioneers of coal mining in the Alais region of south-eastern France, we find that, by the late 1770s, Tubeuf was losing the battle to retain the concession granted to him by Bertin in 1773. Undermined at court by the opposition of the marquis de Castries, who had purchased the *comté d'Alais* in 1777 for the princely sum of 777,000 *livres* in order to control its coal mines, Tubeuf would eventually decide to start a new life in North America. His emigration represented the defeat of a man, chosen by Bertin and Trudaine to lead France into an era of modern coal mining, by a court aristocrat who became minister of the navy, and a favourite of Marie Antoinette.[68] Peter Jones has argued that 'friction within the machinery of government reached a new intensity in the 1770s and 1780s, decades that witnessed mounting political concern over the issue of "despotism", and vigorous attempts to break through the institutional gridlock'.[69] Bertin had been a cautious supporter of the enlightened despotism, a member of Maupeou's 'despotic' administration, and a centralising government reformer. These policies became increasingly unpopular during, and after, the 'Maupeou revolution'.

Bertin's increasing isolation, coupled with successful attempts to break up his ministry, led, inevitably, to his dismissal as secretary of state. During the late 1770s, his enemies at court, as well as in the provinces and the parlements, combined to administer the coup-de-grâce. Their opportunity came when two of his principal lieutenants, Edmé David le Seurre and Melchior François Parent, were accused of defrauding state revenues. Le Seurre, chief clerk and secretary to Bertin since his time as *contrôleur général*, was accused of embezzling money from Bertin's income as Louis XV's *Grand Trésorier*, as well as 200,000 *livres* from the 'Dombes fund', the royal 'private purse', originally created by Louis XV and Bertin to cover the sizeable costs of looking after the king's mistresses and illegitimate offspring.[70] Given Bertin's managerial association with Louis XV's activities in the *Parc aux cerfs*, rumours about financial impropriety relating to the Dombes fund was the last thing Bertin needed as his career began to hit the rocks. Conscious of the damage being inflicted on the monarchy, Louis XVI decreed, in 1779, that income from the fund should immediately be transferred to the public purse, a significant move in modernising the operation of royal finances. The fraudulent activities of Melchior Parent appear to have been just as systemic, but more lucrative, than those perpetrated by le Seurre. Parent had also been one of Bertin's most loyal lieutenants, his service reaching back to the 1750s. It was hardly surprising, therefore, that Bertin should have appointed him as director of the famous royal Sèvres porcelain works in 1772, presenting Parent with a wonderful opportunity for fiddling the accounts of an enterprise that was making massive profits. The dinner service designed for Catherine the Great, and delivered in 1777, cost the Empress 328,188 *livres*.[71] Parent lived on a lavish scale, purchasing expensive properties in Paris and the provinces. Unfortunately, the trail of deceit led back once again to Bertin, who carried the ultimate responsibility for the overall management of the Sèvres enterprise. Charged with 'fraudulent banking, and theft', Parent was imprisoned, briefly, in the Bastille, and asked to repay 240,000 *livres* to the Sèvres company. His family managed to secure his release from prison, but, to end any chance of further legal proceedings, they agreed to his detention in the asylum of Charenton, where he died in 1782.[72]

There can be little doubt that Henri Bertin had failed in his duty as the minister ultimately responsible for the management of the Sèvres company. For many years, his *petit ministère*, which had included so many different briefs, had demanded too much of his time, which explains why 'Bertin's administrative machine operated at the slowest possible speed'.[73] But there was also a worrying naivety, bordering on negligence, in his response to the fraudulent activities of le Seurre, Parent, and, it seems, several junior officials. In his memoirs, his ever-loyal colleague, Jacob-Nicolas Moreau, rejected the claim that Bertin was venal.[74] However, criticism of Bertin's integrity was made, particularly when le Seurre, at his trial before the *grande chambre de la parlement de Paris*, accused Bertin of complicity in his alleged removal of money from the Dombes fund. The scandal associated with le Seurre's trial played a significant part in Bertin's resignation in May 1780, to the delight of his enemies at court, and the jubilation of the marquis de Castries' supporters in the far-off mining region of Alès.[75] Clearly, Louis XVI and his advisers thought it wise to distance themselves both from Bertin and the scandals associated with Louis XV's colourful career in his Deer Park.

The scandal concerning his ministry may have been the immediate cause of Bertin's fall from power in 1780, but Bertin's position had become increasingly precarious as 'the chattering classes', and even the more impoverished section of *le people*, began to exert greater pressure on the government. Sarah Maza has argued that the 1770s and 1780s produced a significant change in the operation and influence of the public sphere, adding that the *'grandes affaires'* of the period that involved political trials focused upon the twin evils of 'despotism' and 'the aristocracy'.[76] The trial of Bertin's lieutenants should be included among the *'grandes affaires'* of the late 1770s. It provided the stage for a parade of ghosts from Bertin's past – Louis XV, Pompadour, and his younger brother who died in the Bastille just a year before Bertin was dismissed. But, by this time, there was another, far more threatening presence on the stage – a 'plebeian Greek chorus' to some of the dramatic events that had been associated with Bertin's career, including the catastrophe of the Seven Years' War, the social consequences of Choiseul's 'free market' policies, the collapse of 'Maupeou's revolution', the shock of the *guerre des farines*, and the cost the American War of Independence.

This popular off-stage chorus could certainly be counted in the hundreds of thousands, if not millions. The introduction of free trade principles after 1763, especially free trade in grain, had totally transformed the relationship between the mass of the population and the government, its politicians and its police: 'The legitimacy of the police was no longer a given fact ... the police service would now have to face a permanent political state of uncertainty: how much time would there be to implement a policy of regulation, government intervention and controls?'[77] Throughout the 1760s and 1770s, the poor and dispossessed, in town and country, had become the guinea pigs for an unprecedented experiment in economic modernisation. Between the early and late 1760s, the price of bread had doubled. In 1789, the *'pacte de famine'*, which resurfaced in the late 1760s and 1770s, would be defined by the *Moniteur Universal* as a plot 'conceived by financiers and courtiers against the food-supplies of an entire nation'.[78] Jean Nicolas' nationwide enquiry into popular movements has established that, although there was no national revolt on the scale of the Great Fear of 1789, anti-seigneurial riots, involving attacks on enclosures, pigeon-lofts and seigneurial agents, increased markedly between the 1760s and the Revolution. John Markoff has identified a rising curve of peasant revolt during the last decades of the eighteenth century: 'From low levels during much of the century ... one sees clearly the curve of conflict starts to rise in the 1760s. There is a sharp peak, the highest in the century so far, at the time of the Flour War of 1775, and although the trajectory falls back afterwards, it remains above its pre-1760s level and then begins *a new, accelerating dizzy ascent in the late 1780s* [emphasis added]'.[79]

This rising curve of rebellion exerted an influence on government policy. Joel Félix's detailed study of *contrôleur général* L'Averdy stresses his concern for the plight of the poor; his eventual successor, the abbé Terray, decided to rescind much of the free trade legislation that had been passed after 1763. He told the comte de Périgord that he still believed that economic reform was necessary, but added that, 'I shall do so because I am always conscious of the interests of the masses (*la multitude*), for whom bread is their main, often their only, source of nourishment, and whose seditious actions, when bread is scarce, can destroy empires.'[80] Terray's comments accurately reflect the fact that the enlightened humanity of ministers was usually laced with a high dose of fear of 'the multitude'. As for Bertin, his career exemplifies the concern for the poor that was one of the characteristic

213

traits of the radical Enlightenment; this trait, a fusion of human concern and realpolitik, may well help to explain the timidity and caution with which he had approached any major free trade reforms. He approached his semi-retirement with a measure of relief. In a letter to a friend living in Chatou, Bertin light-heartedly warned that he should 'take care. It won't be long now before you will have to vegetate like me, an excellent occupation.'[81] In fact, Bertin was still a minister of state who had received permission from Louis XVI to continue, along with Jacob-Nicolas Moreau, his work on the 'Grand Design'. From a personal angle of vision, the last decade of his life would prove to be far more rewarding, and far less stressful, than the time he had devoted to his career as secretary of state.

Notes

1 Bussière, '*Etude sur Henri Bertin*', BSHAP, vol.35 (1908), p.442.
2 Jacques Silvestre de Sacy, *Henri Bertin dans le Sillage de Chine, 1720–92* (Paris, 1920), pp.48–9.
3 *A.N.*, E 3666/7, *registre des renvois des mémoires de Bertin*. The number of *lettres de cachet* issued during the period from 1764 to 1772 was fairly high. Over just one month (May 1766) requests were submitted for warrants to detain eight males and six females.
4 Daniel Charles Trudaine, an *intendant des finances* in the department of the *contrôle général*, was Bertin's indispensable ally in government, the driving force behind so much of the modernisation of French trade and industry that occurred from the 1730s to the 1760s. He had been placed in charge of the influential *ponts et chaussées* section in 1743; his son, Jean Charles, joined him in the *contrôle général* in 1754, the year Bertin was appointed intendant of the Lyonnais.
5 Bussière, '*Etude sur Henri Bertin*', BSHAP, vol.34 (1907), pp.373–88.
6 Bussière, '*Etude sur Henri Bertin*', BSHAP, vol.34 (1907), pp.451–66.
7 Emma Spary, 'Political, Natural and Bodily Economies', in N. Jardine, J. A. Secord and E.C. Spary (eds), *Cultures of Natural History* (Cambridge, 1996), p.179.
8 For the many facets of the Enlightenment, see Dorinda Outram, *The Enlightenment* (Cambridge, 2005), second edn, chap. one.
9 Bussière, '*Etude sur Henri Bertin*', BSHAP, vol.34 (1907), pp.304–6.
10 Foncin, *Essai sur le ministère de Turgot*, pp.134–41.

11 Foncin, *Essai sur le ministère de Turgot*, pp.164–9, pp.316–26 and pp.483–92.

12 Spary, 'Political, Natural and Bodily Economies', p.191; Laurence Brockliss and Colin Jones, *The Medical World of Early Modern France* (Oxford, 1997), pp.455–6.

13 Bussière, '*Etude sur Henri Bertin*', BSHAP, vol.34 (1907), p.306.

14 Foncin, *Essai sur le ministère de Turgot*, p.326.

15 Antoine, *Louis XV*, pp.563–7.

16 Nicole Blondel and Tamara Préaud, *Histoire de Sèvres* (Paris, 1996), p.10–19; *archives de la manufacture royale de Sèvres* (hereafter *A.M.S.*), *cahiers de la céramique du verre et des arts du feu*, no.33, p.34.

17 A.M.S., *cahiers de la céramique*, no.33, p.33.

18 The same letter contains instructions from Bertin to his staff asking them to ensure that the king of Denmark would be given the best possible welcome when he arrived for a visit to Sèvres, so that he that he would leave the factory 'not only content with the beauty of the products, but also with the way the manufacturing process operated'.

19 Daniel Roche, *A History of Everyday Things: The Birth of Consumption in France, 1600–1800* (Cambridge, 2000), p.241 and pp.246–7.

20 A.M.S., A2, dossier 11, *lettres aux intendants sur l'arrêt du conseil du 15 février 1766*.

21 William Doyle, 'The Parlements', in Keith Baker (ed.), *The French Revolution and the Creation of Modern Political Culture* (Oxford, 1987), vol.1, pp.157–67; Julian Swann, '"Silence, Respect, Obedience": political culture in Louis XV's France', in Hamish Scott and Brendan Simms, *Cultures of Power in Europe during the Long Eighteenth Century*, pp.242–7.

22 For a detailed account of Louis XV's infamous liaison with madame du Barry, including an account of her execution during the Jacobin Terror on 11 December 1793, see Goncourt, *Les maîtresses de Louis XV*, pp.587–90, and Antoine, *Louis XV*, pp.959–61.

23 Chaussinand-Nogaret, *Choiseul*, p.299; Antoine, *Louis XV*, pp.885–8.

24 Antoine, *Louis XV*, p.913.

25 Swann, *Politics and the Parlement of Paris*, chaps eleven and twelve.

26 J.-P. Moreau, *Mes souvenirs* (Paris, 1898), vol.1, pp.238–42.

27 Bussière, '*Etude sur Henri Bertin*', vol.36 (1909), pp.245–9.

28 René Nicolas de Maupeou, *Journal historique de la Révolution opérée dans la constitution de la monarchie française* (London, 1774–76), 7 vols, iii, pp.248–50.

29 John Hardman and Munro Price, eds, *Louis XVI and the comte de Vergennes*, (Oxford, 1998), pp.183–4, n.1.

30 Jones, *The Great Nation*, p.288.
31 Antoine, *Louis XV*, p.968; Moreau, *Mes souvenirs*, vol.1, p.307.
32 Moreau, *Mes souvenirs*, vol.2, pp.212–35.
33 See, for example, Hardman and Price, *Louis XVI and the comte de Vergennes*, pp.i–xii.
34 Picciola, *Le comte de Maurepas*, pp.395–416.
35 J. Hardman, *Louis XVI* (London, 1993), p.30.
36 Moreau, *Mes souvenirs*, vol.2, pp.237–8.
37 Hardman, *Louis XV*, p.32.
38 Hardman and Price, *Louis XVI and the comte de Vergennes*, p.29 and p.160, n.2.
39 Foncin, *Essai sur le ministère de Turgot*, pp.51–2.
40 Chaussinand-Nogaret, *Choiseul*, p.298.
41 Baker, *Inventing the French Revolution*, pp.64–5.
42 Swann, *Politics and the Parlement of Paris*, p.367; P. Campbell, 'The Paris Parlement in the 1780s', in P. Campbell, (ed.), *The Origins of the French Revolution* (London, 2006), pp.87–111.
43 Lewis, 'Rising Tides', pp.11–12.
44 Poirier, *Turgot*, chap. eight.
45 Poirier, *Turgot*, p. 103; Hardman and Price, *Louis XVI and the comte de Vergennes*, p.54.
46 Poirier, *Turgot*, p.214.
47 Lewis, *France 1715–1804*, pp.203–4.
48 Jones, *Reform and Revolution*, p.27.
49 Baker, *Inventing the French Revolution*, p.123.
50 A. Batbie, *Turgot, philosophe, économiste et administrateur* (Paris, 1861), p.68.
51 Karl Marx, 'Moralising Criticism and Critical Moralising', in François Furet, *Marx and the French Revolution* (Chicago, 1988), p.177.
52 Darnton, *The Business of the Enlightenment*, p.6.
53 Michael Sonenscher, *Sans-Culottes: An Eighteenth-Century Emblem in the French Revolution* (Oxford, 2008), p.260.
54 Lucien Laugier, *Turgot ou le myth des réformes* (Paris, 1979), p.205; Véri, abbé de, *Journal*, ed. J. de Witte (Paris 1928–30), vol.1, pp.404–45.
55 Moreau, *Mes souvenirs*, vol.2, p.256.
56 Hardman and Price, *Louis XVI and the comte de Vergennes*, p.68.
57 Chaussinand-Nogaret, *Choiseul*, p.259; Dull, *The French Navy*, pp. 249–54.
58 Michael Sonenscher, *Before the Deluge: Public Debt, Inequality, and the Intellectual Origins of the French Revolution* (Princeton, 2007), p.26.
59 Sonenscher, *Before the Deluge*, p.261.

60 Parker, *Class and State*, p.221.
61 Richard Bonney, 'France, 1494–1815', in Richard Bonney (ed.), *The Rise of the Fiscal State in Europe c. 1200–1815* (Oxford, 1999), p.161.
62 Félix, 'The Financial Origins of the French Revolution', pp.35–62; Foncin, *Turgot*, pp.79–80.
63 J. Hardman, 'Decision-making', in P. Campbell (ed.), *The Origins of the French Revolution* (London, 2006), pp.86.
64 Baker, *Inventing the French Revolution*, pp.115–7.
65 Jones, *Reform and Revolution*, p.25.
66 Sacy, *Henri Bertin*, pp.72–84.
67 Bourde, *Agronomie et agronomes*, vol.2, pp.1089–94 and pp.1195–6.
68 Lewis, *The Advent of Modern Capitalism*, pp.100–1.
69 Jones, *Reform and Revolution*, p.46.
70 Sacy, *Henri Bertin*, pp.53–4.
71 Bussière, '*Etude sur Henri Bertin*', *BSHAP*, vol.36 (1909), p.277.
72 *A.M.S., Pâte Dure*, I–III, HI, 2–5. HVI and HVIII provide information on the background to, and resignation, of Bertin. See also Blondel and Préaud, *La manufacture de Sèvres*, pp.9–19.
73 Sacy, *Henri Bertin*, p.56.
74 Moreau, *Mes souvenirs*, vol.2, p.594.
75 Lewis, *The Advent of Modern Capitalism*, p.103.
76 Sarah Maza, *Vies privées, affaires publiques: les causes célèbres de la France prérévolutionnaires* (Paris, 1997), pp.297–300.
77 Steven Kaplan, *Le meilleur pain du monde. Les boulangers de Paris au dix-huitième siècle* (Paris, 1996), p.592.
78 *Moniteur universel*, no.57, 14–15 Sept. 1789.
79 Lewis, *France 1715–1804*, p.207 and p.217.
80 Félix, *Finances et politique*, p.201.
81 B.N., *collection Bréquiny*, vol.296, p.96, reply to a letter of 31 August 1780.

Part Three
The Collapse of the 'Grand Design'

Chapter Six

Monks, Mandarins and the 'Grand Design'

In his overall assessment of Henri Bertin's *petit ministère*, Silvestre de Sacy, having acknowledged Bertin's major contribution to the reform of agriculture and industry, concluded that, 'what stands out as the most solid aspect of all his innovative work is his *Correspondance littéraire* with the French Mission in Peking, which he supported until the end'.[1] At first glance, this claim might appear to be an exaggeration, given the range of responsibilities that Bertin had carried over a long and varied career. The rationale for the statement, however, lies in the true purpose of the *Correspondance littéraire*, which from a political perspective, was an attempt to justify Bourbon absolutism. The Chinese Emperor, Kien-long, was a legendary, absolutist ruler whom Bertin compared with Louis XIV, and many of Bertin's requests for information from his French Jesuit correspondents in Peking, who doubled up as mandarins to Kien-long, were really attempts to discover the key that unlocked the mystery of the Emperor's success. By the 1780s, France had entered the final stage of its ideological battle between Bourbon absolutism and 'Choiseuliste constitutionalism', a French variant of the seventeenth-century, English constitutional struggle between supporters of Stuart absolutism and their parliamentary adversaries. As the pre-Revolutionary political debate became more intense, Bertin would re-orientate the direction of the 'Grand Design' to focus upon the positive values of absolutism, as opposed to its original target, providing a counter-offensive to the challenge from the French parlements.

Jacob-Nicolas Moreau's contribution during the 1780s would centre upon his work as compiler and curator of his unique archival collection, the *Travaux littéraire*, which provided the fledgling French nation with an historical account of how absolute monarchy in France had shaped its history since the time of Charlemagne in the ninth century. As time passed, this endeavour would be accompanied by more public lectures and a reasonably successful attempt to obtain the recognition, and validation, of his achievements by the government of Louis XVI. As Moreau had once explained to Louis' predecessor: 'It has been necessary to collect them [historical records] in order to know them, and it was necessary to know them before acting.' The parlements had been engaged for centuries in the compilation of their massive, legal archive, primarily related to their function as guardians of the legal history of the monarchy. We have noted that, by the end of the Seven Years' War, their version of the history of the French monarchy had emerged as the principal area of contestation with the crown.[2] Moreau's support for the 'Maupeou coup' of the early 1770s had revealed his conviction that Bourbon absolutism would be holed beneath the waterline if the parlements were allowed to press their claim to be the 'guardians of the nation'. Durey de Meinières, a president of the Paris parlement, had already created his own private library, which had been used extensively by Moreau's chief adversary and propagandist for the parlements, Louis Adrien le Paige. The latter's *Lettres historiques sur les fonctions essentielles du Parlement ...* (1753–4) had become essential reading for parlementary magistrates seeking to advance the historic and political claims of the Paris parlement. Moreau's compelling and influential reply was the twenty-one volumes entitled *Principes de morale, de politique et de droit public puisés dans l'histoire de notre monarchie ...* published between 1777 and 1789. From the 1780s to the Revolutionary debates of the early 1790s, Moreau would continue to employ his scholarly and journalistic talents in the defence of Bourbon absolutism.

In their pursuit of what Michel Antoine has described as 'this great work', Bertin and Moreau would pursue different, if parallel, tasks during the 1780s.[3] Bertin would not only supervise the 'Grand Design', he would also increase his correspondence with the French Jesuit mission stationed in Peking. The consequent exchange of ideas and information would produce what might well be regarded as one of the jewels of the global Enlightenment, the *Mémoires concernant l'histoire, les sciences, les arts ... des chinois*, a rich compendium of information about China during the reign of Kien-long (1735–99).[4] By the 1780s, Bertin's fundamental concern would be to filter the information he received about Kien-long's successful regime for the purposes of the 'Grand Design'. As the Revolution approached, the challenge would be to rescue rather than reform Bourbon absolutism. Moreau would also develop his ideological archive: it would eventually match the archival arsenal that the French parlements had not only constructed over many centuries, but had used to great effect in their *remontrances* against royal edicts during the 1750s. Moreau would now use the research from his archive to prepare the public lectures and publications that would play a vital role in his final assault upon the enemies of Bourbon absolutism. He had learned, long before Foucault, that History, as well as Knowledge, was an instrument of power.[5]

There were precedents for the campaign to restore Bourbon power by studying and cataloguing historical archives: for example, a plan to publish a chronological table of royal statutes, dating from the beginning of the tenth-century Capetian dynasty to 1400, had been conceived by Louis XIV's ministers, but only nine volumes had been published in the half century leading up to Moreau's own *Travaux littéraire*. We know that, during the late 1750s, Etienne de Silhouette had played a significant role in the creation of Moreau's original archival collection, the *dépôt de législation*, originally intended as a research facility for royal ministers and officials seeking historical and legal guidance for the preparation of government policy.[6] The *contrôle général* had continued to assume responsibility for the supervision of Moreau's *dépôt de législation* after Bertin had succeeded Silhouette as *contrôleur général* towards the end of 1759, although its holdings were now transferred from Versailles to 'a large site' especially prepared for it in the place Vendôme in Paris. With Bertin's promotion to the office of secretary of state, the collection had been moved once again, on this occasion from the offices of the *contrôle général* to the *Bibliothèque du roi*. However, Bertin had exploited his influence with the king to ensure that Moreau would remain in charge of the collection, which already contained 1,500 volumes and cartons of judicial, administrative and legal charters. This was clearly a major achievement, which not only led to a marked improvement in the administrative procedures of the government, but also constituted the original foundation of the 'Grand Design'. After his release from the heavy burden of responsibility he had shouldered as *contrôleur général*, Bertin was in a better position to provide Moreau with more support for his plan to expand the *dépôt de législation*, which would house copies, and originals, of charters and other documents relating to public law and the history of the French monarchy. With the creation of this new *dépôt de l'histoire et droit public*, the 'Grand Design' had moved from the drawing-board to the building site for the reformation of Bourbon absolutism, which included the political reconstruction of the French parlements.

*   *   *

For the next thirty years, the joint endeavours of Moreau and Bertin would constitute an obsessive effort to control the sources of French history. In the words of Keith Baker, 'fully conceived, the project required a virtual army of local researchers, engaged in identifying and methodically investigating the thousands of public and private archives in France (to say nothing of those in other countries with collections of materials relating to French history). Lists of documents relative to public law once compiled, the local researchers were then expected to send reliable copies of these documents to a central historical bureau, where their evidence could first be scrutinized for its historical, legal, and political implications by a committee of experts and then mobilized in the service of a controlling definition of the nature and implications of French history and politics'.[7] For a relatively brief period, however, Moreau had been forced to wear two hats, the first as archivist of the original *dépôt de législation*, which had remained in the hands of the *contrôle général*, the second as the archivist of the far more voluminous *dépôt de l'histoire et droit public*, which came under the jurisdiction of Henri Bertin's *petit ministère*. The entire venture provides an interesting example of administrative duplication founded upon personal rivalry, jealousy and departmental competition, the very faults that the 'Grand Design' sought to rectify. Bertin's successor as *contrôleur général*, Clément Charles François de L'Averdy, a former magistrate of the Paris parlement, disliked both Bertin and Moreau.

The historical profile of Etienne de Silhouette has remained 'in the shadows', which does little to illuminate his important contribution to Bertin and Moreau's venture. Not only did he appreciate, and reward, the talents of Jacob-Nicolas Moreau, but he also conveyed his keen interest in Chinese politics and culture to Bertin, an interest that had been popularised by the early physiocrats. As early as 1729, Silhouette had published his *L'idée générale du gouvernement et de la morale des Chinois*: 'Government' and 'Morality' were two interrelated concepts that would assume a high profile in Moreau and Bertin's 'Grand Design'. So far as politics and morality are concerned, the 'French Enlightenment' began in the 1720s, not the 1750s: Jonathan Israel has observed recently that, 'The affinities between Spinozism and classical Chinese thought had been widely noted in Europe since Bayle's *Dictionnaire* had first drawn attention to them ...'.[8] The publication of Montesquieu's *Persian Letters* in 1721 provides an early and striking example of the relationship that would develop between political reform in France and the Enlightenment. The *Persian Letters*, one of the first epistolary novels of the eighteenth

225

century, has been described as 'perhaps the first great popular work of the Enlightenment'.[9]

The opaque terminology used to describe the ambitious, essentially political and intellectual projects of both Bertin and Moreau, the *Correspondance littéraire* and the *Travaux littéraire*, had been employed, from the beginning, to deflect the political flak they knew would be targeted at them. The reasons for this deception, which must have fooled relatively few contemporary witnesses, are obvious; they have formed the rationale for arguments introduced in previous chapters of this work – the fear, especially among the parlements, that both Moreau and Bertin were seeking to destroy, or restrict, their powers, which was partly true, but also the more general fear of a 'despotic' government meddling in personal, local and provincial affairs, especially when it involved taxation and official research into land titles, which was true only if we substitute the term 'bureaucratic centralisation' for 'despotic'. It was alleged, for example, that Etienne de Silhouette had 'planned to collect all the property title-deeds that established the king's rights in France', which again was true, but did not, of itself, amount to dictatorship. Memories of Bertin's own attempt to revalue property in the pursuit of a single land tax (*cadastre*) during his spell as Silhouette's successor as *contrôleur général* during the early 1760s were still fresh, and somewhat alarming, for landed elites. The issue here could be construed as an attempt to create a new socio-economic foundation for the Bourbon state, leading to the abolition of the last vestiges of 'feudalism'. It is hardly surprising, therefore, that Bertin and Moreau were both keen to dress their politically charged, centralising and modernising projects in literary and historical robes, although 'priest's robes' would be a more appropriate metaphor, given their decision to recruit monks and priests as their frontline research workers. Moreau would hire his *correspondents* from the ranks of the 'scholar-monks' of the Benedictine Order, whilst Bertin would choose his personal *correspondents* from the French Jesuit priests appointed by Louis XV to the Apostolic mission in Peking. Neither the Benedictines nor the Jesuits raised any strong objections: they were in no position to do so. With radical philosophe critics within the gates, the Benedictines were desperately searching for a new role to play in the more secular environment of mid-century France, another example of the link between the Enlightenment, religion and politics.[10] In the early 1760s, the French Jesuit mission in Peking had been in a state of considerable despair following the suppression of their order in France. The historic conflict leading to this decision between supporters of 'Gallicanism' (control of the Catholic Church by the French state) and 'ultramontanism' (ultimate control of the Church by the papacy) would be mirrored during the 1760s and 1770s some six thousand miles away in Peking as the mission divided into 'French' and 'Roman' camps. In the process of realising some of the more imaginative dreams of the Enlightenment, a few classic *ancien régime* wines would be poured into new secular and national bottles, a metaphor that really does reflect one of the most important processes of historical change during the eighteenth century.

* * *

In 1762, the year that heralded the suppression of the Jesuit order in France, negotiations had begun with the Benedictine order of Saint-Maur, renowned for its scholarship and proven record of historical research. Its *père général*, deeply disturbed by the fate of the Jesuits, was not only eager to cooperate with Moreau's proposals, but he also expressed an interest in the government's reform of the education system, again related to the onward march of the Enlightenment, and the modernisation of the state. The Benedictine order, which included many prominent teachers and researchers, was anxious to increase its credit in the eyes of the public, and, 'The current of intellectual fashion was turning towards history ... the sweep of universal history [was] a theme for the imagination.'[11] Bertin's enthusiasm for history and antiquity, a major theme of Enlightenment scholarship, was to expand the remit of Moreau's work; the *dépôt de l'histoire et droit*

227

public could now be used to satisfy the research requirements of historians and political analysts. Louis XV had apparently been convinced of the necessity for an archive that would contain exact copies of all the undisclosed records, public or private, that were buried in dusty archives, as well as inventories of these documents that would facilitate the work of those who wished to study the history and public law of France.[12] However, Bertin's fingerprints were all over this royal decree; his commitment to the value of historical research; his wish to open up the archives to the wider public. Moreau was more of a political crusader than Bertin. He certainly shared many of Moreau's political ideals, but, as Bertin's career prospects decreased, his commitment to *disinterested* scholarship increased, a commitment that would enrich his prolonged correspondence with abandoned Jesuit priests in Peking.

Instructions to the compliant *père général* of the Benedictine monks of Saint Maur illustrate the breadth of vision that characterised both Bertin and Moreau's challenging project. On 10 May 1763, Bertin had thanked the *père* for sending him, as he had requested, the names and addresses of monks living in the provinces who were prepared to work for the government. On 19 May 1764, Moreau had given the Benedictines a detailed explanation of the scope of the new project – the creation of a repository that would 'include all unpublished charters that could provide information on the public law of France, or on the ancient customs or particular constitutions of its provinces'. He also informed them that, since the *contrôle général* was far too busy to concern itself with this matter, responsibility had been passed to the new secretary of state, Henri Bertin, who had expressed his enthusiasm for the project. Moreau explained that Bertin 'will honour those members of the *congrégation* [of Saint Maur] who made the best contributions with his particular attention'. A subsequent letter explained that the monks should work on 'the archives of the *cours souverains* [used most often to describe the parlements, but covering all royal courts that judged without appeal], local courts and town councils, as well as those belonging to churches, abbeys, monasteries and secular and regular communities'. To complement Moreau's all-inclusive instructions, Bertin had instructed provincial intendants to send him 'the names and addresses of all those *dépôts* containing charters and documents which would be useful for scholars'. He also suggested that they should give their *sub-délégués* the task of listing archives 'belonging to the *cours souverains*, *bailliages* and *sénéchaussés*, etc. etc.' and, very significantly, 'the charters held by individual seigneurs', thus resurrecting the fears of privileged and powerful property owners. This was an extraordinary, nationwide trawl. Did it mask another attempt to resuscitate Silhouette's campaign to introduce a land survey in order to establish the title-deeds of the crown? There had been widespread discontent among the princes of the blood in 1762 when it was revealed that Louis XV had decided not to regard the principality of Dombes, which he had acquired from the comte d'Eu, as crown property, declaring that it was his personal possession. Opposition to 'government interference' would increase pro rata as Moreau's research net was cast even more widely in the 1770s and 1780s, provoking more apprehension among property-owners of all ranks.[13]

Meanwhile, cartloads of charters and other historical documents were rattling their way to Moreau's headquarters in the place Vendôme. By 1766, after pressure from Moreau, a more authoritative 'committee of experts' would be created, composed of scholars in the fields of diplomacy, history and public law. We have unearthed the agenda of a meeting that Moreau had scheduled for Saturday, 30 May 1765, which was sent to Bertin. It was composed of eleven items: item eight, 'to be raised with Bertin', sought 'his opinion on the cabinet de M. le comte de la Launy'; item nine sought Bertin's views on 'copying the charters of Cambray'. Clearly, Bertin had assumed ultimate responsibility for the more delicate decisions that the committee was obliged to take. He also had the last word on a thorny issue that would be raised repeatedly over the next couple of decades – funds to run the increasingly costly enterprise, including payments to individuals for the exacting work they undertook. Originally, Moreau, following an agreement made in August 1762 between Bertin and Louis XV, had been granted an annual sum of 6,000 *livres* 'as payment for the *Travaux littéraire du roi*'. By 1766, Moreau was forced to ask for additional funds, and, again as a result of an agreement between Bertin and the king, he was granted an additional annual sum of 4,000 *livres*. To supplement this source of income, Bertin tried to tap the rich resources of the Catholic Church. In one letter to the bishop of Orléans he explained that he needed more financial support for the *Travaux littéraire* which covered 'public law and the diplomatic and ancient history of the kingdom'.[14]

One of the most respected scholars to join Moreau's revised 'committee of experts' was Louis George Oudart de Bréquiny, an eminent member of the prestigious *Académie des inscriptions et belles-lettres*, who had already participated in the research leading to the long overdue publication of Louis XIV's *Ordonnances des rois de France de la troisième race*. He had also spent a few years in England during the mid-1760s copying charters and other documents relating to the early French monarchy that had been housed in the British Museum and (posing some danger for a Frenchman in the 1760s?) the Tower of London. From the evidence contained in the *Collection Bréquiny*, Moreau's principal researcher emerges as an indefatigable worker, keen to access any documentary source that he stumbled upon. On one occasion, he informed Moreau that he had discovered '15–16 large packets of title-deeds, unknown even to the curators [of the Tower of London]!'.[15]

By the end of the 1760s, Moreau and Bertin must have been more than satisfied with the progress of their expanding *dépôt de l'histoire et droit public*. Although the collection would continue to expand for another twenty years, it already contained around 6,500 copies of charters, a reflection of the professional work that had been conducted by the monks of Saint-Maur. At the end of 1769, Bertin had succeeded in acquiring the *archives de la Dombes*, which probably contained a great deal of information that Louis

XV preferred to keep secret, as well as many priceless documents contained in the *Trésor des Chartes*. On 15 November 1770, the duc de la Vrillière reported that Louis XV had praised Bertin and Moreau's efforts, and, as a token of his appreciation, had asked Armand Bignon, director of the *Bibliothèque du roi*, which continued to house part of Silhouette's original, government archive, the *dépôt de législation*, 'to hand over the title-deeds and original copies of some 30,000 charters housed in the *Bibliothèque*' to Bertin and Moreau.[16]

* * *

Jacob-Nicolas Moreau had discovered his mission in life. Henri-Léonard Bertin had supported him from the beginning, although he had never given his much-esteemed colleague a blank cheque: Bertin had always been in overall charge of their joint 'Grand Design' to reform the Bourbon monarchy. However, his *Correspondance littéraire* with China would increasingly become a personal quest, especially after he was forced to resign as secretary of state in 1780. This is hardly surprising: released from his ministerial duties, he found the time to devote the last phase of his public life to scholarship and intellectual curiosity, whilst Moreau would oversee the expansion and integration of the *dépôt de l'histoire et droit public* into the official structures of government, although still under the watchful eye of the now ex-secretary of state. Bertin had originally received support for his 'Chinese connection' from Louis XV and madame de Pompadour, whose fascination for all things Chinese, especially porcelain, was widely recognised. Bertin's original brief, however, was to discover, through the agency of the group of French Jesuit missionaries in Peking, everything that related to the success enjoyed by one of the greatest of all Chinese emperors, Kien-long. The project was not entirely original: the first French Jesuit presence in China had arrived in Peking in February 1688. Bertin's venture was had been launched in the 1760s with the assistance of one of his disciples, the 'revolutionary' minister we discussed in Chapter Five, Jacques Turgot. They had recruited two young Chinese converts to Catholicism, Louis Ko and Etienne Yang, as their intermediaries with the Jesuit mission in Peking; both had spent a considerable time in France training to be Jesuit priests.

From the beginning, their mission would extend beyond their religious brief to cover political, military, social and, in particular, economic affairs. France was anxious to find compensation for the loss of so many colonial territories as a result of the Seven Years' War, and Bertin, as a minister responsible for the French *compagnie des Indes*, realised that China, under Kien-long, had recovered her role as a world economic power. Turgot prepared a list of fifty-two topics that Ko and Yang were instructed to use as guidelines for their mission; they covered Chinese agriculture, trade and industry, government, public law, and the arts and sciences.[17] Bertin was always keen to offer Kien-long a return for his proposed cooperation. For example, in addition to personal gifts for the Emperor, Ko and Yang were obliged to take lessons on the operation of 'an electric machine that might interest the Chinese', and, having completed an extended educational tour of manufacturing sites in France that included the silk works in Lyon, Ko and Yang praised the introduction of new spinning-mills, adding that 'Chinese workers could, and would, benefit from these ingenious French inventions'.[18] Ko and Yang finally set out on their perilous voyage to Peking on 17 January 1765. The former wrote a farewell letter to Bertin in which he assured the minister 'before heaven and earth, that your Highness will remain an immortal memory in my heart'.[19]

The journey to Peking would take almost ten months, the monsoon seasons dictating the times when ships arrived and departed. Delays of up to a year in the receipt of information between France and China would pose major problems for Bertin and the missionaries in Peking throughout their long relationship. All correspondence would go through the Jesuit *procureur général* in Canton, *père* Lefebvre. Canton was the bonded warehouse for all European commerce; foreigners were not always welcome in Peking. In one of Ko's early letters to Bertin, he explained how difficult their mission would be, given the considerable socio-cultural gap between China and France: 'We were too young when we left China to appreciate all the customs of our own country. Individuals here cannot interfere in matters that do not directly concern them ... affairs are so ordered that one cannot go beyond one's station in life without somebody wanting to know why.' Something of this behaviour, associated with all authoritarian regimes, still manifests itself today. Life was especially dangerous for Catholic missionaries in the field, who periodically faced imprisonment and sometimes martyrdom. Confronted with all these obstacles, one is truly surprised by the huge volume of information and materials that were despatched to Bertin. Part of the explanation lies in the fact that the recipient was a generous human being, but a very hard taskmaster. On 20 January 1767, Bertin had thanked Ko and Yang for all their efforts, but suggested that more could be done: 'Everything that helps us to forge better links between the French and the Chinese should be of interest to you, and I urge you to exploit every opportunity that arises.' In October 1768, Yang reported that he had collected information on canal and road building, as well as 'the machines used by the Chinese for irrigating rice-fields'. But Bertin's *Correspondance littéraire* was not just the personal conceit of a government ex-minister; it provided a rich source of information for the French government, including the development of its twin foreign policies, those of the official government and the King's *secret du roi*.[20] One of the most remarkable, and revealing, consequences of Bertin's relationship with the Jesuits in Peking was that the 'modernisation' of French politics and society would be influenced by reports of policies adopted by an absolute ruler in China. This was the contradiction that lay at the very heart of the 'Grand Design', explaining why, as political reform was replaced by bloody revolution during the early1790s, Bertin and Moreau's hopes would collapse as the barricades were being constructed.

During the decades preceding the Revolution of 1789, Ko and Yang continued to pay their debt to Bertin by providing him with information on the society, economy and governance of China, although their work would become more sporadic as periodic bouts of religious persecution impeded their efforts, and, as was the case with Moreau's *Travaux littéraire*, other religious 'volunteers' would be recruited into the ranks of Bertin's clerical clutch of 'correspondents'. In the Chinese case, they would be the French scholar-priests and 'mandarins of the Emperor Kien-long' belonging to the Jesuit mission of Saint-Sauveur in Peking. By the late 1760s, Bertin had recruited one of the most erudite and remarkable of all these 'mandarins', Joseph Amiot. Amiot, who had arrived in the city of Peking in 1752 and would remain there until his death forty years later, would not only prove to be a loyal friend of Bertin, but one of his most prized correspondents. Thanks to the constant stream of information he provided, Bertin was able to reveal to the savants of the 'French Enlightenment' that, thousands of miles across the ocean, a 'Chinese Enlightenment' was also flourishing.

* * *

The fact was that Ko and Yang, like their superiors, were swimming against the tide. The decade of the 1770s witnessed profound changes in the relationship between France and the wider world, as well as between the French government and the governed. Not only did a new democratic regime, the American Republic, appear in the west, but, in the east, the old autocratic Empire of Russia was flexing its imperialist muscle and expanding beyond its existing boundaries: the threat to Poland in the east and Turkey to the south was particularly worrying for the French, or, to be more precise, to Louis XV's *secret du roi*, which had originally focused on obtaining the Polish crown for the prince de Conti. The French were right to be worried, since external, as well as internal pressures would cause the shaky edifice of Bourbon absolutism to implode in 1789. Both Moreau's *Travaux littéraire* and Bertin's *Correspondance littéraire* would be affected by these momentous changes. At the beginning of the

1770s, events had appeared to be moving in the right direction. Many of the constraints that had restricted Moreau and Bertin's ability to implement the 'Grand Design' had been lifted by what one historian has described as 'the last great demonstration of royal authority in France' – Maupeou's coup against the parlements in 1771. We established in our previous chapter that the coup was a recognition of the fact that a rising tide of democratic and constitutional change, fuelled, in part, by massive social unrest, was undermining the very foundations of Bourbon absolutism, at a time when the reputation of the monarchy was at an all-time low.[21] Little wonder, then, that Louis XV and, to a lesser extent, Louis XVI, continued to favour, and support, the work of Moreau and Bertin, although this support was not always applauded by their ministers.

For example, as a direct result of Maupeou's coup, Moreau was invested with the authority to march his researchers into the very heart of the enemy's defences – the archives of the Paris parlement. They had pursued their work in enemy territory throughout the 1770s, making a major contribution to Moreau's *Plan des travaux littéraires ordonnés par Sa Majesté*, a most confident and impressive statement of the 'Grand Design', whose publication was delayed until 1782, in part as a result of Bertin's customary caution when dealing with politically sensitive issues.[22] At first sight, then, 'Maupeou's revolution' (1771–4) appeared to have realised one of the principal objectives of the project to renovate Bourbon absolutism – the political emasculation of the parlements. As for Bertin, his *Correspondance littéraire* with Jesuit priests in Peking during the 1770s would focus, *inter alia*, on the external threat to France – Russia's advance into Poland and Turkey. He would also extol the virtues of the Chinese 'Enlightened Despot', Kien-long, in Bertin's eyes a Rousseauesque 'Legislator' whose achievements, if imitated by Louis XV and Louis XVI, just might improve the dismal and deteriorating relationship between the masses and the monarchy. Jacques Turgot, as *contrôleur général* in the mid-1770s, had supported both the attack on the parlements and the related attempt to strengthen the authority of the monarchy. His typically confrontational experiment in 'social scientific' government, as we have seen, was founded upon the introduction of a series of rational social, economic and administrative reforms, which, for Bertin and Moreau, went too far, too fast, in the direction of 'participatory democracy'. The distinctly authoritarian message of Confucian political philosophy provided the solution for Bertin. He was worried that the advance of public education, the increasing power of the press, and the political implications of support for the American *republic* were subverting public opinion in France. Both Turgot and, to a certain extent, Bertin, who never under-estimated the complexity of the problems confronting absolute monarchy, fell from power as a result of their failure to repair the 'fault lines' that existed between the conservative foundations of Bourbon absolutism, specifically the role of the monarch, and the radical implications of embryonic, bourgeois, constitutional democracy. Bertin and Moreau did realise, however, that if their 'Grand Design' were to succeed it would have to become more 'democratic', more overt, as opposed to its early, covert operations.[23] But how could one achieve this goal, and maintain the concept of absolute monarchy? A sizeable section of the National Assembly, encouraged and informed by the pamphlets of Jacob-Nicolas Moreau, would try, unsuccessfully, to square this particular circle from 1789 until 1792, the year that the first republican government in French history was announced.

There are other indications that the Maupeou coup enabled Moreau and Bertin to open doors that had originally been closed to them. The Bréquiny collection includes references to two files, dated March 1773: *Observations sur les 20 volumes manuscrits de la Bibliothéque de M. Bertin* (a reference to the *dépôt de l'histoire et droit public*), and *Notes sur les manuscripts de M. Bertin concernant la Cour des Aydes* (*sic*). The first file contained extracts and memoirs from the *Chambres des comptes*, the second, a volume of official reports on the activities of the *cours des aides* covering the period 1360 to 1539. Bréquiny informed Bertin that he was producing 'a table of contents' for the former, and an account of what the latter contained. The significance of this information is that both the *chambres des comptes* and the *cours des aides* were 'sovereign courts', responsible for the supervision of royal finances, the king's domain, and the collection of indirect taxes. They contained information that was of great value to the crown, as well as to the princes of the blood, and we have seen how contentious this issue had become, generating widespread concern amongst the less privileged landowners who worried about the possible introduction of a land survey and a universal single tax. On these very controversial matters, Bertin had form![24]

Finally, it was in 1773 that Moreau, sensing that the tide was flowing in his direction, had published one of his seminal works, the *Leçons de morale, de politique et de droit public, puisées dans l'histoire de notre monarchie*. It was a work that highlighted the main themes upon which the 'Grand Design' was being constructed. Keith Baker summarises them as, 'the constitutional legitimacy and political necessity of *strong monarchical authority* [emphasis added], the evils of the feudal regime, and the intimate relationship between royal power and national liberty'. David Bell has identified several links between Moreau's publications and the development of the relationship between the monarchy and French nationalism, some dating back to his *Observateur hollandais* in the 1750s. Sadly for Moreau, the dismissal of chancellor Maupeou on the 24 August 1774, along with the *contrôleur général*, the abbé Terray, signalled the collapse of this 'last great demonstration of royal authority in France', which included, as David Bell convincingly argues, a pronounced injection of national sentiment.[25] In May 1774, the death of Louis XV, who had maintained his shaky support for Maupeou until the end, precipitated the chancellor's political demise, leading to the return of the ageing Maurepas. For Maurepas, absolute monarchy required at least one of Montesquieu's 'checks and balances', the parlements or the involvement of the nobility, to avoid accusations of 'despotism', a political reality that explains, in large measure, the failure of Maupeou's coup.

Maupeou's dismissal triggered a spate of memoirs and pamphlets that refined the nature of the conflict between the crown and its critics: some of them would furnish much of the script for the final, dramatic events of 1787–9. Critics of the monarchy included Guillaume-Joseph le Saige, whose iconoclastic *Catéchisme du citoyen* was burned in public in 1775 by order of the parlement of Paris as 'seditious, subversive of royal sovereignty, and contrary to the fundamental laws of the state', and Gabriel Bonnot de Mably, whose two-volume work *Observations sur l'histoire de France*, which had originally been published during the 1760s, was revised and published in the immediate aftermath of Maupeou's coup, and would be re-published on the eve of the Revolution.[26] It was this onslaught on Bourbon absolutism, tainted, post-Maupeou, by accusations of 'despotism', that had prompted Bertin and Moreau to publish their *Mémoire sur la constitution politique des ville et cité de Périgueux*, which, reiterated the fundamental, traditional principles they would still be promoting in 1789. A comparison of the basic propositions contained in the Périgueux document with those to be found in the works of Saige and Mably, will reveal where Bertin and Moreau's ideological manifesto, the 'Grand Design', now began to leave the path followed by those critics of Bourbon absolutism who were seeking far more radical solutions.

Périgueux was Bertin's political base, so it is not surprising that when he was asked by the leaders of Périgueux's municipality to support them in a dispute with the intendant of Bordeaux, he had promised to throw his considerable weight behind Moreau's *Mémoire*. The dispute was feudal in origin. The property-owning citizens of Périgueux claimed that, having been granted the status of a 'free city' for services rendered to the king in the Middle Ages, they were not subject to the payment of the *franc-fief*, a heavy tax payable every twenty years by non-noble owners of noble land, and currently being levied by government tax-collectors with the support of the intendant of Bordeaux. Moreau and Bertin seized what they saw as an opportunity to confirm the reformist credentials of the French monarchy that, in their opinion, had their roots in the early Middle Ages. They extended the debate to cover many of the fundamental issues that divided 'republicans', such as Saige and Mably, from born-again absolute monarchists, such as Bertin and Moreau. Moreau tells us that he had consulted the 'immense list of sources' that Bertin's brother, the abbé Bertin, a local historian, had collected over many years, and that he had spent over six months of his precious time writing the Périgueux pamphlet.[27]

The historic role of the French monarchy in what Marxist historians have described as 'the transition from feudalism to capitalism' constituted one of the most important issues that Moreau's Benedictine monks, sifting, quill in hand, through thousands of royal charters since the reign of Philip Augustus (1180–1223) had been asked to address. Feudal/seigneurial laws and property rights in France would continue to operate until the 1790s. There was, for example, the levy, primarily upon the peasantry, of the *corvée* (forced labour on state roads), and the persistent practice of awarding and exchanging feudal fiefs among the monarchy and princes of the realm. On the eve of the Revolution of 1789, two-thirds of the revenue from a fief granted by Louis XVI to the duc d'Orléans came from land rents, the rest from seigneurial dues.[28] Bertin, Moreau and their sometime disciple, Turgot, would all have rejected revisionist arguments that eighteenth-century 'feudalism' was little more than a phantom: in their view, feudal legal and social survivals constituted a serious obstacle to their reform programmes. The privileged orders, including magistrates in the Paris parlement, constantly rejected proposals on the abolition of the 'remnants of feudalism'. When Dupont de Nemours, the renowned *physiocrate/économiste* and ally of Turgot and Bertin, was told that the parlement had blocked the former's reform of the *corvée* in 1776, he almost exploded: 'My old blood boiled in my old veins', he wrote, 'when I learned that the well-heeled courtiers [*escarpins*] of Versailles and Paris had decided to oppose the abolition of this barbaric slavery.'[29] The divide between the 'old order' and the new was widening: Bertin and Moreau were well aware of this, and were doing all they could to close it.

Their principal conclusion was that to save the monarchy, the 'feudal nobility' had to be sacrificed in favour of an alliance of the bourgeoisie and the robe nobility, and they had chosen the history of Périgueux as 'a unique example of a French town that, in order to resist feudal tyranny, had secured its freedom from weak kings'. Unfortunately, 'mediocre monarchs' would prove to be the major fault line of the 'Grand Design' that placed so much emphasis on the necessity for an absolute, as opposed to a constitutional, monarch. Their Périgueux *Mémoire* traced the defence of the town, led by the bourgeoisie, against foreign invaders and predatory feudal lords since the age of Charlemagne. Its heroes are the propertied bourgeoisie; its villains 'anarchic' feudal seigneurs. Reading the Périgueux *Mémoire* reminds one of Pierre de Belloy's patriotic popular play, *The Siege of Calais*, performed in Paris in 1765, whose hero is the town's bourgeois mayor. If Moreau did not actually see the play, he must have heard of its patriotic message, the disasters of the Seven Years' War having pushed patriotism towards the top of the political agenda. Marx's thesis on the link between early modern communes and the 'rise of the bourgeoisie' was taken from early nineteenth-century French liberal historians, Guizot in particular, who had actually studied the historians and pamphleteers of the late eighteenth century.[30]

Both Mably and Saige supported, *grosso modo*, Bertin and Moreau's conclusions concerning the history of *ancien régime* feudalism. Again, this will surprise only those who fail to detect any radical reforming ambition behind their 'Grand Design', or, indeed, those who are unfamiliar with the erudite debate on political and social reform that ran for most of the eighteenth century, from the publication of Fénelon's *The Adventures of Telemachus, Son of Ulysses*, in 1699, through Montesquieu's *Spirit of the Laws* in 1748 and Rousseau's *Social Contract* in 1762, to the second volume of Mably's *Observations sur l'histoire de France*, in

1788. The historical outline in Saige's *Catéchisme du citoyen* (1775) relied heavily on Mably's *Observations sur l'histoire de France*, which, in turn, argued that it was the 'bourgeois' communes that ended the period of 'feudal anarchy' that had developed after the end of Charlemagne's reign.[31] This was precisely the message that Moreau's Benedictine monks were extracting from their laborious study of medieval charters, as Mably, in fact, admitted. He confessed that his *Observations* 'rested on foundations proved by enlightened ministers, who, in their concern to legitimate the authority of absolute monarchy, had invited scholars "to rummage in the dust of our archives, and to publish these precious collections of documents"'. Henri Bertin, obviously the target of this comment, might have thought, 'With friends like this, who needs enemies?', and this was, indeed, one of Bertin's problems. The enemies of the monarchy were increasing in number, and it was all too easy for a moderate reformer like Bertin to find himself rubbing shoulders with more radical critics. However, he must have felt some satisfaction that the campaign for 'open access' to the archives that he and Moreau were assembling was providing results, if not always those he wanted. He had realised, as early as the 1760s, that pressure for more 'open government' could no longer be reserved for dedicated readers of the *Encyclopédie*.[32]

Since Mably, Saige, Bertin and Moreau all adopted an historicist approach to the evolution of contemporary government and society, it is not surprising that we should find more agreement than disagreement between them over the related issue of *ancien régime* class distinctions, especially the distinction between 'nobles' and 'bourgeois'. We know that they agreed, in very general terms, that the 'feudal nobility' had played an anarchic role in the early creation of the French state: by 1789, the abbé Sieyès, in his famous pamphlet, *What is the Third Estate?* would argue that it was the Third Estate, rather than the traditional nobility, that now formed the bedrock of the nation. However, on this extremely controversial issue, Bertin and Moreau once again adopted a more cautious, less radical approach than their critics.

As was the case with so many of their contemporaries, they could not ignore 'the rise of the bourgeoisie', but this did not mean that they had to elevate them to the top of the political and social pyramid. Their compromise solution was to entertain the possibility of a major transfer of political power from a declining feudal aristocracy to a *new elite* that would be dominated by *liberal* nobles and the propertied, industrial, commercial and cultured bourgeoisie, a process that had been weakening rigid class distinctions in French society for centuries.[33]

As we saw in the first chapter of this work, property, industry, commerce and a Catholic culture were the pillars upon which the Bertin family fortune had been constructed. Bertin had also learned from his own experience as a former *contrôleur général* and ministerial supervisor of the *Compagnie de Indes*, as well as from his contacts with '*physiocrat/économistes*' such as Vincent de Gournay, Dupont de Nemours and Turgot, that if France were to prosper it would have to re-invent itself as a global, trading power. Within the context of this debate, Voltaire's disciple, the abbé Gabriel-François Coyer, had already suggested in his *La Noblesse commerçante* (1756) that, 'for the nobility who did not fight', involvement in commerce would prove a better option than constantly begging handouts from the crown.[34] The Périgueux *Mémoire* had provided an historical blueprint for a new elite that would allow the nobility to retain much of its socio-economic and cultural pre-eminence. In an attempt to win over those who believed that the economic and socio-cultural authority of the aristocracy was worth defending, Moreau pointed out that the 'bourgeoisie' in the province of Guienne (which included Périgueux) had always included 'persons of the highest birth … the most illustrious names, including those of princes who did not worry about being called "bourgeois"'. The world was changing, and this change affected government as well as society in general. In January 1783, Louis XVI would propose that a new government committee should be formed, a *comité des finances*. Its remit would be to receive regular financial accounts from individual ministers in an attempt to create a more cohesive and coordinated system of government, a move that had been supported by the abbé de Bernis as early as the 1750s. Marie Antoinette and two of her protégés, the marquis de Castries and the marquis de Ségur, ministers of war and the navy respectively, fought hard to defeat the proposal. Ségur thought that 'this is a fight to the death between the robe [nobility] and [aristocratic] people like us'. He was right, but the remarkable fact is that the marquis de Castries, for example, was 'the most thoroughgoing aristocratic constitutionalist. He had little love for absolute monarchy and none for Louis XVI.'[35]

This was Bertin and Moreau's 'Achilles heel': they wanted a far more flexible noble 'caste' but not one that was prepared to throw out the absolutist baby with the constitutionalist bathwater. We should also note that Charles-Maurice de Talleyrand's aristocratic family, one of the oldest in France, hailed from the Périgord, the same province as Henri Bertin. Louis XVI would be present when his father died in December 1788, but it was the same Charles-Maurice Talleyrand, bishop of Autun by the grace of God, and Louis XVI, who would preside over the National Assembly in 1790, and then lead the campaign that led to the passing of the *Civil Constitution of the Clergy*, one of the most revolutionary and divisive pieces of legislation to be passed during the entire Revolution that placed the Catholic Church, with its vast wealth, in the hands of the French state.[36] By the late eighteenth century, the 'nobility', whether of the sword or robe, had become a distinctly permeable concept.

This process of rapid change can be detected in the work of the abbé Mably. By 1775, never one to miss the chance of predicting Armageddon, Mably had become far less charitable to the parlements than his sometime ally, Guilluame-Joseph Saige. Unique and uncompromising in the application of his main thesis that French history was (is?) composed of repeated bouts of revolution and disorder, he insisted that his reading of the past had convinced him that there had been no stately, evolutionary progress of the parlements and the crown leading to the creation of the mid-eighteenth-century system of Bourbon absolutism (as le Paige in his *Lettres historiques* ... had argued). For Mably, the real lesson to be drawn from the Maupeou fiasco was that the public now realised that the parlements were 'paper tigers' that 'did not have the force that we attributed to them ... [Maupeou] has made us recognize a great truth: that any order of citizens that favors despotism in the hope of sharing it, digs an abyss beneath its feet and draws a storm about its head'.[37] Bertin and Moreau were dismayed by such apocalyptic visions: the parlements had played an historic role in the political and juridical evolution of the French state, as Louis XVI had been obliged to recognise on his accession to the throne in 1774. Neither Bertin nor Moreau objected to the existence of a traditional, noble 'estate'; they just wanted to break its *political* power, just as they wished to break the political, as opposed to the juridical, power of the parlements. They agreed that one had to recognise the fact that social differentiation was increasingly being dictated by the colour of one's money, rather than by the colour of one's blood. Mably described the nobility as 'lacking corporate solidarity'; Bertin wanted to stay with Montesquieu's concept of the nobility as a traditional and institutional constraint on the monarchy. In Roslin's portrait of Bertin, he is seated by a desk that has a copy of Montesquieu's most influential work, *L'esprit des Lois*, prominently displayed upon one of its shelves.[38]

There can be no doubt that for many traditional court nobles, all this verged upon the treasonable, and Bertin was frequently held to account on this very charge by his enemies at Versailles. Moreau, although favoured by Louis XVI and Marie Antoinette, was also treated with suspicion by many court nobles, not just on account of his close friendship with Bertin, but because, throughout his life, he refused to accept, or purchase, any noble title. His personal *mémoires* record that, during the winter of 1773–4, he became completely disillusioned by 'le fanatisme des partis' at Versailles. In his eyes, the Maupeou coup had definitely failed to develop the 'Grand Design'.[39]

What really separated Bertin and Moreau from their more radical critics, however, was, in the first place, the absolutist powers of the Bourbon monarch, and, secondly, the relationship between the absolute monarch and the 'nation', and it was the latter of these two related concepts that now began to occupy the thoughts of radical critics, such as Mably, dealing another hefty blow to the 'Grand Design'. Moreau's ideal monarch was Charlemagne, who had combined 'sovereign will with rational counsel, which he sought not in the stormy confusions of a populous assembly but in the careful deliberations of experienced administrators' (such as his friend Henri-Léonard Bertin!). This had allowed Charlemagne to wield a power that was 'essentially absolute, but essentially enlightened'. This was the formula that Bertin had been developing – absolute government tempered by the reforming zeal of the Enlightenment. The majority of Louis XVI's ministers in the late 1770s were less than impressed by a Charlemagne dressed in the robes of the Enlightenment; for Bertin and Moreau, however, it was essential that the monarchy should be seen as an enlightened force in the evolution of French history. In their opinion, it was the monarchy, not Montesquieu's 'intermediate powers', that had supported the expansion of municipal power; and it was the monarchy, not the nobility or the parlements, that had protected the integrity of the nation. 'Where does the unity of France lie?', Moreau asked. 'It is not in possessions, but in the action of the power that protects them; because this power is a *unitary one*, and its actions must always be guided by justice. Liberty and Property, these are the rights of subjects; Freedom and Direction, these are the rights of the Prince.'[40] Sadly for Moreau, this was proving to be too simple a sermon to preach to an increasingly confused and troubled congregation.

Whether one accepted the desirability of a 'unitary power' or not, the fundamental issue for both Saige and Mably, an issue that would ultimately seal the fate of Bourbon absolutism, concerned the relationship of the sovereign to the people. For the former, it lay with the 'national assemblies' that had restored the Estates General following the feudal anarchy of the Middle Ages. The Estates 'alone had the authority to approve laws, to consent to taxes, to fix the succession to the throne, and even to change the constitution', and the Estates were to be elected, and mandated (Rousseau again), by 'the people'. It is hardly surprising that the parlement of Paris had decreed in 1775 that Saige's *Catéchisme de citoyen* should be burned in public. The truly revolutionary shift of *sovereign* power from the monarchy to the people reflected the zeitgeist of the times, witness the success of the rebels in the 'United States'. It constituted the revolutionary thrust of Mably and Saige's assault upon Bourbon absolutism, whether they were prepared to admit it or not, and Saige would become increasingly ambivalent on this key issue as the Revolution of 1789 beckoned. This explains why Bertin and Moreau would be so reluctant to throw their weight behind the *constitutional* monarchists in 1789. They realised that 'Power to the people' would ultimately strip 'the Prince' of his *sovereign* authority. Many conservative reformers in 1789, including the future counter-revolutionary activist, the comte d'Antraigues, would remind their revolutionary opponents that even Jean-Jacques Rousseau believed that monarchy was the form of government most appropriate to large states.[41] But this was not the main bone of contention between the warring factions during the 1770s and 1780s as the purchase of the monarchy on the people become less effective. Mably's model monarch was a 'democrat' seeking to restore the historic liberties and unity of a *sovereign* people; Saige, also influenced by historical precedence, and profoundly influenced by Rousseau's *Social Contract*, was convinced that 'the nation can create, destroy and change all of the magistracies of the state, modify the constitution, or annihilate it totally, in order to form a new one'.[42] This was not precisely, or even remotely, what Bertin and Moreau had in mind. For them, as for Turgot, men and women in the street had to be educated before they could participate, on a property-owning basis, in the brave new world being constructed by the Enlightenment. Most European rulers of third world countries would adopt this approach in their dealings with their native populations for most of the twentieth and part of the twenty-first century.

Mably's analysis was unquestionably radical, but to understand its *revolutionary* potential, it needs to be placed in a wider context than that allowed by Keith Baker's persuasive, political theories. Certainly, the conflict of political wills that characterise the last decades of the *ancien régime* was an important factor, but, as Mably himself stressed, simmering social revolt, occasioned in part by free market measures such as the re-introduction of the freedom of the grain trade, had injected a popular, revolutionary dynamic into the movement for change. Maupeou had recognised the danger and had supported the abbé Terray's plans to curtail the freedom of the grain trade in 1770, and, subsequently, to declare a partial bankruptcy, but this had done little to resolve the crisis. Turgot had re-introduced the freedom of the grain trade in September 1774, but one year on, the scale of the *guerre des farines* had shaken the government to its foundations. We know that the entire period from 1768 to 1775 encompassed some of the most severe socio-economic crises in French history, comparable with those of 1709–10 and 1788–9. This failed to alter Bertin and Moreau's conviction that economic stability could only be achieved under the paternal leadership of an absolute monarch.

Finally, there was one fundamental issue that united both 'neo-republicans' like Mably and Saige, and 'traditional absolutists', like Bertin and Moreau, and that issue was political morality. From Fénelon's *Telemachus* in 1699 to the 1788 edition of Mably's *Observations sur l'histoire de France*, a spotlight had always been placed on the moral aspects of political and economic theory. Adam Smith thought that his *Theory of Moral Sentiments* (1759) was superior to his more famous *Wealth of Nations*, published eleven years later. In 1750, Rousseau had invoked his 'noble savage' to answer the question posed by the Academy of Dijon – 'whether the restoration of the sciences and arts has contributed to the purification of morals'. In one of his exaggerated attacks on contemporary moral behaviour, the abbé de Bernis blamed the duc d'Orléans (Regent during the early years of Louis XV's life) for having launched 'The spirit of disbelief and dissipation that could be found throughout society. The Regent's lack of religious conviction and his debauchery soon found imitators in a nation whose own character led them to copy, in a servile fashion, the virtues and vices of their masters; corruption became common-place.'[43] Michael Sonenscher has argued that, from the beginning, Physiocracy contained a strong moral message, and 'To contemporaries it was the moral side of Physiocracy that was the more immediately obvious.' Perhaps this is why Bertin never really severed his links with a movement that influenced so many intellectuals in mid-eighteenth-century France. Sonenscher is also of the opinion that the *sansculotte* emblem of republican politics during the French Revolution 'would be connected to a way of thinking about morality and politics that has largely disappeared from view' (until the recent scandal of MPs' expenses in Britain and the European Union?).[44] As for Moreau, from the first drafts of his *Leçons de morale, de politique et de droit public* in 1773 to the unfinished *Principes de morale*, in 1789, morality, political and personal, would play a pivotal role in his analysis of contemporary society and politics.

What was the French monarchy's response to the moral critique adopted by so many eighteenth-century scholars? Keith Baker has argued that, as early as the 1750s, the institutional order of the Old Regime was already 'displaying a series of tensions', one of which 'expressed itself in the inconsistencies and vacillations of government policy; in the inefficiencies, contradictions, and arbitrariness of much of the administrative system; and in the weakening of personal respect for the monarch as a symbol of unity'.[45] We have argued throughout this study that the immoral, almost amoral, behaviour of Louis XV unquestionably weakened personal respect for the monarchy; it was the flaw in Bertin and Moreau's 'Grand Design' from the beginning. In his memoirs, which were written after the Revolution, Jacob-Nicolas Moreau finally felt able to express his personal opinion of Louis XV's actions. He actually dates the beginning of the end of Bourbon absolutism from the time that Louis XV refused to curb his lust for sexual pleasure and leave his mistress after the battle of Metz in 1744 in order to pursue his royal duties. Moreau bemoans his lack of moral fibre: 'Alas, immediately after his return to Paris, we see the first symptoms of that moral contagion that led to the loss of his family and led his nation to an apostasy that sounded the death knell for France', a comment that could have come from the pen of the abbé Bernis fifty years earlier.[46]

There can be little doubt that Bertin came to share this judgement on Louis XV, but how could he express it in open court? Louis and Pompadour had been responsible for his elevation to the highest position at Versailles; he had, in the course of his career, been privy to the more unsavoury secrets of Louis XV's sexual affairs. Then there was the even more intimate and long-running saga of his elder brother, rotting away in a prison. Ironically, the ill-fated marquis de Fratteaux died in the Bastille a few months before Bertin's disgrace. Did the death of his brother help to explain the relief he exhibited when his enemies at court forced his dismissal from the government? Whether it did or not, it is reasonable to suppose that it was Bertin's intimate knowledge of Louis XV's personal life that secured him such a favourable settlement when he finally packed his ministerial bags in May 1780. Although one of his new enemies at court, Jacques Necker, had ensured that he would lose his position as secretary of state and director of the Sèvres factory, he was allowed, as was the custom, to retain his salary as a minister.

But what really pleased Bertin was the fact that he was allowed to continue his *Correspondance littéraire* with China, as well as his membership of the committee of savants that supervised Moreau's *Travaux littéraire*, the nationwide collection of charters and documents that continued to flow into the government's offices in Paris. From 1780, Bertin's energies, after a short interlude of semi-retirement on his estates of Chatou and Montesson, would increasingly be consumed by his personal *Correspondance littéraire* with the Jesuit mission in Peking, or what Bussière referred to as his 'intellectual colony in China'.[47] In other words, Moreau, *historiographe du roi* since 1774, would continue his lifetime career as a government spokesman and curator of the rapidly expanding, future national archives, while Bertin, a member of the *Académie des sciences*, would pursue his career as an Enlightenment scholar and editor of that invaluable collection of publications on Chinese government and society, the *Mémoires conçernant ... les chinois.* He also found time to acquire one of the best personal collections of Chinese antiquities in Europe.

When comparing these two men, very different in character, but totally united in their concern for the fate of the monarchy, we must remember that Bertin, unlike Moreau, was a 'grand seigneur', with a lifestyle to match. Apart from his family possessions in Périgueux and Bourdeille, he had purchased the estates of Benon and des Essarts from the widow of the duc de Trémoille et de Thouars in 1767 for the sizeable sum of 390,000 *livres*. This purchase made Bertin *premier baron* of the province of Saintonge as well as *premier baron* of the Périgord. His income from all these estates, added to his salary as a secretary of state, had helped to fund the construction in the late 1760s of his new, custom-built château of Chatou, on the banks of the Seine, just seventeen kilometres from Paris. His ownership of the seigneurial estates of Chatou and Montesson confirmed his standing as a major landowner and *'grand seigneur'*.

Bertin's modest château no longer exists, but in the spring of 1781, it became his permanent home. Bertin's brother, Louis Augustin, abbé de Brantôme, acted as the family accountant and steward of the estates, while his sister, Marguerite de Creissac, who had settled in the château with her sister Marguerite de Belle-Isle in the early 1770s (she died in 1779), took charge of the household and the gardens. This was a family affair: not one of these four Bertins of Chatou ever married. The château itself was not imposing; the renowned architect Soufflot appears to have received instructions from Bertin that the building should present the aspect of a bourgeois villa, rather than an 'aristocratic pile'. Despite its unpretentious architecture, however, Chatou welcomed guests who were guaranteed good, local cuisine and cosmopolitan conversation, occasionally supplemented by musical and theatrical entertainment. Those who enjoyed a walk around the extensive grounds would have been rewarded with the view of a magnificent grotto (one of Soufflot's principal achievements), and rear gardens that swept down to the Seine, providing access to an island that formed part of the estate. Both of Bertin's sisters were noted for their gardening and agricultural achievements, which included the cultivation and care of vines, orange trees and market produce, including the humble, but very much *à la mode*, potato. This region was 'casserole [*pot-au-feu*] country'; part of its income was drawn from local peasants growing market-garden produce for home consumption and local markets.[48] Chatou may well have provided Bertin with a decade of relative peace and tranquillity before the hammer-blow of the Revolution forced him to emigrate.

Unfortunately for the besieged French Jesuit priests in Peking, however, Bertin's heavy commitments as a minister, followed by the problems associated with his dismissal in 1780, meant that he had been obliged to place his correspondence with the mission on the back burner. The 'decline and fall' of the Bourbon monarchy in France was mirrored by the slow collapse of the French Jesuit mission in Peking. *Père* Amiot (Bertin's most reliable and productive correspondent and a favoured mandarin of the Chinese Emperor, Kien-long) and his handful of loyal priests in the Peking mission had depended upon their annual 'monsoon letter' from Bertin for their survival, just as Moreau's Benedictine monks continued to depend upon him for access to research programmes as well as a role in the introduction of new educational reforms. The Jesuit priests in Peking had survived several major crises during the 1760s and 1770s: apart from the occasional bout of persecution from the Chinese state, they had been forced to accept the suppression of the Jesuit order in France during the early 1760s, then the 'profound sadness' of receiving the news of Pope Clement XIV's world-wide abolition of the Jesuit order on 23 July 1773, and now they were apparently faced with the loss of their saviour at Versailles, Henri Bertin. The shock of being abandoned, first by their mother country in the 1760s, then by Rome a decade later, had already torn the mission apart. The 'cult of the nation' was being worshipped in Peking as well as in Paris.

251

Led by Amiot, some of the French Jesuit priests had fought to defend the interests of France in China; others had decided to retain their allegiance to Rome and join the papal, Portuguese-dominated, organisation for foreign missions, *La Propagande*. The French mission house in Peking became a tiny microcosm of a macrocosmic struggle between national and papal international institutions. This bitter personal battle between 'nationalists' and 'ultramontanes' would not be resolved until 1780s when the French Lazarists performed the last rites and ceremonies over the former Jesuit mission in Peking.[49] The role played by the papacy in weakening the reputation of the French mission in Peking prompted Bertin, whose attachment to the Roman Catholic faith had already been tested by the rationalist message of the Enlightenment, together with Amiot's consistent advocacy of Confucian philosophy, to accuse the Pope of peddling unintelligent and ridiculous policies in China through the agency of *La Propagande*. Ministers raised on the Gallican traditions of Louis XIV had never really worshipped the papacy.[50]

The attack on the French mission in Peking was both a warning sign of France's decline as a great power in the Far East, and a serious blow to Bertin's *Correspondance littéraire*. From the 1760s, the quite extraordinary amount of information on Chinese governance, foreign policy and culture, along with the materials, books and translations of scholarly Chinese publications that he had obtained from his French Jesuit 'mandarins' in Peking, had helped to shape the 'Grand Design' for the reform of Bourbon absolutism. Rowbotham's study of the French mission in Peking led him to the conclusion that Sinophilism in eighteenth-century France 'became the most important element in the larger movement of cosmopolitanism, relativism and universalism'.[51] In other words, the Enlightenment had its satellites across the globe. The scholarly contribution of Bertin's *Correspondance littéraire* to this universalisation of Enlightenment scholarship should receive the credit it deserves. Its reach extended far beyond the specific task of renovating the French monarchy to encompass a truly astonishing array of topics that included a discussion of 36,000 large folio volumes representing 'the largest corpus of traditional learning and literary expression in Chinese history ever assembled in one uniform edition': measures to cure small-pox; Mesmerism, 'la physique des chinois' according to Amiot; as well as botany, astronomy, mechanical engineering and hydraulics. Bertin was always keen to exchange information with Kien-long's Chinese mandarins, via the French Jesuit priests in the mission. In November 1777, he sent one of the French priests a copy of a work he had read by 'an Englishman, M. Priestley, who has become celebrated through his discovery of different kinds of air'.[52]

As a consequence of his long involvement with so many of the aesthetic and intellectual debates associated with the Enlightenment, coupled with the pleasures of semi-retirement, Bertin appears to have adopted something of a new persona as he entered, in 1780, the sixtieth decade of his life. We see the emergence of a more liberal, broad-minded approach to religion and society. One outcome of this aspect of his personal development was a sustained interest in Confucian philosophy, which, as we will see below, offered a powerful perspective on the *moral* philosophy that compensated for his growing disenchantment with Roman Catholicism. It was also a consequence of his life-long attraction for Chinese culture and philosophy. Visitors to Chatou were invited to admire his Chinese pagoda in the grounds and the *cabinet chinois*, complete with a bust of Confucius, in his library. It is quite possible that a copy of *père* Amiot's *Life of Confucius*, which the author completed in 1784, could be seen, strategically placed on one of Bertin's coffee tables. This was no personal whim; it was an acknowledgement of the appeal of Kien-long's China for French intellectuals, especially the physiocrats, since the 1750s.

It is also possible that Bertin's support for Confucius as a moral philosopher was associated with a sense of guilt about his prolonged involvement with Louis XV's quite immoral behaviour, highlighted by the fact that Bertin himself appears to have been almost ascetic in his personal life. Whether this is true or not, Bertin did not allow Confucian precepts on *political* morality to interfere with his dedication to the principle, as opposed to the personal conduct, of Bourbon absolutism as a system of government. Hence the keen interest we find in the *Correspondance littéraire* on military affairs. One of Kien-long's claims to fame was his creation of 'Greater China', achieved, in part, by the defeat of 'the Mongol hordes', a defeat which did not always run parallel with policies being pursued by the French government. However, it was Russian and Turkish ambitions that worried French foreign secretaries: in 1772, Russia's role in the partition of the Polish state had struck 'a major blow for French assumptions in Eastern Europe, because the French had sought a strong Poland and a strong Turkey as a barrier to Russian expansion'.[53]

Two years later, Bertin despatched a letter to two of the founding members of his *Correspondance littéraire*, the Chinese missionaries, Ko and Yang, whom Bertin and Turgot had trained to be their 'men in Peking', instructing them to do all they could to activate 'a regular correspondence' between the courts of Versailles and Peking, citing Russia as a particular problem. Bertin had also asked Ko and Yang to deliver translations of two *mémoires* on military weapons and tactics to the Emperor, the first by the comte de Guibert, the second by the marquis de Puységur, as well as Saint-Rémy's three-volume *Traité de l'artillerie*.[54] By the 1780s, however, the incoherence and contradictions that characterised French foreign policy, the *secret du roi*, the failure to sustain the Franco-Austrian alliance, and the decision to participate in the War of American Independence, for example, meant that the Russian threat, which was very real in the early 1780s, lost much of its urgency. As it turned out, the fatal flaw in French foreign policy by the eve of the Revolution proved to be the Pyrrhic victory over Britain during the American War of Independence, and France's relations with Prussia and Holland, not the threat from Russia.[55]

By the 1780s, however, Confucian ideas on the personal role of the sovereign proved to be of greater interest to Bertin than the threat of Russian expansion, a myopic view that may have reflected the impact of growing internal dissension within French government and society. One Chinese historian who has recently sought 'to re-define the concept of Enlightenment from a global perspective' has argued that the seventeenth-century ideological pillar of despotism, the Chen-Zhu neo-Confucianist school of philosophy, was partly responsible for the fall of the Ming dynasty in 1644, and that 'a group of giant thinkers', reacting to this tragedy, had purged Confucianism of its 'despotic' tendencies.[56] 'Confucianism purged of its despotic tendencies' was precisely what Bertin was seeking; it might succeed where 'Maupeou's despotism' had failed. *Père* Amiot, a fellow-traveller on the road that Bertin had chosen to walk, encouraged his patron to look again at Confucius, 'who not only advocated simplicity, candour, moderation, and respect for old age and wisdom, but *"submission to legitimate authority"* [emphasis added]'. Bertin thought that this principle of submission to legitimate authority just might provide the 'missing link' for the 'Grand Design', that it might replace Bossuet's sanctification of the monarchy – 'kings as vicars of God on earth' – with something more in touch with the increasingly secular ethos of late eighteenth-century French society – 'kings as enlightened representatives of the people'.[57]

Should we dismiss all this as evidence of Bertin's naiveté? By no means: a recent popularisation of Confucian philosophy by a Chinese academic, Yu Dan, sold more than 10 million copies, while, in 2005, the president of the Chinese Republic, Hu Jintao, reminded his audience that it was Confucius who said that 'Harmony is something to be cherished'.[58] This is an interesting comment in the light of Bertin's search for a political philosophy that would unite the nation under the Bourbons.

Jacob-Nicolas Moreau had less time, and inclination, than Bertin for all this philosophising. A letter he wrote to one of his researchers, who had evidently expressed some criticism about the purpose of the *Travaux littéraire*, provides us with an excellent account of his more mundane responsibilities in 1780s: 'We meet once or twice a week in the minister's office to deal with the *Travaux littéraire*. We have been gathering material for the past

255

fifteen years. The place that houses our collection is, to coin a phrase, my historiographical workshop. It contains a great many books, copies of inventories relating to documents from the *Chambre des comptes*, and catalogues of all known historical records, together with an immense number of copies of charters and diplomas, unknown until now. On top of all this, I catalogue all the holdings in my *cabinet de l'histoire et droit public*, following the same system adopted by M. Buffon for his *cabinet de l'histoire naturelle* in the Jardin du Roi.'[59]

In fact, Moreau was engaged in far more important matters than those he was willing to explain to his correspondent. Partly as a consequence of Bertin's semi-retirement, he was making an abortive attempt to create a literary academy founded upon the work of his *Travaux littéraire*. This was followed by a successful attempt to combine the *dépôt de législation* that Moreau had originally launched with Silhouette's encouragement in 1759 and which had remained under the jurisdiction of the *contrôle général*, with the massive *dépôt de l'histoire et droit public*, which had been placed under Bertin's *petit ministère* since its creation in the early 1760s. The new amalgam would be known as the *Bibliothèque de législation, administration, histoire et droit public*. Much to Moreau's delight, the *Travaux littéraire* had been greatly enriched since the Maupeou coup of the early 1770s by the deposit of copies of charters that Moreau's researchers had unearthed in the archives of the parlement of Paris. The 36,000 unpublished charters in the *Bibliothèque du Roi*, together with the smaller, but priceless, collection housed in the *Trésor des chartres*, would retain their separate identities.[60]

Moreau's idea of transforming his *Travaux littéraire* into an academy appears to have been related to the opposition that he, and many of his Benedictine researchers, had faced from the owners or stewards of private and public archives. Criticised on many fronts, he was convinced that his work did not enjoy the public esteem that it merited. The *collection Moreau*, which includes many letters of complaint to Moreau, provides considerable evidence for his unhappiness on this score. There was the cleric who explained that, although he wanted to send him the title-deeds of individuals who had received gifts of property from the crown, there would be a big fuss if he forced them to make inventories of their properties before a notary. Far more disturbing was the demand from one of the comte d'Artois' officials that he be given access to Moreau's *dépôt de l'histoire* in order to retrieve information on the rights that Artois enjoyed on his estates, especially those in the Ponthieu region. The original intention of the *dépôt* was to identify the rights of the crown not the royal princes. Many correspondents were prepared to co-operate, but sought payment for their trouble. M. de Montenault from Puteaux near Neuilly-sur-Seine explained to Moreau that he had sent Bertin eight manuscript folios relating to the royal domain that his father had worked on for thirty years: 'one would think that they would have made my fortune,' he added, 'but they were just deposited in your collection. What reward can I expect from the king?' The answer appears to have been 'nothing'.[61]

These were sensitive issues, matters that Moreau's Benedictine monks had to deal with on a daily basis. Moreau's response was to seek more official government support for his *Travaux littéraire*, confident that he had the support of the head of the Benedictine order. There was also a personal motive behind the request that Moreau's work should be given a higher status: his well-founded fear that he would never gain entry to the prestigious *Académie française*.[62] He tells us that it was the publication, in 1757, of his savage, satirical attack on '*Philosophes et Encyclopédistes*', the *Mémoires pour servir à l'histoire des Cacouacs*, that had ruined his chances of becoming an academician.[63] Bertin, a member of the *Académie des inscriptions et belles lettres*, an institution that Moreau criticised as 'antiquated', was reluctant to give his support, primarily because he thought it was inappropriate. By the 1780s, one detects certain strains and tensions in the relationship between Moreau and Bertin, although Moreau would remain loyal to Bertin until the latter's death.

Given their failure to attract enough official support, Moreau and his Benedictine monks had to be satisfied with a reconstituted '*comité d'histoire et de droit public*'. From 1781 to 1784, it would hold its fortnightly meetings in the office of the Keeper of the Seals, Hué de Miromesnil, who had been appointed to his post after the fall of Maupeou in 1774. The *Travaux littéraire* had finally been given the official blessing of the monarchy, confirmed by a royal edict of 3 March 1781. Despite the fact that Miromesnil was an old enemy of Bertin (as *premier président* of the parlement of Rouen, he had frequently crossed swords with him in the early 1760s when Bertin was *contrôleur général*), he nevertheless agreed that he should continue to serve on a committee that now included some powerful figures. In addition to the marquis de Paulmy, whose personal library was one of the best in France, we find Moreau's right-hand man, the long-serving and indefatigable Louis Georges de Bréquiny, alongside two of the best historians in France, both Benedictine monks, Dom Michel-Jean-Joseph Brial, who was just over forty years of age in 1784, and Dom François Clément, who was seventy.

With the encouragement of both Bertin and Miromesnil, Moreau now felt that it was time to publish 'a general collection of all the records relating to French history and public law' in his possession. It would represent the realisation of a dream he had cherished since the beginning of his extraordinary personal odyssey – to do for France what the English *historiographe royal*, Thomas Rymer, had done for England, only better.[64] On 11 October 1788, a final reorganisation of Bertin and Moreau's work confirmed the official take-over by the state: 'Meeting with the chancellor every two weeks, this body was expected to confer with him regarding "all of the useful work destined to aid the legislation, purify the history [*sic*], and maintain and preserve the essential principles of the monarchy".' This was a fitting tribute to a man who, with Bertin's encouragement and leadership, had already constructed his own monument for posterity. By 1786, Moreau's 'ideological archive ... had grown to the extent of 46,432 copies and 1,042 original documents, together with an inventory of 19,150 pieces and summary abstracts of another

21,758'. The archive would continue to expand until 1789, when it was placed at the disposal of the nation.[65] Bertin and Moreau would continue to defend the 'essential principles of the monarchy' through the early phase of the Revolution of 1789: having nailed their colours so firmly to the mast, they had little choice but to fight on. For Bertin, the fight would end with his death, in exile, on the very day the First French Republic was announced (22 September 1792). Moreau, on Bertin's advice, did not emigrate, but would live long enough to experience the 'enlightened military despotism' of Napoleon Bonaparte – a form of government that was not a million miles away from Kien-long's regime in China.

Notes

1 Sacy, *Henri Bertin*, p.155.
2 Baker, *Inventing the French Revolution*, p.32. See also Richard Bonney, 'Absolutism: What's in a Name?', *French History*, vol.1 (1787), pp.93–117.
3 Michael Antoine, *Le secrétariat d'Etat de Bertin 1763–1780* (Paris, 1948), pp.17–18.
4 Published in 17 vols. (Paris, 1777–1814), the last two volumes published after Bertin's death.
5 Baker, *Inventing the French Revolution*, p.84.
6 Moreau, *Mes souvenirs*, vol.1, pp.67–8.
7 Baker, *Inventing the French Revolution*, p.40.
8 Jonathan Israel, *Radical Enlightenment: Philosophy and the Making of Modernity, 1650–1750* (Oxford, 2001), pp.544–5.
9 Montesquieu, *Persian Letters*, trans. by Margaret Mauldon (Oxford, 2008). Montesquieu's work reveals a similar interest in the links between religion, politics and history that would characterise the work of Bertin and Moreau.
10 Nigel Aston tells us that, 'The 26,500 monks, and to a lesser extent, the 37,000 nuns, were easy targets for Enlightenment writers. They tirelessly rehearsed the salacious stories that sold pamphlets and squibs rather than reported up-to-date news at odds with the mythology.' *Religion and Revolution in France* (London, 2000), p.20.
11 John McManners, *Church and Society in Eighteenth-Century France* (Oxford, 1999), vol.1, p.524.

12 Moreau, *Mes souvenirs*, vol.1, pp.130–1.

13 B.N., *collection Bréquiny*, vol.155, pp.226–39 and pp.247–8.

14 B.N., *collection Moreau*, vol.290, p.4 and p.53; Baker, *Inventing the French Revolution*, pp.78–80.

15 B.N., *collection Bréquiny*, vol.75, p.220, *Mémoire sur l'état actuel des recherches dans les archives de Londres*.

16 Baker, *Inventing the French Revolution*, p.84; Moreau, *Mes souvenirs*, vol.1, p.217; B.N., *collection Moreau*, vol.296, p.27.

17 For the historical significance of Turgot's list, see Poirier, *Turgot*, pp.102–14.

18 *Bibliothèque de l'Institut de France*, mss.1515–26, *correspondance des RR. PP. Jésuites missionnaires en Chine* avec H. L. J. Bertin (hereafter C.L.). 12 vols., ed. Henri Cordier, vol.6, p. 23. *Mémoire sur ce qui les chinois doivent voir en France avant de retourner en Chine*. We have drawn extensively on this quite remarkable collection of documents.

19 Lewis, 'Henri Bertin and the Fate of the Bourbon Monarchy', p.75.

20 Lewis, 'Henri Bertin and the Fate of the Bourbon Monarchy', pp.75–6.

21 Sonenscher, *Before the Deluge*, pp.31–2.

22 Baker, *Inventing the French Revolution*, p.75.

23 For a comprehensive account of Turgot's reforms see Foncin, *Essai sur le ministère de Turgot*, pp.545–74.

24 B.N., *collection Bréquiny*, vol.75, p.192.

25 Baker, *Inventing the French Revolution*, pp.79–81; David Bell, *The Cult of the Nation in France: Inventing Nationalism, 1680–1800* (Cambridge, Mass., 2001), pp.63–6, pp.87–91 and p.247, n.90.

26 Baker, *Inventing the French Revolution*, p.111.

27 Moreau, *Mes souvenirs*, vol.2, p.304.

28 Miller, 'Modern Bureaucracy or Feudal Bricolage', p.29.

29 Foncin, *Essai sur le ministère de Turgot*, pp.422–3. Dupont's blood was not that old. Born in 1739, he had another forty years to live, and a fortune to make – in America!

30 Furet, *Marx and the French Revolution*, p.177 and p. 52. David Bell argues that Belloy's play could be defined as more patriotic than nationalistic, representing a relatively early stage in the complicated evolution of French nationalism. *The Cult of the Nation in France*, p.45.

31 Baker, *Inventing the French Revolution*, pp.144–50.

32 Baker, *Inventing the French Revolution*, pp.46–7.

33 Lewis, 'Rising Tides', p.7.

34 Sonenscher, *Sans-Culottes*, pp.290–1.

35 Hardman and Price, *Louis XVI and the comte de Vergennes*, pp.20–2.

36 J. F. Bernard, *Talleyrand: a Biography* (London, 1973), pp.58–92.

37 Baker, *Inventing the French Revolution*, p.49.

38 Lewis, 'Rising Tides', p.12.

39 Bussière, *'Etude sur Henri Bertin'*, *BSHAP*, vol.36 (1909); Moreau, *Mes souvenirs*, vol.2., pp.327–8.

40 Baker, *Inventing the French Revolution*, p.53; Bell, *The Cult of the Nation in France*, pp.136–9; Moreau, *Mémoire sur la Constitution politique de la ville de Périgeux* (Paris, 1775), p.310.

41 Gordon McNeil's 'The Anti-Revolutionary Rousseau', *American Historical Review*, vol.58 (1953), pp.808–23, still provides one of the best accounts of this facet of the multifaceted Rousseau; Baker, *Inventing the French Revolution*, pp. 123–6.

42 Baker, *Inventing the French Revolution*, p.53 and p.124.

43 Sonenscher, *Sans-Culottes*, p.134; Bernis, *Mémoires et lettres*, i, p.41.

44 Sonenscher, *Before the Deluge*, p.190; *Sans-Culottes*, p.61.

45 Baker, *Inventing the French Revolution*, p.115.

46 Moreau, *Mes souvenirs*, vol.2, pp.564–5.

47 Bussière, *'Etude sur Henri Bertin'*, *BSHAP*, vol 36 (1909), p.133.

48 Bussière, *'Etude sur Henri Bertin'*, *BSHAP*, vol.33 (1906), pp.236–44.

49 Lewis, 'Henri Bertin and the Fate of the Bourbon Monarchy', p.81.

50 C.L., vol.10, 21 Oct. 1768.

51 A. Rowbotham, *Missionary and Mandarin: The Jesuits at the Court of China* (Berkeley, 1942), p.280.

52 C.L., Bertin to Cibot, 30 Nov. 1777.

53 Black, *From Louis XV to Napoleon*, p.121.

54 C.L., vol.8, 1 Jan. 1774.

55 Black, *From Louis XIV to Napoleon*, pp.134–7; Munro Price, *The Fall of the French Monarchy: Louis XV, Marie Antoinette, and the Baron de Breteuil* (London, 2002), pp.8–17.

56 Zhang Zhilian, 'Unfinished Enlightenment: the Chinese Experience', in *Centres and Margins: Enlightenment from Belfast to Beijing* (Paris, 2003), pp.214–5.

57 Lewis, 'Henri Bertin and the Fate of the Bourbon Monarchy', p.88.

58 Timothy Garton Ash, 'Confucius Can Speak to us Still', *The Guardian*, 9 April 2009.

59 B.N., *collection Moreau*, vol.296, p.102. For Buffon, 'classification served merely to comfort the mind; it did not correspond to anything real'. This conviction confirmed his belief that 'science was tending to become the catalogue of an inventory'! See Jacques Roger, *The Life Sciences in Eighteenth-Century French Thought* (Stanford, 1997), ed. Keith Benson, trans. Robert Ellrich, p.166.

60 Moreau, *Mes souvenirs*, vol.2, p.321; Baker, *Inventing the French Revolution*, pp.73–4.

61 Moreau, *Mes sourvenirs*, vol.2, p.160.
62 Moreau, *Mes souvenirs*, vol.2, pp.296–7.
63 Moreau, *Mes souvenirs*, vol.1, pp.53–4.
64 Moreau, *Mes souvenirs*, vol.2, pp.339–40; Baker, *Inventing the French Revolution*, pp.80–2 Antoine, *Louis XV*, pp.859–61. Antoine suggests that, over the years, the 'grand design' of Bertin and Moreau gave birth to 'a kind of ministry of scholarship [*érudition*]', and that Louis XV gave his complete support to the venture. Rymer's renowned twenty-volume collection, the *Foedera, conventions, literae et cuius-cunque général acta publica* ..., had been published in London between 1704 and 1732. Rymer, who had conceived the project, died in 1713.
65 Baker, *Inventing the French Revolution*, pp.83–4.

Conclusion

Endgame

On Sunday morning, 10 May 1789, the church bells of Chatou summoned parishioners to an ordinary meeting; unfortunately, these were not ordinary times. If some villagers thought the meeting had been arranged to choose their tax collector for the year, others were afraid that the bells tolled to warn them that 'the brigands are coming'. Throughout the village, there was a sense of excitement and apprehension generated by the unprecedented political upheaval of '1789'. Bertin and the guests who had joined him for a quiet weekend in his modest château must have been aware of the revolutionary events that were transforming the Estates General of the realm into a National Assembly, officially recognised on 17 June, as well as the sporadic violence that was sweeping through many regions of the country, violence that would spiral into the most dramatic and revolutionary popular rebellion in the history of eighteenth-century France – the Great Fear of the spring and summer of 1789. If by some quirk of fate, one or two of them had not registered the revolutionary potential of what was happening around them, then the presence of a detachment of mounted police at the gates of the château, despatched in response to a request from Bertin, would have left them in no doubt of immediate danger. For some reason, however, the mounted police left Chatou the following day, providing an opportunity for an angry crowd of men, women and children to demolish part of the impressive wall that Bertin had recently constructed (at a cost of 32,000 *livres!*) to keep poachers out of his seigneury of Chatou and Montesson. The construction of the new wall involved the closure of traditional pathways, maintained by local inhabitants, that had been used to reach their fields, or take their produce to market, which explains why, when a few of Bertin's guests summoned up the courage to remonstrate with the crowd, they were attacked with 'hatchets, picks, and halberds' amid shouts of, 'We want our old road back!' and 'Long live the Third Estate!'. The revolutionary politics of Paris and Versailles had arrived at the small village of Chatou.[1]

The *journée* of 11 May, Bertin's personal 'Bastille Day', marked the culmination of a campaign of popular resentment, beginning in the 1760s, against the modernising zeal of Henri Bertin, the *grand seigneur*. Relieved of his national responsibilities as a member of Louis XV's government, Bertin was now implementing, at village level, the reforms he had introduced on a national level as a minister responsible for agriculture in the 1760s and 1770s.[2] As we noted in earlier chapters, he had faced fierce, national resistance from the working population during these decades, especially in the agricultural and mining sectors. A detailed explanation of the violent resistance he faced in his own back yard during the late 1780s throws a more focused light on the socio-economic and political reasons for the failure of the 'Grand Design' he had constructed with his friend, Jacob-Nicolas Moreau. Bertin would learn that the 'missing link' between the major aims of this thirty-year project and the causes of the Revolution of 1789 was not to be found in China, but at home, in Chatou. What had always been missing from the 'Grand Design' was an intelligent analysis of the *social* grievances that had fuelled popular rural and urban rebellion from the 1760s to the Revolution. The *Grande Peur* of 1789 would force both reformers to realise that the replacement of the 'feudal nobility' by a new elite that included liberal nobles and bourgeois, but excluded even the higher echelons of the peasantry, was far too restrictive.

264

They should have cast their sociological net wider, to include, at least, the sizeable property-owning peasant. From 1789 to De Gaulle's Fifth Republic of 1958, successive governments would learn to recognise, and fear, the political and economic significance of the 'coq du village'. Peter McPhee has reminded us that, 'Until 1791, the Revolution was overwhelmingly popular: sweeping changes occurred within a context of mass optimism and support.'[3] The early, radical course of the Revolution of 1789 would be determined by peasants and artisans, not the bourgeoisie and the nobility, and the 'Grand Design' had little to offer this disenfranchised majority.

*　*　*

However, this is to fall back, prematurely, upon the historian's first response, and all too frequently his or her last resort, when confronted with complex historical problems – hindsight. During the pre-Revolutionary period of the late 1780s, Bertin and Moreau were busy making history, not reflecting upon it, and they were doing so in 'times that tested men's soul's' as Tom Paine described them. They would fight to the bloody end, effectively, the creation of the First French Republic in September 1792, to preserve what they could of their thirty-year long campaign to rescue Bourbon absolutism from the serried ranks of its enemies, which included Tom Paine. We must, therefore, record their stubborn devotion to what was rapidly becoming a lost national cause, before returning to our local study of Bertin's personal, but related, campaign during the 1780s to 'modernise' the small village of Chatou, which will focus, primarily, upon the socio-economic consequences of modernisation as conceived by ruling elites.

As for Bertin's right-hand man, Jacob-Nicolas Moreau, he had continued to dedicate his life during the 1780s to the implementation of the programme set out in his *Plan des travaux* of 1782, which focused upon archival research into the history of the French monarchy, conducted, in large measure, by hand-picked historians and the Benedictine monks of Saint Maur and Saint Vannes. The information that Moreau and Bertin were gathering from their exhaustive investigation would prove to be of increasing interest to monarchist supporters (*monarchiens*), such as Jean-Joseph Mounier, as the Revolution of 1789 approached. Mounier would launch a last-ditch campaign to defend a 'long constitutional tradition, emphasizing the continuity of the fundamental laws of the monarchy', which precisely mirrored the agenda of 'Grand Design'.[4] As late as 1789, the vast majority of deputies and their constituents would see themselves as monarchists of varying hues, and Moreau, again loyal to his *Plan des travaux*, did more than anyone during the 1780s to promote this image by publishing articles and delivering lectures throughout the country, highlighting the role played by the (undefined) 'people' in the evolution of the Bourbon monarchy. In February 1783, a local official in the town of Corlay in Brittany had thanked Moreau for sending him a copy of his *Plan des travaux*, adding that, having read it, he had decided to set up 'a society of letters, science and history, which would operate under the title of the Patriotic Society of Brittany'. In November 1784, an admirer from Chartres told Moreau that 'everyone here is full of admiration' for his 'lecture on the history of France', adding that he would be most grateful if he would accept 'the feeble analysis that I have just made of it'. In May 1786, an official of the presidial court of Valence told Moreau that his recent lecture on the monarchy had made a very big impact on those who had heard it, or read the printed version. He concluded that they had 'every right to hope that your scholarly researches, and the wise conclusions you derive from them, will prove useful in correcting the present disregard for the truth, and the errors which have necessarily ensued'.[5] But, although these were comments that reflect the degree of success that Moreau had achieved as a royalist propagandist, they were reactions from the bourgeois boulevards, not from the fields and workshops of the 'lower orders'.

Nonetheless, Moreau found that appeals for his assistance increased as the immediate Revolutionary crisis, which began with the convocation of the first Assembly of Notables on 22 February 1787, gathered momentum. His sympathisers could draw upon his 'apparently endless series of instalments of the *Principes de morale, de politique et de droit public puisés dans l'histoire de notre monarchie, ou discours sur l'histoire de France*. They could also consult the '50,000 documents, drawn from 350 different archives, an inventory of 41,000 pieces, and many other volumes of manuscripts'.[6] Never before in the history of the French monarchy had so many appeals been made to Clio, the muse of history, in so short a time. Moreau also played a prominent role in the 'pamphlet war' that sharpened the political rivalries of the late 1780s. He tells us in his memoirs that as a 'Constitution de France did not exist ... we had to work on historical documents to make one', and this is precisely what he did. His pamphlet rejecting radical proposals on the creation of a constitution, the first part of which was published before the end of 1789, was entitled *Exposition et défense de notre constitution monarchique français.*[7] On 1 October 1789, a constitutional act that provided a blueprint for a constitutional monarchy was introduced. Many of its provisions were acceptable to *monarchiens* like Moreau and Mounier. Unfortunately for Moreau, the constitutional act was only the beginning of a two-year debate on the fate of the Bourbon monarchy. The radicalisation of the Revolution, accelerated by the outbreak of war with Francis II of Austria on 20 April 1792, would ensure that the process would end with the abolition of the monarchy and the establishment of the First French Republic in September 1792.

In the same month of that same year, Henri Bertin died in exile. He had worked as hard as Moreau to defend the idea of a reformed Bourbon monarchy, although, like his close friend and colleague, and, indeed, the marquis de Castries, his respect for the personal contributions of Louis XV and Louis XVI had diminished as time passed. Both kings had contributed to the collapse of absolutism in France. During the final years of the 1780s, a disillusioned Bertin would concentrate more on his personal *Correspondance littéraire* with the beleaguered French Jesuit monks in Peking than on the political repercussions of the pre-Revolutionary crisis in Paris, a sure indication that he had become semi-detached from his association with Louis XVI. He was not alone in adopting this stance: for the majority of the French people in 1788 'the monarchy seemed morally and financially bereft, the economy was in trouble and Bourbon diplomacy was in utter disarray, bordering on paralysis'. Mably, in Cassandra mode, had predicted, as early as 1779, that, 'The reign of France, the house of Austria and England is over.'[8] It is not surprising, then, that Bertin's relationship with the French Mission in Peking had begun to deteriorate during the early 1780s. His dismissal as secretary of state in 1780 had obviously undermined his authority over the former Jesuit priests in the Mission, who needed all the help they could get, given the suppression of their order by the French state in the 1760s.

In November 1783, Bertin had received a letter from his most loyal supporter in the Mission, *père* Amiot, which revealed the sense of abandonment that he, and the handful of ex-Jesuits who had decided to stick it out in Peking, were experiencing: 'We once had great hopes for the Mission, but now our enemies are rejoicing because it is three years since we received any news from Europe.' Amiot's 'enemies' were those priests in the Mission who had cut their links with France to support the *Propagande*, the missionary organisation directed from Rome. Explaining that 'things were pretty bad in the Mission', he went on to ask if, 'now that His Highness has renounced the great affairs of state, he has also given up the small inconvenience of writing once a year to Peking?'[9] It appears that the consequences of Bertin's dismissal – the court case over the alleged fraudulent activities of his staff, the decision to settle down with his brother and sister in Chatou – had pushed his *Correspondance littéraire* onto the back burner. There is, however, another possible explanation for Bertin's apparent failure to contact the French Mission, and that was the lengthy delays in the delivery and receipt of mail from Paris to Peking, occasioned by uncertain weather conditions, wars, and fluctuations in trade patterns between Europe and China. In a letter written in December 1784, Bertin assured Amiot that he had only received his three letters of 25 July, 5 and 16 September 1779, towards the middle of 1784.[10]

One thing is absolutely clear: as soon as he had dealt with his legal and domestic problems, Bertin did everything he could to strengthen his association with Amiot and his colleagues, placing renewed emphasis on two of the objectives he had pursued from the 1770s – the acquisition of *curiosités Chinoise*, which included books, furniture and musical instruments, for his personal *cabinet Chinois*, and the compilation of material for the sixteen volumes of *Mémoires concernant les Chinois*. The first volume had been edited, under Bertin's supervision, by the abbé Batteaux in 1776. The fifteenth would be published in 1791, the last volume after Bertin's death.[11] Bertin, who had already spent many years acquiring valuable Chinese antiquities, furniture and merchandise, continued to ask Amiot and his fellow priests to send him the best examples of Chinese literature, sculpture, arts and crafts that they could find. In 1784, Bertin thanked Amiot for promising to send him a copy of his *Life of Confucius* as soon as it was finished, assuring him that 'it would take pride of place in my *cabinet Chinois*'. The following year, he informed Amiot that he had now received his study of Confucius, as well as a Chinese musical instrument called a 'Lo'. As a sign of his gratitude, Bertin said that he was sending Amiot a few cases of wines and liqueurs. Two years later, we find Bertin acting as a broker for the duc de Chaulnes, who, Bertin explained in a letter to Raux, was sending 3,000 *livres* for 'some purchases intended for his *cabinet Chinois*'.[12] All this was, literally and metaphorically, a world away from the Revolutionary turmoil in France.

However, the increased flow of *la chinoiserie* into Bertin's cabinets around this time suggests that he may have realised that the opportunity for expanding his personal collection was finally coming to an end. Far more worrying for Bertin was the fate of the French Jesuits in the Peking Mission, effectively secularised by the abolition of the Jesuit order. Their final surrender would not only have affected the standing of the French monarchy in the eyes of the Chinese Emperor, Kien-long, it would also have curtailed the flow of information on Chinese politics and society that Bertin directed, in the first place, towards relevant government ministers, and in the second, towards the editor of the *Mémoires concernant les Chinois*, Bertin's major contribution to late eighteenth-century knowledge of China. As early as the end of 1783, a very long letter he had written to *père* Bourgeois (responsible for all correspondence with the French priests) revealed that he was concerned about the eventual fate of the Mission, given the profound rivalry that now separated those priests who chose to obey the Pope's orders from those who tried to remain loyal to the French state. He reassured Bourgeois that money to pay 'correspondents' attached to the Mission, notably, Ko and Yang, the first emissaries despatched to Peking by Bertin in the 1760s, had recently been allocated by the government. He then referred to his 'chief correspondent' in the Mission, *père* Amiot, who was not enjoying the best of health, explaining to Bourgeois that he had no wish to put too much pressure on Amiot, but 'I would like to know more about a kind of encyclopaedia that he is preparing for the Emperor, as well as information on the Chinese government's relations with foreign powers'.[13]

Two years later, the promise of money in return for information from his *correspondents* formed the substance of another long, personal letter to *père* Amiot, in which he promised to send him an annual sum every year, 'as a proportion of the money I receive from the king for our *Correspondance*'. He followed this up by pressing him for more information on Chinese religious life, civil affairs, and '*antiquités*'.[14] Bertin's frequent references to religion reflect the turmoil that characterised the daily life of priests in the Peking Mission, as well as his own personal battle with spiritual issues. He had absolutely no time for the way the Vatican ran its Missions in China. In 1786, he launched a bitter critique of the trouble caused by 'stupid cardinals' from Rome: 'I predict that not only will Christianity make no further progress in China, but that it will be increasingly despised. If Saint Francis Xavier had preached the cult of Rome ... he would have been driven out of

China.' These were the opinions of a man who was drifting away, on waves of Gallican and Enlightenment distrust of the papacy, from institutional religion to a more personal, intellectual system of belief, a process that was national in scope. He concluded his letter to Amiot with these words: 'It is the intelligence of the European in Peking that impresses the Emperor, not religion. I have been persuaded that our *Correspondance* and the new understanding of Europe that it brings to China ... is more important for religion than all the correspondence of the [papal] *Propagande.*'[15] Interesting, but was this really what the founders of the 'Grand Design' should have been engaged with in the late 1780s? It appears that Bertin, more than Moreau, had 'lost the plot', along with an increasingly large proportion of the French people.

The late 1780s was a time when the economic and political world was turning on its axis, not a time to be ruminating about Gallicanism, the Roman Catholic Church and Confucius. Louis Dermigny was right to argue that the attraction of the 'Chinese connection', which had influenced French philosophes and physiocrats for over half a century, faded 'as the ethics and exigencies of commercial capitalism began to make a real impact during the second half of the eighteenth century. Imitating China had made some sense during the age of Louis XIV's confessional absolutism, but it was of decreasing value in the age of Louis XVI, when the "rights of merchants" were increasingly being identified with the "Rights of Man", and when French absolutism was being undermined by the rise of "public opinion".'[16] From the 1770s, English tea traders had been pushing the French out of their warehouses in Canton, the bonded warehouse for European trade in China. On 2 February 1787, the renowned French explorer, La Pérouse, informed a French naval official in Macao: 'I cannot hide from you the fact that there is not a single individual representing the French nation here who gives me confidence to put this little *dépôt* back on its feet.'[17] French trade with China would collapse during the 1790s, along with the French Mission in Peking. Bertin had done what he could during the previous

271

decade to assist the flow of French trade, but his claim to fame would rely more on his wide-ranging *Correspondance littéraire*. As one admirer of Bertin's career concluded: 'If France, and through her the West, was able to enter the nineteenth century with an informed sympathy for the China of that time, the credit must given to Bertin's discrete and courageous initiative.'[18]

In this twenty-first century, the word 'globalisation' is frequently employed to explain patterns of economic and climatic change. Before we end our study by focusing upon what appears to be a parochial quarrel, but which was really a microscopic reflection of a national upheaval, Bertin's 'Bastille Day' in May 1789, we should remember that Bertin, despite his apparent lack of concern for political realities in the pre-Revolutionary period, had lived through, and contributed to, the eighteenth-century Enlightenment, a time when the word 'progress' was a word employed as liberally, and often as injudiciously, as 'globalisation' in our own times. Throughout his career, he had been eager to explore new ways of thinking about the wider world at a time when explorers were discovering 'new worlds' across the globe, enabling international commerce to expand and savants to speculate about the impact of global climatic change upon their lives. During the late 1780s, the political and economic crisis that would culminate in the Revolution of 1789 in France did actually prompt Bertin to compare what was happening in his own country with the serious crises that characterised the final years of Kien-long's long reign in Peking. Over the years, Bertin had asked Amiot to send him excerpts from the main Chinese official newspaper, the *Gazette Chinois*. In 1788 and 1789, Amiot supplied Bertin's tireless researcher, Oudart de Bréquiny, with his comments on information contained in the *Gazette*. Brequiny's analysis of these comments provides us with material for a quite remarkable comparative study of France and China during one of the greatest periods of global change. It is clearly beyond our remit to undertake this challenging project here, but in order that we might pay proper respect to the historical value of Bertin's *Correspondance littéraire*, and the debt Bertin owed to *père* Amiot, we should single out the key issues and important data that Bréquiny compiled for Bertin's perusal and subsequent inclusion in the *Mémoires concernant les Chinois*.

In a letter of 12 November 1787, Bertin commented upon the three major themes that regularly made an appearance in Amiot's correspondence around this time – the outbreak of rebellions in many parts of China, economic collapse, and the severe weather conditions that led to famine and suffering on a huge scale in many Chinese provinces. Volume 10 of the *Collection Bréquiny* includes a great deal of information on rebellions in many different provinces of China, focusing in particular on the massive revolt that occurred during the late 1780s on the island of Formosa. Today, of course, Formosa is an independent territory, known as Taiwan, but its independence has never been recognised by the leadership of mainland China. In terms of 'globalisation', the economic crisis facing Kien-long's regime on the eve of the French Revolution was associated with the collapse of trade between China and several European countries, as we noted above. Amiot's excerpts from the *Gazette* concentrate on the internal causes for the economic collapse that led, on 28 February 1788, to an official announcement in the *Gazette* (only distributed to 'grand mandarins', and other top government officials) that the coffers of the Imperial Treasury were empty. Finally, Bréquiny's collection makes it abundantly clear that the famine and revolts that characterised the *Grande Peur* in France during the late the 1780s were also characteristic of the political and economic crisis that occurred during the same period in China, and that adverse climatic conditions contributed to the severity of the crisis that affected both countries. Between them, Bertin, Amiot and Bréquiny were supplying future historians with invaluable information on late eighteenth-century Franco-Chinese relationships.[19] Unfortunately, they failed to realise its relevance to the French political scene in 1789.

* * *

In this study, we have followed Bertin's career on the national, and international, stage from the 1750s to the Revolution of 1789. We end with a brief account of his localised conflict with the inhabitants of Chatou (population – 215 households) and neighbouring Montesson (233 households), which was attached to the seigneury of Chatou until 1789. This historic conflict between a *grand seigneur* and his vassals, repeated in a thousand traditional peasant and artisan communities scattered throughout France, and many parts of Europe and the wider world, was a major factor in the crisis that led to '1789'. Its historical significance lies in its relationship to the increasing alienation, and politicisation, of traditional peasant and artisan communities from the 'new seigneurialism'. It has a particular significance for us, since it provides another socio-economic explanation for the failure of the 'Grand Design', which had been focused upon the creation of the new noble/bourgeois elite that was being formed by the expansion of a more capitalist and commercial society, but which had little to say about mass poverty and unemployment.

In his illuminating comparative study of six French villages, Peter Jones rejects de Tocqueville's suggestion that 'seigneurs had evacuated the local power arena by the end of the *ancien régime* ... On the contrary, the arresting fact that emerges is the continuing relevance to village life of seigneurialism in all six localities. Not only did the seigneurie continue to function as a regulatory institution, but in several instances the titular seigneurs were personalities in their own right.' We can add the seigneury of Chatou and Montesson to Jones' list, with Henri Bertin fulfilling the role of 'a very important personality in his own right'. There were, of course, certain facets of the political, economic and social life of Bertin's seigneury that were unique, as was the case with all six of the villages studied by Jones, the most important being its proximity to the massive Parisian market, just fifteen kilometres to the east. Jean-Marc Moriceau' s exhaustive study of farming in the Ile-de-France, the province that included Chatou and Montesson, explains why we referred above to the '*new* seigneurialism' that was characterised, above all, by the injection of capitalist methods of production. For Moriceau, this modernisation process, which began to accelerate in the Ile-de-France between 1670 and 1720, continued to produce capitalist transformations in the scope and orientation of large-scale farming throughout the eighteenth century. It also led, predictably, to the 'bipolarisation of social structures', and it was this 'bipolarisation' that produced the increasing local animosity towards the Bertin family from the 1760s to the attack on their château in May 1789.[20]

Bertin's personal modernisation programme had begun with the purchase of several properties during the 1760s and 1770s, making him one of the biggest landowners in the Ile-de-France. In this regard, he was obviously following in the footsteps of his ambitious and acquisitive father, Jean Bertin II. In 1759, when he was appointed to the lucrative position of *contrôleur général des finances*, Henri already controlled extensive estates associated with his titles of *baron de Bourdeille, comte de Benon and seigneur de Brantôme, Belisle et autres lieux*, but, for obvious reasons, Bertin wanted to introduce his agricultural reforms on estates nearer Versailles and the expanding Parisian markets. In September 1761, he acquired the domain of Barnwall for 13,000 *livres* from a Scottish captain of the guards who had supported the Jacobite cause of James II. This was followed, in March 1762, by the purchase of the one thousand-acre seigneury of Chatou and Montesson for the bargain-basement price of 160,000 *livres*. The previous owner had allowed much of the estate to fall into ruin, including the château of Chatou, which is why Bertin decided to build a modest new manor house within the perimeter of the old grounds. Periodic purchases of real estate, from Chatou along the Seine to Carrières-Saint-Denis, were made during the 1770s and 1780s: in April 1772, the relatively small fief (just twenty acres) of Malnoue; in 1776, a property in Montesson, followed by more purchases in 1777, 1778 and 1785.[21] Jean Bertin II would have been very proud of his second son.

It was not so much the extent of Bertin's property portfolio, however, that eventually provoked a hostile response from his local community, especially from small owners and market-gardeners, but the methods he adopted to modernise the running of his estates, which, all too often, meant squeezing greater profits from them. Bertin was not a 'feudal noble', but his reforming zeal did more to alienate the farming communities of Chatou and Montesson than many a traditional 'feudal' seigneur. One could say, as Le Roy Ladurie has said of the Burgundian peasantry, that these communities were 'anti-feudal because they were anti-capitalist'.[22] For example, Bertin was keen to implement legislation, such as the *Triage* edict of 1669, which had enabled seigneurs, under certain conditions, to partition common lands. In other words, the new seigneuralism exploited feudal law to implement capitalist projects. As a reforming minister, he had persuaded Louis XV in September 1763 to pass a decree forcing peasants to justify in law their rights to pasture animals on common lands. In 1775, he invoked article four of the *Triage* edict, which allowed him to claim one-third of the common lands of Chatou, since local farmers had not protected their common law rights by registering them in accordance with his 1763 decree. As a result of this decision, a ditch was dug to separate Bertin's acquisition (around 40 acres) from the remaining eighty acres of Chatou's common lands.[23] The ditch became a symbol of the widening gap that separated poor peasants from modernising landowners, prompting local inhabitants to ask what was the difference was between 'feudal seigneurs' and 'capitalist seigneurs'. The Revolution of 1789 answered such questions, often with bold and bloody consequences.

There *was* a difference of course, and Henri Bertin, during his ministerial career, had tried to deal with it. He had argued that the issue was not simply about the levying of feudal dues, such as the *cens* (the quitrent peasants were obliged to pay their lords) or the *champart* (a variable due, paid in kind), since many a bourgeois landowner who purchased a seigneury, or 'feudal estate', continued to levy such dues, or sought to transform them into money payments. The essential difference was that entrepreneurial owners, like Bertin, were prepared to invest considerable sums of money in their estates, replacing traditional methods of farming, alongside traditional personal relationships, with modern systems of cultivation and exploitation. We are passing through an era when cash was becoming far more important than paying 'in kind', and Bertin was very keen to practise on his estates in the Ile-de-France what he had preached as a government minister in the 1760s. Between 1763 and 1766, he had introduced legislation relating to tax exemption on reclaimed land and the partition of common lands; he had also instructed members of his new Agricultural Societies that they should introduce reforms to end, or curtail, the traditional rights of *vaine pâture* (allowing villagers to pasture livestock on common lands) and *parcours* (reciprocal stubble and fallow grazing between neighbouring villages). He had always believed that no serious land, or tax, reform should be introduced without first compiling a land register that recorded the size and value of holdings held by village communities (a *cadastre*, not a *terrier*, which was more focused on the payment of feudal dues). Bertin's 1780 register covering the seigneury of Chatou and Montesson was 52cm wide and 65cm high.[24] It estimated that Bertin owned a total of over one thousand acres. However, the *cadastre* was a double-edged sword for many landowners; it was obviously invaluable for those seeking to make greater profits on their estates, but it was also very useful to governments seeking greater efficiency in collecting taxes. We must remember that when he had pressed the case for the introduction of more land registers in the early sixties, he had been in charge of government finances. During the Great Fear of 1789, peasant communities would queue up to burn these registers, examples of illegal evidence, according to their belief in a 'moral economy', of oppression and extortion. Moreau's *Principes de morale* never really engaged with this fundamental issue.

One final, and very important, issue contributed to the long-term opposition to Bertin, which culminated in his 'Bastille Day' – his public profile as a reforming secretary of state and favourite of Louis XV. The Ile-de-France had always been an attractive province for rich landowners, given its proximity to Parisian markets and the palace of Versailles, and many of them saw the reformist Bertin as something of a role model. Members of the sword and robe nobility owned forty-five per cent of the seigneuries in the Ile-de-France. As late as 1791, the biggest property-owner in Chatou, after Bertin, was the comte d'Artois, and it was d'Artois' agent who had contacted Bertin in 1781 to ask, or rather demand, that M. Boncerf, *Inspecteur des domaines de Monsieur*, be allowed access to the charters in Moreau's *dépôt de l'histoire* so that he could ascertain 'the dues owing to the count in the different parts of his domain'.[25] Louis XVI had recently gifted d'Artois with the château and forest of Saint-Germain, a few kilometres from Chatou, and it was not long before d'Artois's agents were enclosing forest land that the local community had long used for hunting game, 'provoking consternation among the local market gardeners, for whom Paul Gautier, the previous owner of the domain, had shown such concern'.[26] Pierre-François Boncerf was renowned for the publication of his pamphlet, *Les inconvénients des droits féodaux* (1776), and was much in demand by landowners who sought to 'modernise' their estates by denying local communities their traditional rights to hunt game on their property, and by squeezing more income from their 'vassals'.

In other words, by the 1780s, Henri Bertin had become one of the leaders of the new commercial and capitalist seigneurialism, often referred to in the past as the 'seigneurial reaction'of the late eighteenth century. To provide a striking example of his influence, we can cite the case of a bourgeois, Jean Chanorier, who, like the Bertins, had climbed the social ladder by purchasing a noble fief. He had decided to move to Croissy-sur-Seine from the province of Burgundy 'to live near his protector and friend, Henri Bertin, seigneur of Chatou ... He dreamed of turning his fief into an experimental farm, following the example of what Turgot had done when he became Intendant of the Limousin, and as Bertin, seigneur de Chatou, and minister for agriculture during the reigns of Louis XV and Louis XVI, had done on his estate.'[27] As a first step in the modernization of his estate, and following Bertin's example, Chanorier had employed an expert in feudal law to compile a register of the land owned and the dues to be paid on his property.[28]

We can now begin to understand the mounting anger of the farm labourers, wine-growers (vineyards covered one-third of the cultivable land of Chatou), carters and market gardeners, for whom 'capitalism' was a poor substitute for old 'feudalism'. This popular 'plague upon both your houses' led directly to the demolition of the walls of Bertin's modest château on 4 May 1789. Their toleration had been already been tested to the limit by the adverse weather conditions of 1787 and 1788, which had driven up grain prices by two-thirds. To add insult to injury, a destructive hailstorm of 13 July 1788, which ruined the vineyards of peasants in Chatou and Montesson, led to serious acts of violence, as was the case in many parts of the country. Many families began to make ends meet by poaching game in reserves that were now the property of 'modernising' seigneurs; some were involved in the pillaging and distribution of grain in the markets of Saint-Germain-en-Laye. One grain merchant, accused of hoarding grain, was killed. Reports of this increasing resort to violence, the prelude to the *Grand Peur* of the spring and summer of 1789, were recorded in many other regions of France.[29]

From the beginning of 1789, responding to government legislation relating to the meeting of the Estates General on 5 May, villagers throughout France began to meet and draw up their lists of grievances (*cahiers de doléances*). The process concentrated the minds of disgruntled peasants wonderfully. The village *cahier* for Chatou was drawn up on 4 April by an anti-Bertin lobby of twenty-three inhabitants, headed by Jean-Pierre Nicole, a spokesman for the carters and market gardeners of Montesson and Carrières. We noted above that, during the early1780s, Bertin had constructed a new wall, accompanied by a new road and barrier that made it almost impossible for local inhabitants to use the shortest, traditional route to the bridge over the Seine at Chatou, and thence to vital Parisian markets. The village *cahier* demanded, *inter alia*, that a single tax should be introduced to replace all seigneurial dues, but it also included a direct attack upon Bertin's new wall and road, which, the *cahier* argued, had only been constructed to facilitate the delivery of Bertin's merchandise to Saint-Germain-en-Laye and Paris. Bertin claimed that the wall had been built to protect his crops from the devastation caused by burrowing wild mammals. Whatever the reason, the new wall was demolished on 11 May as Bertin and one of his disciples, Jean Chanorier, who was spending the weekend with him, looked on. The demolition marked the first of a sequence of events that forced Bertin to emigrate in 1790.[30] The 'Grand Design' had done little to prepare him for the tragedy that afflicted his last, apocalyptic years.

It was from his place of exile in Aix-la-Chapelle that Bertin advised his loyal friend and colleague for thirty years, Jacob-Nicolas Moreau, not to follow in his footsteps. Moreau, who had been driven out of his home town of Ville d'Avray the day after the fall of the Bastille on 14 July 1789, was warned that the grass was not necessarily greener across the French border: 'You are in France among tigers who are tearing themselves apart, but in Coblenz [head-quarters in 1791 of Louis XVI's exiled brothers, the comte d'Artois and the comte de Provence] butterflies burn themselves on a candle. Stay on your own patch and say to yourself, France no longer exists ... Empires, like individuals, die when their time has come. If struck down by illness, the lives of men can be quite short: empires often exist for many centuries. France's time has come.' Moreau followed Bertin's advice, dining quite happily in Paris and Versailles from 1790 to 1791, then settling down in Chambourcy, despite the fact that the National Assembly had decreed, on 14 August 1790, that he should be relieved of all his duties, without any financial compensation. He blamed the collapse of the monarchy on the immoral actions of Louis XV and the weakness of his successor, as well as on 'the abbés Mably and Raynal', whose 'project to wipe out Christianity in France was more general than that of destroying the monarchy'. Despite the many tribulations he had endured, including a spell in the Recollets prison from 20 March 1794 to 7 August 1796, Moreau lived long enough to see the rise of Napoleon Bonaparte, dying in

1803 at the ripe old age of 86. His memoirs end with an expression of gratitude to God 'for allowing me to retain that old-fashioned *gaieté* that enabled the comtesse de Noailles to say on her death-bed, "I am laughing as I am dying"'.[31]

We do not know if Bertin imitated the enviable example of the comtesse de Noailles, whom he also knew quite well, but it is unlikely. There was a gravitas about Bertin's personality that moved him in the direction of Confucian stoicism and the fatalism of Gibbon's *Decline and Fall of the Roman Empire*: 'France crumbles like the Roman Empire under the last emperors,' he told Moreau, 'under its own weight, its own faults, and its own corruption' – Bertin's historic *Liaisons dangereuses*.[32] Reports about the last years of his favourite 'correspondent' in Peking, *père* Amiot, whom he never saw in the flesh, would have done little to evoke laughter. In October 1792, the French Mission in Peking was closed down, and, just one year later, Pierre Jules Amiot passed away at the age of 76, having spent almost half a century in China as a priest, scholar and mandarin to the 'Celestial Emperor', Kien-long. His will stipulated that his few possessions should be distributed among the poor.[33] Amiot died without knowing that Bertin's death had preceded his by almost a year. On 25 August 1791, Bertin had sold the seigneury of Chatou for 280,000 *livres* to Anne-Thérèse de Pelser-Berensberg, the wife of the marquis de Feuquières, who was arrested by Chatou's *comité de surveillance* and executed by the infamous Revolutionary Tribunal on 30 June, 1794, a fate that would undoubtedly have befallen Henri Bertin had he not decided to emigrate in 1790.[34] As it was, he passed away peacefully in Aix-la-Chapelle on 16 September 1792, an appropriate place, given his historicist approach to the study of the Bourbon monarchy and his admiration for the legendary emperor, Charlemagne, for whom the last rites had been recited in the Imperial Palace at Aix-la-Chapelle on 24 January 814.

Bertin and Moreau's 'Grand Design' had failed to prevent the collapse of Bourbon absolutism, flawed as it was by its refusal to accept that 'sovereignty' had, for a brief period, passed from kings to communities. Nevertheless those who have dedicated much of their working lives to the study of French history should be grateful to Henri Bertin and his loyal colleague, Jacob-Nicolas Moreau. If their 'Grand Design' ended in failure, the value of their thirty-year long collection of historical and legal documents, charters and memoirs that formed the basis of that enterprise increased over time. Apart from Bertin's contribution to the foundation of the *Archives nationales* and the *Bibliothèque nationale*, the seventeen volumes of *Mémoires concernant les Chinois*, which constituted an essential part of Bertin's *Correspondance littéraire*, would provide future scholars with a rich source of information on China. One renowned social and economic historian of France concluded that Karl Marx's references to 'the asiatique mode of production' could not have been made without the information contained in this collection. Silvestre de Sacy, writing in 1920, argued that 'if culti-vated circles in France today interest themselves in serious studies of [eighteenth-century] China, they owe it to Bertin'. All this is undoubtedly true, although, as one historian has noted, from a personal standpoint his success was undermined by his failure to 'produce the descendants who, by the third generation, would have ensured the subtle transmutation of all the material values he had accumulated as a noble'. For some, this barren legacy represented the ultimate revenge of the marquis de Fratteaux, his older brother who had died in the Bastille.[35]

Notes

1 Marie-Christine Davy and Paulette Blampin, *Vivre à Chatou à la fin du XVIIIe siècle: le village retrouvé* (Paris, 1989), pp.22–30; Paul Bisson de Barthélemy, *Histoire de Chatou et de ses environs* (Paris, 2002), p.24. *Vivre à Chatou* provides us with a wealth of detailed information on the village.
2 Moriceau, *Les fermiers de l'Île-de-France*, pp.779–83.
3 Peter McPhee, *Living the French Revolution* (New York, 2006), p.95.
4 Baker, *Inventing the French Revolution*, p.259.
5 B.N., *collection Moreau*, vol.291, p.269, and p.364; vol.297, Le Boucg to Moreau, 22 Nov. 1784.

6 Baker, *Inventing the French Revolution*, p.85 and p.40.

7 Moreau, *Mémoires*, vol.2, p.343 and p.41.

8 Jones, *The Great Nation*, p.378; Sonenscher, *Before the Deluge*, p.251.

9 C.L., Amiot to Bertin, 22 Nov. 1783.

10 C.L., vol.10, 31 Dec.1784.

11 Following the death of Oudart de Bréquiny (responsible for editing most of the volumes) in 1815, 23 cartons of memoirs, papers and other documents, together with twelve volumes of Bertin's correspondence, were placed in one collection, which is now housed in the library of the *Institut de France*.

12 C.L., vol.10, letter of 31 Dec. 1784; letter of 21 Dec. 1785; Bertin to Raux, Dec. 1787.

13 C.L., vol.10, 14 Dec. 1783. Bertin wrote most of his lengthy missives around Dec./Jan.

14 C.L., vol.10, 21 Dec. 1785.

15 C.L., vol.10, 21 Oct. 1786.

16 Louis Dermigny, *La Chine et l'Occident: Le commerce à Canton au XVIIIe siècle*, 3 vols (Paris, 1964), vol.1, p.55.

17 Lewis, 'Henri Bertin and the Fate of the Bourbon Monarchy', p.85.

18 Sacy, *Henri Bertin*, p.175.

19 Vol.9, pp.40–146 of the *collection Bréquiny*, held in the *Bibliothèque nationale,*, includes daily records of meteorological conditions in Peking from 1 Jan. 1786 to 31 May 1789. Was there a global climatic catastrophe that might help to explain the severe weather conditions that affected both France and China during the late 1780s?

20 Peter Jones, *Liberty and Locality in Revolutionary France* (Cambridge, 2003), p.63; Moriceau, *Les fermiers de l'Ile-de-France*, p.613.

21 Paul Bisson de Barthélemy, *Histoire de Chatou et des environs*, second ed. (Paris, 2002), pp.115–6; *Vivre à Chatou à la fin du XVIIIe*, p.17.

22 Cited by Peter Jones, *The Peasantry in the French Revolution* (Cambridge, 1988), p.51.

23 Bisson de Barthélemy, *Histoire de Chatou*, p.119.

24 *Vivre à Chatou*, pp.35–9.

25 The letter ended with a scarcely veiled threat – 'I am sure that you will waste no time in carrying out these orders'!

26 Jacques Catinat, *C'est arrivé à Croissy-sur-Seine* (Paris, 1971), pp.122–3.

27 Catinat, *C'est arrivé à Croissy-sur-Seine*, pp.124–6.

28 Catinat, *C'est arrivé à Croissy-sur-Seine*, pp.148–50. Unlike Bertin, Chanorier, who was imprisoned for a short period during the Jacobin Terror of 1793–4, survived to become a member of Napoleon Bonaparte's Council of 500.

29 *Vivre à Chatou*, pp.29–30; Jones, *The Peasantry in the French Revolution*, pp.61–2.
30 Bisson de Barthélemy, *Histoire de Chatou*, pp.137–45.
31 Moreau, *Mes souvenirs*, vol.2, pp.497–575.
32 Lewis, 'Henri Bertin and the Fate of the Bourbon Monarchy', p.90.
33 C.L., vol.4, *Notice sure M. Pierre Jules Amiot*, n.d.
34 Bisson de Barthélemy, *Histoire de Chatou*, p.24.
35 Bourde, *Agronomie et agronomes*, vol.2, pp.1078–80; Sacy, *Henri Bertin*, p.169; Chevé, *La noblesse du Périgord*, p.141.

Bibliography

Manuscript sources

Archives nationales
Série E, Conseil du Roi, minutes d'arrêts.
2660–2661, minutes d'arrêts se rapportant au département du Bertin, 1764–1782.
2661A, correspondance de Bertin.
2784, minutes d'arrêts du Conseil ... rapportant au département de Secrétaire d'Etat Bertin, et relatifs au pays de Dombes, 1764–1779.
3666/7 registre des aide-mémoires de Bertin.
3701, analyse de la correspondance du Secrétaire d'Etat Bertin, 1772–73.
Série H1, 1624–27, mémoires et correspondance sur l'agriculture, 1761–1788; sociétés d'agriculture.
Série F4, 1938–9, plans et projets financiers présentés par des particuliers, XVIIIe siècle.
F11/265, correspondance de Bertin à Turgot.
F12/151–2, correspondance de Turgot, 1774–6.
F14, 1301, 1304, 7833.

Bibliothèque nationale
Collection Bréquiny, vols 75, 155, 290–91, 296 (Vol. 9 of this collection includes the meteorological records for Peking between 1 January 1786 and 31 May 1789).
Collection Moreau, vol. 290, travail de Moreau avec le Ministre.
291, correspondance de Moreau avec Bertin.
295, receuil de lettres de Moreau relative au Cabinet de Chartres.
296–7, lettres du Ministre sur le Cabinet de Chartres, 1765–87.
1090, mémoires historiques sur les Parlements et le Secrétaire d'Etat.
Mss, *Nouvelles acquisitions françaises,* vols 1000, 6498.

Printed sources

Histoire de M. Bertin, marquis de Fratteaux avec des éclaircissements sur son enlèvement de Londres et les nom de ceux qui y ont participé, par le comte d'H*** (Paris, 1756).

Jacob-Nicolas Moreau, *Mémoire sur la constitution politique de la ville et cité de Périgueux* (Périgueux, 1775).

Bibliothèque de l'Institut de France

Mss, 1515–26, *correspondance des RR. PP. Jésuites missionnaires en Chine avec H.L.J. Bertin, 1744–1798*, ed. H Cordier, 12 vols (A source of prime importance for Bertin's 'Chinese connection').

Archives départementales de la Dordogne

2E 130–37.

2E 203 (*dossiers* 1–17 relate to Henri Bertin and his family).

2E 725; 763, *dossier* 2; 1803, *dossier* 146 (primarily concerned with the purchase and sale of Bertin's properties).

'La Mémoire du Périgord', *Bulletin de la société historiographique et archéologique de la Dordogne* (a most valuable collection that identifies over 100 significant manuscript and printed sources, many of which cover the life and career of Henri Bertin).

Georges Bussière, *Henri Bertin et sa famille, Bulletin de la société historique et archéologique du Périgord*, tome 22 (1905), pp.216–44, 381–418; tome 23 (1906), pp.72–113, 211–43, 311–31; tome 24 (1907), pp.53–83, 272–314, 337–88, 451–66; tome 25 (1908) pp. 274–316, 437–64; tome 26 (1909), pp.133–62, 210–81.

Série 6C/5, répertoire ... des cahiers de doléances et procès-verbaux d'assemblées primaires de la Dordogne.

Archives de la manufacture royale de Sèvres.

Série B, nos 506, 1019, 1046, 3542.

Série 43 J, dossiers 1–13.

Cahiers de la céramique du verre et des arts du feu, no. 33.

Pâte Dure, I-III, HI, II-V, HVI and HVIII.

Secondary printed sources

Ackroyd, P., *London: the Biography* (London, 2000).

Algrant, C., *Madame de Pompadour, Mistress of France* (London, 2003).

Antoine, M., *Le secrétariat d'Etat de Bertin, 1763–1780* (Paris, 1948).

Antoine, M., *Louis XV* (Paris, 1989).

Ardacheff, M., *Le secrétariat d'Etat de Bertin* (Paris, 1909).

Argenson, marquis d', *Journal et mémoires du marquis d'Argenson* (Paris, 1866).

Aston, N., *Religion and Revolution in France 1780–1804* (London, 2000).

Baker, K., *Inventing the French Revolution* (Cambridge, 1990).

Bamford, P., *Privilege and Profit: A Business Family in Eighteenth-Century France* (Philadelphia, 1988).

Batbie, A., *Turgot, philosophe, économiste et administrateur* (Paris, 1861).

Batut, Guy, de, ed., *Louis XV* (Paris, 1933).

Bell, D., *The Cult of the Nation in France: Inventing Nationalism, 1680–1800* (Cambridge, Mass., 2001).

Benabou, E.-M., *La prostitution et la police des moeurs aux XVIIIe siècle* (Paris, 1987).

Bernis, F.-J. de Pierre, *Mémoires et lettres de François-Joachim de Pierre, Cardinal de Bernis 1715–78*, 2 vols (Paris, 1878).

Bisson de Barthélemy, P., *Histoire de Chatou et de ses environs* (Paris, 2002).

Black, J., *From Louis XIV to Napoleon: The Fate of a Great Power* (London, 1999).

Blondel, N. and Préaud, T., *Histoire de Sèvres* (Paris, 1996).

Bonney, R., 'Absolutism: What's in a Name?', *French History*, vol.1 (1987), pp.93–117.

—— 'Early Modern Theories of State Finance', in R. Bonney (ed.), *Economic Systems and State Finance* (Oxford, 1995), pp.163–229.

—— 'France, 1494–1815', in R. Bonney (ed.), *The Rise of the Fiscal State in Europe c. 1200–1815* (Oxford, 1999), pp.123–76.

Bourde, A., *Agronomies et agronomes en France au XVIIIe*, 2 vols (Paris, 1967).

—— *Le comte de H****, *Histoire de M. Bertin, marquis de Fratteaux* (*Imprimerie nationale*, 1994).

Bourdon, L.-G., *Le Parc au cerf, ou l'origine de l'affreux déficit. Par un zélé patriote* (1790).

Braudel, F., *Civilisation and Capitalism, 15th-18th Century* (London, 1985), vol. 3, *The Perspective of the World*.

Briggs, R., *Early Modern France, 1560–1715* (Oxford, 1998).

Brockliss, L. and James, C., *The Medical World of Early Modern France* (Oxford, 1997).

Campbell, P., *Power and Politics in Old Régime France, 1720–1745* (London, 1996).

—— 'The Paris Parlement in the 1780s', in P. Campbell (ed.), *The Origins of the French Revolution* (London, 2006), pp.87–111.

Castries, duc de, *La Pompadour* (Paris, 1983).

Catinat, J., *C'est arrivé à Croissy-sur-Seine* (Paris, 1971).

Chaussinand-Nogaret, G., *Choiseul, Naissance de la Gauche* (Paris, 1998).

Chevé, J., *La noblesse du Périgord* (Paris, 1998).

Chiappe, J. F., *Louis XV* (Paris, 1996).

Combeau, Y., *Le comte Pierre-Marc d'Argenson, ministre de Louis XV* (Paris, 1999).

Darnton, R., *The Business of Enlightenment, 1775–1800: A Publishing History of the Encyclopédie* (Cambridge, 1979).

Darrow, M., *Revolution in the House: Family, Class, and Inheritance in Southern France, 1775–1825* (Princeton, 1989).

Davidson, I., *Voltaire in Exile* (London, 2004).

Davy, M.–C. and Paulette Blampin, *Vivre à Chatou à la fin du XVIIIe siècle: le village retrouvé* (Paris, 1989).

Dermigny, L., *La Chine et l'Occident: Le commerce à Canton au XVIIIe siècle*, 3 vols (Paris, 1964).

de Sacy, J. S., *Henri Bertin dans le Sillage de Chine, 1720–92* (Paris, 1920).

Dickinson, H.T., *Liberty and Property. Political Ideology in Eighteenth-Century Britain* (London, 1979).

Doyle, W., *Jansenism* (London, 2000).

—— 'The Parlements', in Keith Baker (ed.), *The French Revolution and the Creation of Modern Political Culture*, vol.1, *The Political Culture of the Old Regime* (Oxford, 1987), pp.157–67.

Dugrand, R., *Villes et compagnes en Bas-Languedoc* (Paris, 1963).

Dull, J., *The French Navy and the Seven Years' War* (London, 1905).

Dumaine, J., *Louis XV et le Parc-aux-Cerfs* (Paris, n.d.).

Farge, A., *Vivre dans la rue à Paris au XVIIIe siècle* (Paris, 1992).

Félix, J., *Finances et politique au siècle des Lumières: le ministère L'Averdy, 1763–1768* (Paris, 1999).

—— 'The Financial Origins of the French Revolution', in P. Campbell (ed.), *The Origins of the French Revolution*, pp.35–62.

Fleury, comte, *Louis XV intime et les Petites Maîtresses* (Paris, 1933).

Foncin, P., *Essai sur le ministère de Turgot* (Geneva, 1976).

Furet, F., *Marx and the French Revolution* (Chicago, 1988).

Goncourt, E. and J., *Les maîtresses de Louis XV et autres portraits de femmes* (Paris, 2003).

Hardman, J., *Louis XVI* (London, 1993).

—— 'Decision-making', in P. Campbell (ed.), *The Origins of the French Revolution*, pp.63–86.

Hardman, J. and Price, M., *Louis XVI and the Comte de Vergennes: Correspondence* (Oxford, 1998).

Hausset, Madame, d', *Mémoires* (Paris, 1824).

Hudson, D., 'The Parlementary Crisis of 1763 in France and its Consequences', *Canadian Journal of History*, vol.7 (1972), pp.97–117.

Israel, J., *Radical Enlightenment: Philosophy and the Making of Modernity, 1650–1750* (Oxford, 2001).

Jones, C., *The Great Nation: France from Louis XV to Napoleon* (London, 2002).

—— *Madame de Pompadour: Images of a Mistress* (London, 2002).

Jones, P., *Liberty and Locality in Revolutionary France* (Cambridge, 2003).

—— *The Peasantry in the French Revolution* (Cambridge, 1988).

—— *Reform and Revolution in France: The Politics of Transition, 1774–1791* (Cambridge, 1995).

Kaplan, S., *Le complot de famine: histoire d'une rumeur au XVIIIe siècle* (Paris, 1982).

—— *Le meilleur pain du monde. Les boulangers de Paris au dix-*

huitième siècle (Paris, 1996).

Kwass, M., 'A Welfare State for the Privileged?' , in Mark Ormrod, Margaret Bonney and Richard Bonney (eds), *Crises, Revolutions and Self-Sustained Growth: Essays in European Fiscal History* (Stamford, 1999), pp.344–76.

Labatut, J.-P., 'La revendication du pouvoir noble en France aux XVIIe et XVIIIe siècles', *Fédération historique du Sud-Ouest. Actes du colloque franco-britannique, 27–30 septembre 1976* (Bordeaux, 1979).

Le Goff, T., 'How to Finance an Eighteenth-Century War', in Mark Ormrod *et al.*, *Crises, Revolutions and Self-Sustained Growth* (Stamford, 1999), pp.377–414.

Lever, M., *Louis XV, libertin malgré lui* (Paris, 2002).

Lewis, G., *France 1715–1804: Power and the People* (London, 2004).

—— *The Advent of Modern Capitalism in France, 1770–1840: The Contribution of Pierre-François Tubeuf* (Oxford, 1993).

—— 'Rising Tides. The Rise of the Bourgeoisie and the Fall of the Bourbon Monarchy', *Socialist History*, vol.33 (*Origins of the French Revolution*), pp.1–21.

—— 'Henri Bertin and the Fate of the Bourbon Monarchy: the Chinese Connection', in *Enlightenment and Revolution. Essays in Honour of Norman Hampson* (Aldershot, 2004), M. Crook, W. Doyle and A. Forrest (eds), pp.69–90.

Marx, K., 'Theories of the Plus Value', in François Furet, *Marx and the French Revolution* (Chicago, 1988), pp.217–19.

—— 'Moralising Criticism and Critical Moralising', in François Furet, *Marx and the French Revolution* (Chicago, 1988), pp.172–77.

Mathias, P. and O'Brien, P., 'Taxation in Britain and France, 1715–1810: A Comparison of the Social and Economic Incidence of Taxes Collected for the Central Governments', *Journal of Economic History*, vol.5 (1976), pp.601–50.

Maupeou, R.N. de, *Journal historique de la Révolution opérée dans la constitution de la monarchie française* (London, 1774–76), 7 vols, vol.3.

Maza, Sarah, *Vies privées, affaires publiques: les causes célèbres de la*

France prérévolutionnaires (Paris, 1997).

McLynn, F., *1789, the Year Britain Became Master of the World* (London, 2004).

McManners, J., *Church and Society in Eighteenth-Century France* (Oxford, 1999), vol. I: *The Clerical Establishment and its Social Ramifications*.

McNeil, G., 'The Anti-Revolutionary Rousseau', *American Historical Review*, vol.58 (1953), pp.808–23.

McPhee, P., *Living the French Revolution, 1789–99* (New York, 2006).

Mercier, S., *Paris Le Jour, Paris La Nuit* (Paris, 1990).

Meyrac, A., *Louis XV, ses maîtresses, le Parc aux Cerfs, d'après le journal-mémoires de d'Argenson, les chansons du temps et les mémoires du duc de Richelieu* (Paris, 1914).

Miller, S., 'The Absolutist State of Eighteenth-Century France: Modern Bureaucracy or Feudal Bricolage?', *Socialist History*, vol.33 (*Origins of the French Revolution*), pp.22–45.

Montégut, M. H. de, *Histoire d'un vieux logis en Angoumois: le château des Ombres* (Paris, 1922).

Montesquieu, C.L. de Secondat, *Persian Letters*, trans. by Margaret Mauldon (Oxford, 2008).

Moreau, J.-P., *Mes souvenirs*, 2 vols (Paris, 1898).

Moriceau, J.-M., *Les fermiers de l'Ile de France, XVe–XVIIIe siècle* (Paris, 1994).

Mouffle d'Angerville, *Vie privée de Louis XV, ou principaux événements, particularités et anecdotes de son règne* (London, 1781).

Nolhac, P. de, *Louis XV et Madame de Pompadour* (Paris, 1928).

Outram, D., *The Enlightenment* (Cambridge, 2005; second edn.)

Parker, D., *Class and State in Ancien Régime France: The Road to Modernity* (London, 1996).

Parker, H., *The Bureau de Commerce in 1781 and its Politics with Respect to French Industry* (Durham, Carolina, 1979).

Picciola, A., *Le comte de Maurepas: Versailles et l'Europe à la fin de l'ancien régime* (Paris, 1999).

Pillorget, S., *Claude-Henri Feydeau de Marville, lieutenant général de la police de Paris, 1740–47* (Paris, n.d.).

Poirier, J.-P., *Turgot* (Paris, 1999).

Porter, R., *Enlightenment: Britain and the Creation of the Modern World* (London, 2000).

Price, M., *The Fall of the French Monarchy: Louis XV, Marie Antoinette, and the baron de Breteuil* (London, 2002).

Richelieu, duc de, *Mémoires du maréchal duc de Richelieu* (Paris, 1792), vol.9.

Riley, J., *The Seven Years War and the Old Regime in France: the Economic and Financial Toll* (Princeton, 1986).

Roche, D., *La France des Lumières* (Paris, 1993).

—— *A History of Everyday Things: The Birth of Consumption in France, 1600–1800* (Cambridge, 2000).

Roger, D., ed. Keith Benson, trans. Robert Ellrich, *The Life Sciences in Eighteenth-Century French Thought* (Stanford, 1997).

Rowbotham, A., *Missionary and Mandarin: The Jesuits at the Court of China* (Berkeley, 1942).

Sonenscher, M., *Before the Deluge. Public Debt, Inequality, and the Intellectual Origins of the French Revolurion* (Princeton, 2007).

—— *Sans-Culottes: An Eighteenth-Century Emblem in the French Revolution* (Oxford, 2008).

Spary, E., 'Political, Natural and Bodily Economies', in N. Jardine, J. A. Secord and E.C. Spary (eds), *Cultures of Natural History* (Cambridge, 1996), pp.178–96.

Swann, J., *Politics and the Parlement of Paris under Louis XV, 1754–1774* (Cambridge, 1995).

—— '"Silence, Respect, Obedience": Political Culture in Louis XV's France', in Hamish Scott and Brendan Simms (eds), *Cultures of Power in Europe during the Long Eighteenth Century* (Cambridge, 2007), pp.225–48.

Young, A., *Travels in France During the Years 1787, 1788, and 1789* (Gloucester, Mass., 1976).

Zhilian, Z., 'Unfinished Enlightenment: the Chinese Experience', in *Centres and Margins: Enlightenment from Belfast to Beijing* (Paris, 2003), pp.213–18.

Index

Lightning Source UK Ltd.
Milton Keynes UK
UKOW020810111011

180112UK00001B/50/P